BASIC STUDIES ON READING

BASIC STUDIES ON READING

EDITED BY

HARRY LEVIN

AND

JOANNA P. WILLIAMS

Basic Books, Inc., Publishers · New York · London

© 1970 by Basic Books, Inc.

Library of Congress Catalog Card Number: 76–116851

SBN 465–00578–0

Manufactured in the United States of America

THE AUTHORS

TOMI D. BERNEY is a doctoral candidate at the Ferkauf Graduate School of Social Sciences and Humanities, Yeshiva University. She has published numerous articles and is coauthor, with Dr. Vera P. John et al. of a forthcoming book, *Early Childhood Bilingual Education.*

GASTON E. BLOM is a psychoanalyst and Professor of Psychiatry and Education at the University of Colorado Medical Center. He is also Director of the Day Care Center, a psychoeducational facility with outpatient and day services for emotionally and educationally handicapped children. The center also functions as a training, research, and community school consultation unit.

THOMAS G. R. BOWER is Lecturer in Psychology at the University of Edinburgh. His major interest is psychological development in infancy, a topic on which he has published numerous articles.

ROGER BROWN is Professor of Social Psychology at Harvard University. He is the author of *Words and Things, Social Psychology,* and *Psycholinguistics.*

NOAM CHOMSKY is Professor of Linguistics at MIT. His books include *Syntactic Structures, Aspects of the Theory of Syntax, Language and Mind,* and, with Morris Halle, *Sound Pattern of English.*

W. NELSON FRANCIS is Professor of Linguistics and English and Chairman of the Department of Linguistics at Brown University. He is the author of the *The Structure of American English* (1958), *The English Language, an Introduction* (1956), and, with Henry Kucera, *Computational Analysis of Present-Day American English* (1967).

ELEANOR J. GIBSON is Professor of Psychology at Cornell University, where she does research concentrated on perceptual development and the basic learning processes in acquisition of reading skill. She is author of *Principles of Perceptual Learning and Development.*

JULIAN HOCHBERG, Professor of Psychology at Columbia University, is author of *Perception* and many articles in the field of visual perception and communication.

VIVIAN M. HORNER is Assistant Professor of Psycholinguistics and Education in the Department of Educational Psychology and Guidance of the Ferkauf Graduate School of Social Sciences and Humanities, Yeshiva University. She was co-Director, with Vera P. John, of the Early Childhood Bilingual Education Project and is currently Acting Director of Ferkauf's interdisciplinary Language and Behavior Program.

VERA P. JOHN is Associate Professor in the Department of Educational Psychology at Yeshiva University. Coauthor, with Vivian Horner, of a book titled *Early Childhood Bilingual Education* (forthcoming), she writes mostly about the field of language development.

ELEANOR L. KAPLAN was a graduate student at Cornell University and a postdoctoral fellow at Stanford University. She is now Assistant Professor of Psychology at Hayward State College. Her research interests are in cognitive development.

PAUL A. KOLERS, Professor of Psychology at the University of Toronto, has worked extensively on cognitive aspects of visual perception, including form perception, illusions, and the perceptual processing of printed text.

WILLIAM LABOV is Associate Professor of Linguistics at Columbia University. He is the author of *The Social Stratification of English in New York City* and many articles dealing with the structure and evolution of language in its social context.

HARRY LEVIN is Professor and Chairman of the Psychology Department at Cornell University. He was Director of Project Literacy. His research interests are concerned with the reading process.

DAVID W. REED was formerly Professor of Linguistics at the University of California, Berkeley. He is now Professor of Linguistics at Northwestern University and Director of the Linguistic Atlas of the Pacific Coast. He has contributed several articles on linguistics and reading to both journals and collections of essays.

ARTHUR SHURCLIFF was a graduate student at Cornell University and is currently a Lecturer at The Flinders University of South Australia.

RICHARD L. VENEZKY, Associate Professor of Computer Sciences at the University of Wisconsin, is author of *The Structure of English Orthography* and of numerous articles on reading.

RICHARD R. WAITE is Clinical Associate Professor of Clinical Psychology at the University of Colorado Medical Center. Currently, he is Director of the Denver Model Cities Mental Health project, Human

Relations: Pride and Respect; this is administered by the Denver Department of Health and Hospitals and Consultants in Human Resources, Inc., an interethnic corporation concentrating on cultural and racial issues and solutions.

ROSE-MARIE WEBER, formerly a Research Associate at the Laboratory for Research on Language Skills at Cornell University, is now Assistant Professor of Linguistics at McGill University.

JOANNA P. WILLIAMS is Associate Professor of Education at the University of Pennsylvania. She has published numerous articles on children's learning and on reading.

ALBERT YONAS is Assistant Professor at the Institute of Child Development and Training Director at the Center for Research in Human Learning at the University of Minnesota. He has published studies on perceptual learning and perceptual development.

SARA G. ZIMET is an Instructor in Psychiatry at the University of Colorado Medical Center and co-Director of a research program entitled, Influence of Content of Primers on School Children. She is the author and coauthor of numerous articles describing the content of readers.

PREFACE

This volume is a collection of studies designed for linguists, psychologists, and educators who are interested in basic research on reading. The theme that runs through many of the chapters is that reading is a complicated process about which we know too little. The emphasis should be on the word *process* in that little or no attention in this book is given to the pedagogy of reading. We deliberately inflated the title with the word *basic* in order to make it clear that this volume is not another touchstone about how to teach children to read. We have nothing to add to the fantastically large, and for the most part ineffective, literature on teaching people to read. That is not our purpose, and, except for an occasional speculative foray by an author, these studies are not concerned with practical issues of reading instruction. Indeed, the relationship between understanding the nature of a complex skill and teaching that skill is not at all clear. Chomsky, for example, asserts strongly that the study of linguistics has little to offer the reading teacher. Other authors, as you will see, are more hopeful. In the final chapter, Williams discusses how the practitioner might use fundamental research.

The chapters fall under three rubrics. The first section concerns linguistics and reading, and Francis' comments on these chapters point up certain general ideas among the authors. Chomsky and Reed take up the important problem of how language is represented in writing. These issues are important and provide a focus for future linguistic inquiry.

Several of the chapters cover various psychological processes and reading. With the exception of Weber's work on children's reading errors and Gibson's on deaf people, the studies are about mature, skilled readers. In commenting on these chapters and reviewing some of their common themes, Brown points out that these studies have put reading research into the broader context of psycholinguistics and information processing.

Three chapters relate to social variables in reading research. Blom and his coworkers have content analyzed children's readers for, among other things, the social values that they communicate. The chapters by John and by Labov are concerned with minority groups and, in fact, Labov's chapter might easily have been included in the section on linguistics.

Taken together, all these chapters—each of which was specially prepared for this collection—give a reasonably complete picture of current theory and research about how people read. Many, though not all, of the studies were instigated and discussed over a five-year period by Project Literacy. The project, under the auspices of the U.S. Office of Education, was designed to support in various laboratories basic research on reading and to bring together and disseminate the results of the research. The initial impetus for Project Literacy came from Francis Keppel, then U.S. Commissioner of Education, and Francis A. J. Ianni, formerly chief of the research branch of the Office of Education. We admire their vision of such a coordinated research program and their focus on long-term gains of substance rather than on immediate and obvious payoff.

Both Project Literacy and this volume owe much to the help, encouragement, and prodding of a most extraordinary secretary and aide, Mary Blomgren. We are grateful to her. We also thank Virginia Powers, who competently typed the various versions of the manuscript, and Lynn Levin, who did the final editing chores.

H.L.

July, 1970   J.P.W.

CONTENTS

BASIC STUDIES ON READING

1 NOAM CHOMSKY

Phonology and Reading

Before entering into a discussion of how the study of sound structure might contribute to research on problems of literacy, I would like to emphasize two points that can be easily overlooked. The first is that the study of sound structure is in a state of intensive development; no one can say with any security what will be the fate of the conventional wisdom of today. The subject is alive, exciting, and changing. The second point is that, even if we had achieved near certainty on some basic issues of phonology, it is by no means obvious that conclusions of any importance would follow for the study of reading and teaching of reading. There is a natural enough tendency for teachers to turn to the fundamental disciplines (psychology, linguistics) for guidance, but they should do so with skepticism and a critical attitude. The insights that have been achieved into behavior and mental function are limited. Furthermore, there is little reason to doubt that the dominant factor in successful teaching is and will always remain the teacher's skill in nourishing, and sometimes even arousing, the child's curiosity and interest and in providing a rich and challenging intellectual environment in which the child can find his own unique way toward understanding, knowledge, and skill. It is difficult to imagine that psychology or linguistics or any other academic discipline will make much of a contribution to this end; correspondingly, it may be that their contribution to education will be quite restricted. The final judgment on this matter must be that of the teacher in the classroom. More generally, it is quite clear that the professional psychologist, linguist, mathematician, and so on has no particular competence, as a professional, to determine the educa-

3

tional goals that provide the framework for the choice of a curriculum or the manner of its implementation.

With this qualification, I would like to turn to the problem at hand. It seems to me that the most direct contribution that contemporary linguistics can make to the study of literacy is in clarifying the relation of the conventional orthography to the structure of the spoken language. This relation is, I believe, much closer than is ordinarily supposed. So much so, in fact, that conventional English orthography in its essentials appears to be a near-optimal system for representing the spoken language; it is to a large extent merely a direct point-by-point transcription of a system that the speaker of English has internalized and uses freely, a system that I will refer to as "lexical representation." Furthermore, it seems to be the case not only that lexical representation is a basic element in the system freely used by the speaker-hearer, but also that it varies very little from speaker to speaker, even across major dialect boundaries. Correspondingly, conventional orthography is highly appropriate, with little modification, for a wide range of dialects. To the extent that this point of view can be substantiated, it would follow that the teacher of reading is not introducing the child to some new and obscure system that is only distantly related to the spoken language he has, to a substantial degree, already mastered. Rather the teacher is engaged in bringing to consciousness a system that plays a basic role in the spoken language itself. Beyond this, the study of sound structure has important implications for cognitive psychology and may, in this connection, be of interest in the study of specific topics, such as literacy. These are the general points I will try to explain in the following remarks.

The conception of sound structure that I will use as a background for this discussion is one that Morris Halle and I have been developing for several years and have applied in detail to the study of English structure. A detailed presentation appears in Chomsky and Halle (1968), and certain theoretical conclusions are outlined in Chomsky (1967).

When we consider the structure of a language, we are, fundamentally, concerned with a relation of sound and meaning. The rules of the language relate certain physical signals to certain semantic interpretations. It is these rules that the native speaker-hearer intuitively commands and that the linguist tries to discover and express in a precise way. To carry out this task, the linguist must have a way of characterizing physical signals and semantic interpretations and a theory that permits him to formulate the rules that relate them. In principle, he wishes to carry out this task for any possible human language, just as any normal child, it is safe to assume, has the ability to represent for himself the sounds and meanings and the rules expressing their interconnection for any human language. A general task of linguistics, then, is to develop a universal phonetics, which serves to represent in a psychologically appropriate way the physical signals used in human languages; a universal semantics, which plays the same role with respect to the semantic aspect of language; and, more generally, a universal grammar, which specifies the kinds of rules that are used in natural languages, the representations of sound and meaning and formal structure to which they apply, and the principles of organization that they must obey.

Considerable progress has been made, over the years, in developing a universal phonetics that meets empirical conditions of adequacy. The problems of semantic representation, needless to say, are in a much less satisfactory state. There has, however, been some success in recent years in specifying the kinds of rules that relate phonetic representations to abstract structures—let us call them "structural descriptions" of sentences—that seem highly appropriate for semantic interpretation. A structural description that is adequate to express the semantic content of a sentence must contain, at least, a representation of the meaning-bearing units of which the sentence is composed and the arrangement of these units at various levels of organization, in particular their arrangement into phrases. Thus, the structural description of the phrase *American history teacher* must indicate that it contains the units *America, -an, histor-, -y, teach-, -er,* and it must indicate that these units are organized into the words *American, history, teacher.* Furthermore, this structural description must associate these words in one of two possible ways, to indicate which of two possible semantic interpretations is expressed. The phrase can be analyzed as *American-history teacher* 'teacher of history who is an American' or *American history-teacher* 'teacher of American history.' Thus, there are two possible structural descriptions of the phrase *American history teacher,* each underlying one semantic interpretation. The structural descriptions in question must indicate the proper phrasing and must also express the deeper relations among the units that determine the meaning and that underlie the form of the phrase. Similarly, the word *theatricality* must have structural description indicating that it is a noun derived from the adjective *theatrical,* which is in turn derived from the noun *theater.* Thus, at the very least, the grammar of a language must contain syntactic rules that determine phrasing and a lexicon that contains the semantically and syntactically functioning units, as well as rules that relate structural descriptions to phonetic representations.

One kind of linguistic representation that surely has psychological significance, both on the perceptual and motor levels, is phonetic representation, in the sense just mentioned; another is representation in terms of structural descriptions. For present purposes, we may limit ourselves to one subsidiary aspect of structural descriptions, namely, the specification of the meaning-bearing elements and their arrangement into phrases. Thus we are concerned with the lexicon and with the rules that relate a bracketing such as (1), (2), or (3) (where the labels on the brackets indicate the category to which the bracketed phrase occurs) to a phonetic representation. This aspect of structural description is called "surface structure." Our evidence leads us to postulate, tentatively, that it is only surface structure that is relevant to determining the form—the phonetic representation—of a sentence, although it is far from adequate for the determination of semantic interpretation.

(1) $[[[America]_N\text{-}an]_A[[[histor\text{-}]_S\text{-}y]_N[[teach]_V\text{-}er]_N]_N]_{NP}$[1]
  'teacher of history who is an American'

(2) $[[[[America]_N\text{-}an]_A[[histor\text{-}]_S\text{-}y]_N]_{NP}[[teach]_V\text{-}er]_N]_{NP}$
  'teacher of American history'

(3) $[[[theater]_N\text{-}ical]_A\text{-}ity]_N$

Observe that (1) and (2) are pronounced slightly differently; specifically, they differ in stress contour. Using the numeral "1" for primary stress, "2" for secondary stress, and so on, the stressed syllables of (1) have the contour 213, whereas the stressed syllables of (2) have the contour 313. These contours, as well as the stress contours of (3)—and other aspects of the phonetic representation, in these and other cases—are determined by the surface structure of the phrase.

Consider now the character of the lexicon. It is easy to justify the assumption that each lexical item is represented (in part) as a sequence of "segments." Each item has a unique such "spelling" in the lexicon. This spelling must contain all information not predictable by the phonological rules. These rules apply to surface structures, such as (1) through (3), which contain the lexical items. Thus the lexical representation of the common item of *histor-y, histor-ical, histor-ian,* or of *anxi-ous, anxi-ety,* or of *courage, courage-ous,* or of *tele-graph, tele-graph-ic, tele-graph-y,* and so on must be selected so as to contain just what

---

[1] N = noun, A = adjective, S = stem, NP = noun phrase, V = verb.

is not predictable in the variant phonetic realizations of these items. It is evident that the speaker of the language has an intuitive control of the information presented in the lexical representation, though he may not be able to give conscious expression to this knowledge; correspondingly, the psychological reality of lexical representation, in this sense, is hardly open to question.

Observe that a lexical representation, in this sense, provides a natural orthography for a person who knows the language. It provides just the information about linguistic forms that is not predictable by phonological rules or by the syntactic rules that determine the surface structure of the expression in which the item is embedded, that is, just the information about the item in question that is needed by a person who knows the language and wishes to use this item properly. Conventional orthography, in the case of English (or any other language of which I have any knowledge), is remarkably close to optimal in this sense. For example, the spellings *histor-, anxi-, courage, telegraph* are (minor notational conventions aside) essentially what would appear in the lexicon of spoken English. Conventional orthographies tend to differ systematically from lexical representation only in that true irregularities[2] (for example, *man, men; run, ran*) are differently represented, as is quite natural. Apart from this, the symbols of conventional orthography correspond fairly closely to the segments of lexical representation, and the lexical representation of an item tends to be rather close (under this correspondence) to its orthographic representation.

The phonological rules determine the phonetic representation of an expression from a surface structure that contains the lexical representation of each meaning-bearing item, its representation as a sequence of segments. The phonological rules are perfectly automatic; there is no reason why the speaker-hearer should have any awareness of the nature or organization of these rules, and, in fact, introspection tells us next to nothing about them. The effect of these rules may be to modify lexical representations quite drastically, as the examples given indicate. For example, the item *courage* is phonetically [kárəǰ] in isolation and [kəréyǰ] in the context ——*ous;* the item *anxi-* is [æŋgzáy] in the context ——*ety,* and [ǽŋkš] in the context ——*ous.* As noted earlier, the phrase *American history teacher* may have one or another stress contour depending on its surface structure. And so on. English phonology contains

---

[2] The notion "true irregularity" is a bit vague. Careful analysis shows surprising subregularities even in such cases as *run, ran, cling, clung,* and *satisfy, satisfaction.*

hundreds of rules, arranged and organized in accordance with complex patterns and conditions, and it is to be expected that the effect of such rules on abstract lexical representations will often be quite drastic. Investigation of English sound structure amply confirms this expectation. It is important, however, to be aware of the fact that these modifications are, for the most part, quite regular and automatic. In particular, the examples given in this paragraph are moderately complex cases where very simple and general rules applying in sequence to an abstract lexical representation convert it, in successive stages, into a phonetic representation that bears little point-by-point resemblance to the underlying abstract form.

Space does not permit a persuasive analysis of this matter, but I think that even some informal comments may at least give some of the flavor of the effects of phonological rules on lexical representations. Consider, for example, the word *courage*. The evidence seems to me strong that the underlying lexical representation is /koræge/.[3] Consider the processes that apply to the word *courage* in isolation. We can describe these in terms of the following "derivation" of the phonetic form [kʌrəj̆] from the lexical representation /koræge/.

(4) koræge   lexical representation
    kóræge   stress rule
    kóræ̆je   velar softening
    kʌ́ræ̆je   unrounding
    kʌ́ræj̆   e-elision
    kʌ́rəj̆   vowel reduction

The top line of derivation (4) is the underlying lexical representation. A rule of stress assignment assigns primary stress to give the second line of the derivation. This rule is one part of a complex and interesting system that determines stress contours, a residue of a set of historical processes, some of Romance and some of Germanic origin. The rule is based on the fundamental notions "weak cluster" and "strong cluster."

---

[3] The symbols are intended in their ordinary phonological interpretation. Thus, /k/ and /g/ are unvoiced and voiced velar stops, respectively; /o/ /æ/, and /e/ are, respectively, mid-back-rounded, low-front-unrounded, and mid-front-unrounded vowels. I will follow the convention of using /,/ for underlying lexical representations and [,] for the realizations given by application of phonological rules, including, in particular, the phonetic representations that result from application of all phonological rules.

Putting some details aside, we can think of a strong cluster as a sequence consisting of a vowel followed by zero or more consonants, either where the vowel is tense (as the vowels of the words *bait, bite, boat, boot*) or where the consonant cluster in question consists of two or more consonants (as in *bilk, bust, bend*). A weak cluster, then, will consist of a nontense vowel followed by no more than one consonant (as in *bit, bet, bun*). The stress rule specifies, in particular, that in a noun ending in a weak cluster, the stress is placed on the penultimate cluster if that cluster is strong or the antepenultimate cluster if the penultimate is weak. In the case in question, stress is placed on the antepenultimate cluster, because both the final cluster [e] and the penultimate cluster [æg] are weak.

The next process to apply is velar softening. This rule softens the velar stop [g] to [ǰ] before the nonlow front vowel [e], but leaves the velar stop [k] before the back vowel [o].

We next apply the rule of unrounding to give the fourth line of the derivation. This rule is one component of a process of very great generality in English, a process that is, for example, involved in giving the phonetic realization [aw] from the underlying /ū/ (a tense vowel) in the word *profound*, which has the underlying representation /pro-fūnd/. In the word *profundity* the underlying /ū/ becomes nontense [u] by a rule that applies in a syllable followed by an unstressed nonfinal syllable; it then lowers to [o] and unrounds to [ʌ] just as the /ū/ of *profound*, after dipthongizing to /ūw/, lowers and unrounds to [a]. If this underlying /ū/ were realized directly as a phonetic segment, it would be pronounced like the vowel of *shoe*. Instead, it is either [aw] as in *profound* or [ʌ] as in *profundity*, and the same process of unrounding gives [ʌ] from /o/ in *courage*. The rule that untenses underlying /ū/ in *profundity* before an unstressed nonfinal syllable has other interesting consequences; for example, it accounts for the fact that the first syllable is tense (namely, [rīy]) in *relaxation* but nontense (namely, [re]) in *registration*, the second syllable being unstressed in the latter case but not the former. Rules of tensing, untensing, lowering, raising, rounding, unrounding, and others interweave to determine complex relations between the abstract underlying forms and the phonetic output.

The fifth line of derivation (4) results from a rule that elides [e] in the final position of an item. The final line results from a very general process that reduces unstressed vowels to [ə].

Consider next the form *courageous*, represented lexically as /kor æ geɔs/. We have the following derivation:

(5) korǽgeɔs   lexical representation
    korǽgeɔs   stress rule
    korǽ̌jeɔs   velar softening
    korǽjeɔs   tensing
    korǽyjeɔs   diphthongization
    koréyjeɔs   vowel shift
    koréyjɔs   e-elision
    kəréyjəs   vowel reduction

Derivation (5) proceeds as follows. The top line, again, is the lexical representation: the item /korǽge/ followed by the adjectival ending /ɔs/, which under stress would appear phonetically as [as] in General American, as in *curiosity*. Notice that the latter realization again involves unrounding, as in the examples discussed in connection with (4). The rule of stress assignment again places stress on the antepenultimate cluster, the penultimate cluster ([e] in this case) being weak just as the final cluster ([ɔs] in this case) is weak. The third line, once again, results from velar softening. The process of tensing that gives the fourth line applies to a stressed vowel followed by a single consonant, which is in turn followed by a nonlow front vowel (in this case, [e]) followed by another vowel. This is the same process that gives a tense diphthongized vowel in the stressed position of such words as *ministérial, harmónious,* and *funéreal.* Tense vowels diphthongize, as we have already noted in the case of *profound;* a front vowel, such as [ǽ] in (5), receives the front glide [y], whereas a back vowel, such as [ū] in *profound,* receives the back glide [w]. We now have line 5 of derivation (5).

By "vowel shift" we refer to the process that in the case of (5) raises the low tense vowel [ǽ] to [ē]. Exactly the same process raises the underlying low vowel of *sane* (represented lexically as /sǽn/) to [ē], so that with diphthongization we have phonetic [sēyn]) from underlying /sǽn/. Observe that in the form *sanity* (with the lexical representation /sǽnity/), the same vowel first untenses to [æ] by exactly the process mentioned earlier that untenses the underlying /ū/ of *profound* to [u]; being nontense, it does not diphthongize or undergo vowel shift, so that the first syllable of *sanity* retains the low vowel [æ]. Although far from obvious, it is a fact, nevertheless, that the process of vowel shift that raises the stressed vowel of *courageous* and *sane* is fundamentally the same process as the one that lowers the stressed vowel in the second syllable of *profound* and *profundity,* along lines described earlier. This general process of vowel shift is, in a sense, the fundamental phonological process involved in English vowel system.

Returning to derivation (5), we next apply the process of e-elision and the process of vowel reduction, exactly as in the case of derivation (4), giving the final line of (5) as the phonetic representation.

Summarizing, the underlying form /koræge/ becomes [kʌrəǰ] in isolation and [kəréyǰ] when followed by -*ous*, by processes that make essential reference to the abstract segments of the underlying representation. This representation includes such segments as the final /e/, which never appears in the phonetic representation of the various forms of *courage* but which plays an essential role in determining placement of stress, tenseness of vowels, and point of articulation of consonants. Thus, the final /e/ of /koræge/ predicts the stress pattern of *courage* on the analogy of *cinema, animal;* the stress pattern of *courageous* on the analogy of *melodious, Canadian;* the tenseness of the stressed vowel of *courageous* on the same analogy; and so on. The alternation *courage, courageous* would be entirely unique and inexplicable were we not to postulate the abstract underlying form as in (4) and (5). Evidence of the sort just summarized indicates that the underlying lexical representation for the form *courage* is, in fact, /koræge/; it is this form that is internalized, as part of his knowledge of English, by the speaker-hearer who is acquainted with this word. A linguist knowing nothing of English orthography would be led to postulate this underlying form from consideration of the evidence just cited. Turning to conventional orthography, we observe that it is near optimal for the spoken language, in this case, differing only in that it has *ou* where we would expect ɔ or *o*, and that it uses *c* for the occurrences of *k* in words that undergo velar softening—a rather natural notation. Neither stress placement nor the phonetic form of the vowels and consonants is directly indicated in the orthography, for the very good reason that these details are determined by rules of great generality that apply as well to a mass of other forms.

The marvelous intricacy of the workings of a real phonological system can barely be suggested by such a brief and compressed account. The examples, however, are not untypical. A great many examples of this sort lend much weight to the hypothesis that there is a highly abstract system of lexical representation that functions in the use and understanding of English sentences and that is related to the phonetic representation (which, in turn, has both a motor and sensory aspect) by general rules that apply in a precise and well-defined way. Furthermore, this underlying representation for the spoken language is surprisingly close to conventional orthography. In short, conventional English orthography is much closer than one might guess to an optimal orthography, an orthography that presents no redundant information and that indicates directly, by a direct letter-to-segment correspondence, the underlying lexical form of the spoken language.

It seems fairly well established that the level of lexical representation is highly resistant to change and persists over long historical periods. It follows, then, that it should be common to a wide range of dialects. The evidence now available, though scanty, is certainly consistent with this conclusion. Correspondingly, one finds that conventional orthographies remain useful, with minor changes, over long periods and for a wide range of dialects.

Tentatively, we might propose that the process of reading aloud would take place along the following lines, for a person who knows the language as a speaker-hearer and who has learned the letter-segment correspondence of an orthography. Given a string of written letters, the reader converts it to a lexical representation, the task being eased to the extent that the orthography is optimal at this abstract level. The same processes that enable him to understand spoken speech enable him to associate a structural description—in particular, a surface structure—with this lexical representation. Using the rules that govern ordinary speech, he then converts this surface structure, with the given lexical representation, to a phonetic representation, ultimately, a physical signal.

Of course this schematic picture leaves out factors of basic importance—the effects of set and attention, perceptual strategies, the role of eye movements, and the use of deeper linguistic knowledge in identifying the written symbols in the first place on the basis of expectations that may in themselves involve abstract syntactic and semantic processes. However, it seems clear that an optimal orthography, one that would facilitate the use of available perceptual strategies and deeper linguistic knowledge, would be one that has as close a correspondence as possible, letter-to-segment, to the abstract lexical forms. Such an orthography leads directly to the semantically and syntactically significant units, abstracting away from all phonetic properties that are determined by general rule.

I have suggested that the level of phonetic representation and the level of lexical representation are psychologically real—that they correspond to significant stages in the process of use and understanding of ordinary speech. Our research into sound structure has led us to the conclusion that there is no linguistically significant level of representation intermediate between phonetic representation and the lexical representations to which conventional orthographies closely correspond (apart from the matter of true "irregularities"). Rather, there is a complex correspondence between lexical and phonetic representation, mediated by phonological rules of the sort illustrated earlier. Furthermore, dialects that differ quite widely in phonetic realization of particular forms appear to share common lexical representations.

Let me emphasize once again the advantages of an orthography that corresponds to lexical representation—for a speaker who knows the language as a spoken language. For such a speaker, an orthography corresponding to lexical representation omits redundant phonetic information and permits the most rapid transition to the semantically significant units. In contrast, broad phonetic (or possibly, so-called phonemic) representation is the only kind of spelling that would be of any use to someone who knows nothing of the syntax of the language but who wishes to produce a noise that is close to the phonetic form of a sentence—for example, an actor who has to produce a sentence of a language that he does not know. Referring again to the examples (4) and (5), an actor who knows general phonetics but knows no English (or who knows only low-level phonetic rules of English such as those governing aspiration of stops) would require a so-called phonemic representation such as [kʌrəj], [kəréyj], in order to pronounce the words *courage, courageous* acceptably. But these phonemic representations would be extremely inefficient for the speaker of English, because he would have units. In contrast, broad phonetic (or possibly so-called phonemic) representations on the basis of the single underlying lexical structure /koræge/, which in isolation becomes [kʌrəj] and before *-ous* becomes [kəréyj], as we have seen. The reader who knows English would be best served by an orthography that leads him directly to the single syntactic-semantic unit *courage* that appears in these two phonetic forms and that eliminates all irrelevant phonetic detail that is determined by automatic processes of the spoken language. Conventional orthography, in this as in many other cases, serves this function quite well, whereas phonetic or phonemic notation would be quite inappropriate.

A few additional remarks may be in order regarding phonemic representation in the sense of modern linguistics. A phonemic system is one that, in effect, extracts all regularities from the sound system that can be detected with no consideration of higher level structures.[4] There are no extralinguistic grounds for supposing that such a system exists. For example, there is no reason to suppose that a child learning a language begins by constructing a system of this sort and only then proceeds to the problem of acquiring syntax or semantics, and there is no evidence, to my knowledge, suggesting that there is a level of perceptual processing (or motor performance) that corresponds to phonemic representation in any of its modern sense. Furthermore, it has been argued—persuasively, I believe—that a phonemic level can be incorporated into a full grammar only if certain otherwise valid and quite significant generalizations are abandoned. If correct, these arguments (to date, unanswered) show that there is no linguistic justification for such a level and more that there are internal linguistic arguments indicating that it does not exist. It seems to me, therefore, that phonemics in the sense of modern linguistics is perhaps nothing more than a methodological artifact.

Discussion of problems of literacy quite naturally turns to problems of dialect variation and to the question of "phoneme-grapheme" correspondences. As to the former, dialect variation is of importance to the study of reading and teaching of reading only to the extent that dialects differ on the syntactic and lexical levels. Differences in phonological rules are irrelevant, because orthography corresponds to a level of representation that abstracts away from the effects of phonological rules, assuming that what has been said earlier is correct. Although the dialects of modern English differ enormously in their "phonemic" structure, they seem quite similar, so far as we know, at the level of lexical representation that is directly related to orthography.

---

[4] This is the most "austere" form of phonemics, and the one worked out in the classic papers of Bernard Bloch and a number of others. In other versions of phonemics, certain higher level information is permitted, for example, information regarding word boundaries. I do not wish to enter here into a discussion of various forms of phonemic theory. My own view, to summarize briefly, is that the methodological studies of Troubetzkoy Bloch, Harris, and many others were of fundamental importance in clarifying basic problems of sound structure and that not the least of their contributions was the clear and responsible way in which they followed assumptions to their logical conclusions, at which point, I believe, the assumptions can be shown to be untenable. For further discussion, see my *Current Issues in Linguistic Theory* (1964). I also feel, and have argued elsewhere (see references above), that recent work that attempts to "defend phonemics" does so by eliminating precisely the clarity and consistency that were its real merit. For additional discussion of these matters, see Postal, *Aspects of Phonological Theory* (1968), and references cited here.

As to the question of phoneme-grapheme correspondence, it may be that this is something of a pseudoissue. If by *phoneme* is meant the unit constructed in accordance with modern principles, then there is little reason to expect that phoneme-grapheme correspondences will be of much interest because it appears that phonemes are artificial units having no linguistic status. Hence, it is not clear why one should investigate phoneme-grapheme correspondences at all. If the phonemes are taken to be the units at the level at which all predictable differences are extracted (hence, for example, the level exemplified by the topmost lines of the derivations (4) and (5)), then the phoneme-grapheme correspondences seem quite simple, by and large—they are very close to one-one, given certain notational conventions and disregarding a class of true exceptions and a set of oddities. On the other hand, if the term "phoneme-grapheme correspondence" is taken to refer to sound-letter correspondences, then the study of such correspondences is, in effect, ordinary phonology. Or, to be more precise, the only reasonable way to study sound-letter correspondences seems to be to acknowledge the fact that orthography corresponds closely to a significant level of linguistic representation that is, furthermore, related to sound by general rules. Thus, to repeat, letters correspond closely to segments of the underlying lexical representations, and the rules that relate these segments to sound are the phonological rules, which are part of the system for producing and understanding ordinary speech. Hence the study of sound-letter correspondences can be divided into three parts: phonology; the systematic (near one-to-one) relations between phonological segments and letters (or conventional letter sequences); and a residue of exceptions (some of which exhibit subregularities of various sort).[5] But the vast central domain of this study is simply investigation of the phonological pattern. For the reasons that have been suggested, this study may have no particular relevance to the teaching of reading, because the processes and principles that it reveals, though of great interest to the study of human cognition, can be presupposed without comment (or understanding) by the teacher of reading.

If this much is correct, then it would seem to follow that the rules of sound-letter correspondence need hardly be taught, particularly, the deepest and most general of these rules. Consider again examples (4) and (5). It would hardly make sense to introduce the beginning reader to such basic principles of sound-letter correspondence as the vowel shift,

---

[5] See footnote 2.

the principles of stress assignment, and so on; nor is there any particular reason why the teacher should be aware of these processes or their detailed properties. These rules, it appears, are part of the unconscious linguistic equipment of the nonliterate speaker. He uses them freely in interpreting what is said to him and forming new utterances, though quite without awareness. What the beginning reader must learn (apart from true exceptions) is simply the elementary correspondence between the underlying segments of his internalized lexicon and the orthographic symbols.

The real interest and importance of the study of phonology—hence the study of sound-letter correspondence, when this notion is properly interpreted—seem to me to lie in a rather different area. Current work suggests that the principles that relate sound and lexicon (more generally sound and surface structure) are in themselves quite interesting and obey some highly restrictive and quite complex conditions. It is difficult to imagine how abstract principles of this sort can be learned. Certainly there is no concept of "induction" or "conditioning" or the like that shows the slightest promise of leading from experience to the postulation of principles of this sort. Therefore, if the linguistic evidence really does show that these principles function in the ordinary use of language, we must conclude that they reflect, in some way, the basic mental endowment that the normal human brings to the problem of language learning, the schematism that enables him to interpret experience and to construct his knowledge of language in a specific way on the basis of the fragmentary evidence available to him. It follows, then, that the principles must be universal; in principle, counterevidence from any language will serve to refute them. Considerations of this sort lead to a host of interesting problems regarding human cognitive processes and their innate basis, but I do not see the direct relevance of these matters to the practical problem of the teaching of reading, except insofar as advances in our understanding of cognitive processes may be informative and suggestive in this domain.

There is, however, one very important qualification that must be added to these remarks. The conventional orthography corresponds closely to a level of representation that seems to be optimal for the sound system of a fairly rich version of standard spoken English. Much of the evidence that determines, for the phonologist, the exact form of this underlying system is based on consideration of learned words and complex derivational patterns. This is clear from the examples presented earlier. Both the derivations (4) and (5) and the examples cited in explaining and commenting on them involve a learned stratum of vocabulary and processes that are based on properties of such items. It is by no means obvious that a child of six has mastered this phonological system in full. He may not yet have been presented with the evidence that determines the general structure of this system. A similar question arises in the case of an adult who is not immersed in the literary culture. It would not be surprising to discover that the child's intuitive organization of the sound system continues to develop and deepen as his vocabulary is enriched and as his use of language extends to wider intellectual domains and more complex functions. Hence, the sound system that corresponds to the orthography may itself be a late intellectual product. Furthermore, we have no understanding of how tentative conclusions about the sound system, constructed by the child at one stage of his development, may affect the interpretation he gives to data and his effort to deepen this analysis as his knowledge of language grows.

What is more, it seems that children are much more attuned to phonetic nuance than adults—they "hear phonetically" rather than "phonologically," to a considerable extent. I have no systematic evidence about this matter, but I have observed a number of cases in which children developing their own alphabet or learning to read insisted on a much narrower representation of the sound than would seem plausible to the adult. To mention one case, my oldest daughter at age five objected to using the same symbol for the two stops in the word *cocoa*. It turned out on investigation that the difference in aspiration between the initial and medial [k], a difference that is barely perceptible to the adult ear, seemed to her sufficiently significant to require a different symbolization. She insisted that the medial stop be represented with the same symbol as the medial [k] of *pumpkin*, not the initial stop of *kitten*, for example. Such reactions suggest that the child, at an early age, is concerned with a level of phonetic detail that is of no interest to the adult. Though this is hardly better than a guess, it is not a particularly surprising one. Thus, it is a familiar observation that children can mimic and can acquire a new pronunciation much more readily than adults, and this ability may be based on their use of a more superficial (narrower) level of organization of the phonetic material.

For various reasons, then, it may turn out that the psychologically real representation for the child changes and deepens with age, approaching the adult phonology with increasing maturity and experience with language. Serious investigation of these questions is far from easy, but it should shed much light on problems of speech perception and production and general problems of how language is used and, perhaps, indirectly on the problems of literacy as well.

For the moment, our understanding of sound structure does not, so far as I can see, lead to any very surprising conclusions regarding the problems of literacy or teaching of reading. It may very well be that one of the best ways to teach reading is to enrich the child's vocabulary, so that he constructs for himself the deeper representations of sound that correspond so closely to the orthographic forms. At the earliest stages, one would obviously make use of materials that do not involve abstract processes and do not depart too far from the surface phonetics. Beyond such relative banalities, I do not see what concrete conclusions can be drawn, for the teaching of reading, from the study of sound structure, although, as noted, this study may have profound implications for human psychology.

This work was supported in part by the U.S. Air Force (ESD Contract AF19(628)–2487) and the National Institutes of Health (Grant MH–13390–01).

REFERENCES

Chomsky, N. *Current Issues in Linguistic Theory.* The Hague: Mouton, 1964.

Chomsky, N. Some general properties of phonological rules. *Language,* 1967, *43,* 102–128.

Chomsky, N., & Halle, M. *Sound Pattern of English.* New York: Harper & Row, 1968.

Postal, P. *Aspects of Phonological Theory.* New York: Harper & Row, 1968.

2 DAVID W. REED

Linguistic Forms and the Process of Reading

In order to discuss reading from a linguistic point of view, it is important to distinguish between the elementary aspects of reading (termed here "the process of reading") and what reading specialists are accustomed to think of as more advanced aspects of the same subject (which may be termed "the uses of reading"). Children with normal physical and mental capacity, whose sociocultural backgrounds are not severely disadvantaged, ought to master the process of reading by the end of their second year in school. That is to say, such children ought to be able by that time to identify, through viewing the graphic symbols by which linguistic forms are conventionally represented in writing, all the linguistic forms that they can identify through hearing the phonological symbols by which the same forms are represented in speech. In contrast, no one fully masters the uses of reading in a lifetime devoted to that discipline. The uses of reading and, indeed, the uses of speech are concerned with the enlargement of one's knowledge of the universe, of himself, and of the language in which these kinds of knowledge are embodied and communicated. In this chapter, I shall be concerned exclusively with the process rather than the uses of reading.

The process of reading was defined above, by implication, as the identification of linguistic forms through viewing the graphic symbols by which they are conventionally represented in a given language. To appreciate this definition fully, it will be necessary to secure a more precise notion of the nature of linguistic forms and of the writing system by which

19

they are represented in English. I have borrowed the term "linguistic form" from Leonard Bloomfield's *Language* (1933, pp. 158 ff.). Bloomfield defined linguistic forms as the grammatical units of a language, consisting of morphemes (the smallest meaningful units) and what he called taxemes of order, selection (primarily of form classes and constructions), phonetic modification (by which the forms of the morphemes are modified when they enter into combination with other morphemes), and modulation (that is, intonation). The Bloomfieldian analysis of grammar is now recognized to be unworkable in several important respects, but it seems to be possible to rescue the concept of linguistic forms and apply it to any mode of grammatical analysis that is currently in favor.

Thus, in generative-transformational grammar, the linguistic forms are elements of the deep structure of a language and consist of (1) the nodes, such as NP and VP, that are represented in a tree diagram of a sentence, (2) lexical formatives, such as *boy*, or *recite*, which correspond fairly well to the class of simple and derived words of structural linguistics, and (3) grammatical formatives, such as "perfect" or "question," which resemble inflection plus some of the taxemes in the Bloomfieldian model.

To illustrate what has been said about the process of reading as identification of linguistic forms such as those listed above, let us consider what it means to read the sentence *Does the boy recite the poem?* To read such a sentence is to determine from the graphic symbols by which it is represented that the sentence has the deep structure shown in Figure 2–1.

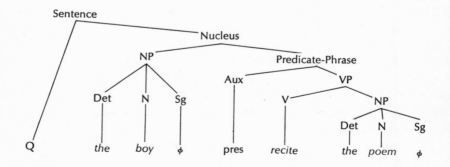

Figure 2–1

* The system of symbolization employed here is like that in Katz and Postal (1964) and in Chomsky (1965).

To state the matter more conventionally, one who reads this sentence must identify at least the following linguistic facts that underlie it: (1) that the sentence is a question, (2) that the sentence consists of a subject and a predicate, (3) that the subject is definite and singular, (4) that the predicate is present tense, (5) that the predicate consists of a verb and a direct object, (6) that the direct object is definite and singular, and (7) that the lexical formatives *boy, recite,* and *poem* derive from the subject, the verb, and the direct object respectively.

It would be well to observe at this point that, although the elements of deep structure identified above are closely associated with the meaning of the sentence, they are not elements of meaning. "Question," for example, is a linguistic form rather than a meaning. The meaning might be paraphrased somewhat as follows: "This sentence asks for a linguistic response of *yes* or *no* or some qualified type of affirmation or negation" (in contrast to declarative sentences, which merely ask for evidence that the hearer is attending—*I see, well,* and so on—and also in contrast to imperative sentences, which ask for some type of practical action rather than for a purely linguistic response). A linguistic form such as "question" serves to link a meaning of the sort paraphrased above to a set of directions or rules for representing the form in the concrete symbols of speech or writing.

Reading specialists have for a long time attempted to explain reading exclusively in terms of meanings and the concrete symbols of speech and writing. This has led to the extreme of "look-say," in which reading is defined as getting meaning from written symbols, or to the opposite extreme of "phonics," in which reading is defined as associating written and spoken symbols. Without the mediation of linguistic forms, the process of reading will never be correctly understood.

The output of the deep structure for the sentence symbolized by the tree diagram (Figure 2–1) is "Q *the boy* ø pres *recite the poem* ø." Obviously, certain changes must be introduced into the sentence before it attains the surface form with which we are familiar in speech or in writing. One set of changes underlying both speech and writing comprises the grammatical transformations. After these changes have been effected, phonological rules will convert the terminal string into a spoken sentence or orthographic rules will convert it into a written sentence.

Grammatical transformations are obligatory, given certain deep structures. Thus, the presence of Q in the deep structure of the illustrative sentence requires inversion of the elements deriving from NP (*the boy* ø) with the initial element(s) deriving from Aux (in the illustrative sentence, "pres" is the only derivative of Aux). Thus, the Q transformation produces "Q pres *the boy ø recite the poem ø*." Further transformations delete the element Q; supply *do* because "pres" does not occur immediately before a verb, *be, have,* or a modal auxiliary; replace "pres" with -*s* in the context N Sg; and delete the two elements ø. These changes produce the terminal grammatical string *do-s the boy recite the poem.* Working on this output of the grammar, the phonological rules produce the correct pronunciation (including intonation) of the sentence, or, alternatively, the orthographic rules produce the correct spelling (including punctuation and capitalization).

Three sets of interesting problems remain to be discussed regarding the process of reading: (1) What evidence can one give that he has read a sentence? (2) What clues are present in the written form of a sentence like the example given above that enable the reader to identify the nodes and grammatical formatives in the tree diagram (Figure 2–1)? (3) How are the letters of the orthographic system related to the lexical and grammatical formatives, which may in turn be represented by phonetic features in speech?

As to the first question, the only evidence that I can think of that demonstrates the reading of a sentence is the representation of that same sentence in some other symbol system. For the ordinary reader, this would mean "reading aloud"—that is, reencoding the sentence in the symbols of speech. For deaf mutes, to whom the symbols of speech are not available, evidence of reading might be given by reencoding in the gesture system employed by the deaf. Other readers with different impairments might make still different reencodings.

These considerations call for a brief digression on the differences between reading and understanding—a difference that is closely linked to the distinction between linguistic forms and meaning. It is easy to imagine a sentence that one can read adequately without understanding it. Most people can even compose such sentences. Here is an example, composed on the spot: *Space is finite and curved, but unbounded and constantly expanding.* Notice that when I say I can compose and read such a sentence without understanding it, I am claiming far greater competence than that of a phonograph needle that reacts in a predictable, mechanical way to the grooves of a record, or than that of a parrot who might be trained to mimic the same sentence perfectly. I am saying that I can give a reasonably detailed analysis of the syntax and word composition of this sentence according to any of several systems that may be selected and give dictionary-type definitions of all the words.

Most native speakers of English who are not linguists would possess all or most of this knowledge intuitively, but might be unable to discuss it. Both the linguist and the nonlinguist native speaker can read the sentence without understanding it, as witnessed by their inability to discuss its content in a way that would be remotely satisfactory to a physicist.

The second set of problems is of more general interest and is often not recognized for what it is: how does the reader identify the nodes and grammatical formatives from a written sentence? For example, if a child reads every word in a sentence as if it were an item in a list, a linguist would say that he has not identified such linguistic forms as noun phrases, verb phrases, and sentence adverbials. Reading teachers seem to make one of two assumptions: either that the problem is one of elocution, in which case the child will be exhorted to "read more naturally" or to "read the words as if talking to a friend," or else that the problem is one of understanding, in which case the advice will be to "think what the words mean as you read." Both these assumptions are correct so far as they go. The child's oral reading is faulty as regards intonation, and he probably has failed to understand any sentence that he reads as if it were a list of syntactically unrelated items. But both these facts are merely superficial symptoms of an underlying cause—failure to identify linguistic forms.

Linguistic forms are often signaled differently in speech and in writing. Sometimes a structure is signaled consistently in one mode of representation but not in the other. Let us take as an example the English question. All adult speakers of English will acknowledge that some English sentences are questions—that is, sentences that require a different kind of response from statements, commands, and exclamations. Therefore, it is essential to be able to identify those sentences that are questions, whether one is listening to spoken English or reading written English. In reading a sentence aloud, one must be able first to determine from graphic signs whether or not it is a question; then he must, assuming that it is a question, be able to encode this information into suitable phonetic signals as he reads. At the heart of the matter is the recognition of the question as a linguistic form. Secondary are the associated graphic and phonetic signals.

Let us consider how the fact that a sentence is a question is signaled in English writing and speech. First, because words almost always occur in the same order in both systems of representation, most devices of word order are the same in both. (One type of exception is *$5.00,* which is read *five dollars.*) Most English questions employ one of the following devices: (1) Inversion of subject and auxiliary (or a finite form of *be* or *have*): *Is the boy hitting the ball?* (2) Insertion of *do* before the subject: *Does the boy hit the ball?* (3) Replacement of the subject with *who* or *what: Who hits the ball? What causes rain?* (4) Replacement of modifiers of the subject with *which* or *what: Which* (or *What) boy hit the ball?* (5) Replacement of an element other than the subject by a word beginning with *wh-* (also how). The *wh-* word then begins the sentence and the auxiliary (or a finite form of *be* or *have*) is inverted with the subject, or else *do* is inserted before the subject: *What is the boy hitting? What does the boy hit? When does the boy hit the ball?* and so forth. It is interesting to note that with three rather unimportant exceptions, one is able to determine from the first two words of spoken or written English whether or not a sentence is one of these five types of question. That is to say, sentences that begin either with an auxiliary or a finite form of *be* or *have* followed by a noun phrase (the beginning of which is always consistently signaled) or else with a *wh-* word followed by an auxiliary or a verb are almost always questions.

These definitive beginnings of questions might be diagrammed as

Table 2–1.

FIRST ELEMENT	SECOND ELEMENT
$\left\{\begin{array}{l}\text{Aux}\\ do \\ be \\ have\end{array}\right\}$	NP
$\left\{\left.\begin{array}{l}\left\{\begin{array}{l}which\\ what\end{array}\right\}+\text{NP}\\ \text{other } wh\text{- word}\\ how\end{array}\right\}\right.$	$\left\{\begin{array}{l}\text{Aux}\\ do \\ be \\ have \\ \text{V}\end{array}\right\}$

shown in Table 2–1. The first of the three minor exceptions to this diagram that I have encountered is when the sentence begins with a directly quoted question, or in grammatical terms, when an initial clause that is a question is embedded in a main clause that is not. For example,

"Who hit the ball?" he asked. In writing, the fact that the whole sentence is not a question is immediately signaled by the opening set of quotation marks. In speech, this fact is not signaled until the word *he* is reached. Then, if the question clause is imbedded in a main clause, *he* begins on the same pitch level with which *ball* ended (that is, pitch 1, or the lowest pitch, for the example sentence and all other questions of types 3, 4, and 5 above, but normally pitch 3, high pitch, for questions of types 1 and 2 above). If, however, *he* begins a new sentence, it gets a different pitch (level 2), which is the normal starting point for sentences. *"²Who hit the ³ball¹?" ¹he asked.¹* and *²Who hit the ³ball¹? ²He didn't ³know.¹* A doctoral dissertation by Samuel Stone (1961) under the direction of Walter Loban at Berkeley several years ago demonstrated that if these two utterances are pronounced naturally and recorded on tape, and then everything after *he* is erased from both utterances, tenth-grade children can unerringly determine whether or not *he* begins a new sentence. It should also be noted that in normal speech there is no difference in the length of pause between the two utterances.

The second minor exception to the observation that a native speaker can identify sentences as questions after hearing or reading the first two words occurs only with the questions of types 3 and 4 above—questions in which the subject is replaced by *who* or *what* or else a modifier of the subject is replaced by *which* or *what*. Sentences beginning in this manner may have the initial clause imbedded as an indirect question in a main clause—for example, *Who hit the ball is of no consequence. Which boy hit the ball is unimportant.* In listening to speech, one cannot tell until he hears the intonation of *ball* whether or not the first clause is an independent question. If the pitch drops all the way to level 1 (characteristic of sentence endings), the clause is an independent question. If it drops only to pitch level 2 (characteristic of the ending of sentence parts), the clause is an indirect question imbedded in a main clause. In reading, one must wait to see whether there is a question mark, on the one hand, or a verb or an auxiliary, on the other, to know whether the first clause is an independent question or an indirect question imbedded in a main clause. The very infrequent occurrence of this postponed identification of the sentence as a question is seen in the fact that postponement is not necessary for questions of types 1, 2, and 5. With types 1 and 2, the independent question begins with an auxiliary or a finite form of *be, have,* or *do.* The corresponding indirect questions imbedded in main clauses begin with *whether.* Thus, *Can the boy hit the ball?* but, *Whether the boy can hit the ball is doubtful.* In independent questions of type 5, the *wh-* word is followed immediately by an auxiliary or a finite form of *be, have,* or *do.* The corresponding indirect questions begin with a *wh-* word followed by the subject. Thus, *What did the boy hit?* but *What the boy hit is unimportant.*

The third and final minor exception to the ability of the native speaker to identify questions after hearing or reading the first two words occurs in sentences beginning with *do* or *have* (but not with other inflected forms of these words) followed by a noun phrase headed by a plural noun (but not a pronoun). Certain commands may begin in the same way. *Do your lessons seem difficult?* vs. *Do your lessons.* In such cases it is necessary to postpone identification of the sentence type until it is noted whether the noun phrase is followed by a verb (in which case the sentence is a question) or whether it ends the sentence or is followed by something not a verb (in which case the sentence is a command). A more elaborate diagram (Table 2–2) will provide for these exceptional cases.

Table 2–2.*

FIRST ELEMENT	SECOND ELEMENT	INTONATION (OR) PUNCTUATION

$$\left\{ \begin{array}{l} \left\{ \begin{array}{l} \text{Aux} \\ \left\{ \begin{array}{l} be \\ do \\ have \end{array} \right\} \left\{ \begin{array}{l} -s \\ \text{past} \end{array} \right\} \text{NP} \\[6pt] \left\{ \begin{array}{l} do \\ have \end{array} \right\} \qquad \phi \qquad \text{Npl} + \text{V} \\[10pt] \left\{ \begin{array}{l} who \\ what \quad (\text{NP}) \\ which + \text{NP} \end{array} \right\} \left\{ \begin{array}{l} \text{Aux} \\ do \\ be \\ have \\ \text{V} \end{array} \right\} \text{Pitch } 1\# \\[14pt] \left\{ \begin{array}{l} \text{other } wh\text{- word} \\ \\ how \end{array} \right\} \left\{ \begin{array}{l} \text{Aux} \\ do \\ be \\ have \\ \text{V} \end{array} \right\} \end{array} \right\} \left\{ \begin{array}{l} +\alpha \text{ Pitch}\# - \alpha \text{ Pitch} \\ \text{Pitch } 3\# \text{ Pitch } 31 \end{array} \right\} \#-\text{``}-\text{''} + ?\#$$

* The α refers to any particular pitch. The notation "$+\alpha$ Pitch $-\alpha$ Pitch" means that if a particular pitch occurs before a clause boundary, the pitch immediately following the boundary must be different—that is, not α. The formula for punctuation is to be read, "quotation marks may not follow the initial clause boundary nor precede the final clause boundary, but a question mark must precede the final boundary."

We have now seen that, both in listening to spoken English and in reading, it is possible in most cases to identify these types of sentences as questions (which probably account for 99 per cent of all English questions) solely on a basis of word order and usually after noting the first two words. Only rarely is it necessary to resort to punctuation or intonation, although these devices are often present as redundant features that permit identification of questions if the word order cues have been overlooked.

Before leaving the subject of question identification, it would be well to examine the function of punctuation and intonation and their interrelations, which are by no means as simple as is often supposed. The function of the question mark in written English, however, is simple and straightforward. The question mark is used at the end of independent questions and, along with quotation marks, at the end of directly quoted questions imbedded in major clauses. It is not used at the end of any other type of sentence or clause, including indirect questions. The function of intonation is a trifle more complicated. The general public as well as English and reading teachers often suppose that any sentence or clause punctuated with a question mark is read with rising intonation. This is most emphatically not the case. Questions beginning with *wh*-words (types 3, 4, and 5) are normally read with falling intonation in all dialects with which I am familiar. Questions of types 1 and 2—those that may be answered *yes* or *no*—are read with rising intonations by most speakers of American English, but again with falling intonation by a majority of speakers in the northern Midwest. In these yes-or-no questions, intonation may also be used nongrammatically to express the attitude of the speaker toward the situation about which he is communicating. Thus, in most of the country, the use of falling intonation on a yes-or-no question is considered brusque. Northern Midwesterners are often taken to be impolite in other parts of the country when they use their normal intonation on these questions. Conversely, rising intonation on yes-or-no questions in the northern Midwest is used to express hesitancy or tentativeness, and auslanders who use it normally are considered to lack self-confidence.

Finally, the question mark in writing and rising intonation in speech may be used to convert sentences that are not otherwise yes-or-no questions into yes-or-no questions. For example, *The boy hit the ball?* Such questions usually mean something like *Did you say that* . . . or *Do you mean that* . . . or even *Would this be an example?* In speech, rising intonation may also be used with questions that normally require falling intonation to convey a similar added meaning. Thus, *Who hit the ball?* with rising intonation may mean *Did you ask who hit the ball?* Because such sentences are already punctuated with question marks, there is no simple graphic device for them that corresponds to rising intonation. To communicate the same meaning in writing, one must write something like *Did you ask who hit the ball?*

I hope that this long excursion into the problem of how listeners and readers identify questions will have served to reinforce certain observations already made under the heading of linguistic forms. First, the question is a linguistic form. In asking whether a person can read English we want to know, among other things, whether he can identify questions from the clues he finds in writing, as evidenced by his use of oral intonation patterns that he has already learned are associated with questions in speech. Second, it would be fruitless to try to make direct connections between punctuation and intonation, because such connections as exist do so indirectly through the fact that both punctuation and intonation are devices employed in different ways to represent questions.

The third and final set of problems with which I set out to deal concerns the relationship of the lexical and grammatical formatives to the orthographic and phonological systems. Because I have treated this subject in some detail elsewhere (Reed, 1965), the discussion that follows will be in the nature of a summary. Just as we have seen in the case of intonation and punctuation, the letters of the alphabet and the sounds of speech represent linguistic forms (lexical and grammatical formatives) rather than being directly related to one another. The letters of the alphabet are clearly segmented and sequential in nature, although some devices of writing, such as capitalization and italics, may be thought of as simultaneous components or features. The sounds of speech, on the other hand, are best analyzed as consisting of simultaneous components or distinctive features, but may, with some loss of economy, be analyzed as segments. Because we wish to drive both speech and writing from lexical and grammatical formatives, it seems best to treat these linguistic forms as composed of segments. The procedure, then, is to postulate for each formative in the language a segmental structure from which writing and at least the major dialectal varieties of speech can be derived by application of the smallest possible number of rules.

The segments of which linguistic forms are ultimately composed, which I have termed "linguons" elsewhere (Reed, 1965), are more abstract than phonemes, being at one and the same time morphophonemic and diaphonemic. The first of these characteristics implies, for example, that the second syllables of *nasal, rebel, civil, Mongol,* and *cherub* contain five different linguons—even though they are all pronounced /ə/ in most dialects—in order to account for the stressed pronunciations of these vowels in the related words *nasality, rebellion, civilian, Mongolian,* and *cherubic.* The diaphonemic characteristic of linguons may be illustrated by the composition of the words *cart, cot, caught.* In some dialects, like that of western Pennsylvania, these words are all pronounced with the same vowel. In the majority of American dialects two different vowels are employed; but in some dialects *cart* and *cot* have the same vowel, whereas in others *cot* and *caught* have the same vowel. In Standard Southern British, three different vowels are used in these three words. The words therefore have three different vowel linguons, because it is much simpler to devise rules that will produce coalescence of classes for the American dialects than it is to devise rules that will differentiate classes for Southern British. An extra dividend from the linguon approach to both morphophonemic and diaphonemic variation is that linguons correspond more closely to spelling than the phonemes of any dialect would.

It seems indisputable that the concept of linguistic forms, separate from meaning and from the concrete symbols of speech and writing, can clarify the relationships among meaning, speech, and writing and serve as a useful tool for research in the process of reading.

REFERENCES

Bloomfield, L. *Language.* New York: Henry Holt, 1933.

Chomsky, N. *Aspects of the Theory of Syntax.* Cambridge, Mass.: M.I.T. Press, 1965.

Katz, J. J., & Postal, P. M. *An Integrated Theory of Linguistic Descriptions,* Research Monograph No. 26. Cambridge, Mass.: M.I.T. Press, 1964.

Reed, D. W. A theory of language, speech, and writing. *Elementary English,* 1965, *42,* 845–851.

Stone, S. B. A structural comparison of the speech and writing of selected average tenth grade pupils. Doctoral dissertation, University of California, Berkeley, 1961.

3 RICHARD L. VENEZKY

Regularity in Reading and Spelling

A craving for order has characterized man's intellectual appetite from as far back in time as man's thoughts can be traced. Hesiod's Greek cosmogony placed the beginning of all things in the formless, inpenetrable darkness of chaos, from which order rather violently evolved. Ancient and modern astronomers have labored over the cosmic confusion, imposing order with cycles and epicycles, spheres, elipses, and negative space curvatures, but still several minutes of an arc of disorder remain, and there are many sleepless nights on account of it.

For the linguist, order is judged by the elusive measure of regularity, making the most prized trophy of any philological foray a demonstration of order rescued from the debris of irregularity. Grimm, in positing a regular relationship between the sounds of various Indo-European languages, brought a semblance of order out of many centuries of chaos, but still left a substantial marginal mess for Verner and others. The concept advanced by Chomsky of a finite set of generative patterns for deriving an infinite set of sentences imposed a higher degree of theoretical regularity on language capabilities than had existed previously. And the isolation of acoustical correlates of speech by Liberman and others at the Haskins Laboratories (Liberman, 1957) further orders a previously chaotic system. What is regular in one system may be irregular in another, and what one analyst sees as order, another sees as disorder. This results not so much from such problems as the nonuniqueness of phonemic solutions or the varying tenets of different models of language as it does from elusiveness of the concept of "regularity."

30

The remainder of this chapter concerns the designation of regularity—especially as it applies to the selection of regularly and irregularly spelled words for the teaching of reading. Because English orthography is both phonemically and morphemically based, not only graphemic patterns, but also morphophonemic and phonemic patterns will be considered. Once the terms "regular" and "irregular" are properly pilloried, a more practical classification scheme is offered.

Attempts to define linguistic regularity have appealed either to the internal structure of the linguist's description or to the (assumed) language processing habits of the native speaker. Harris (1951) defined descriptive linguistics as a search for regularities, but only hinted at how one separated the regular from the irregular.

> Descriptive linguistics, as the term has come to be used, is a particular field of enquiry which deals not with the whole of speech activities, but with the regularities in certain features of speech. These régularities are in the distributional relations among the features of speech in question, i.e., the occurrence of these features relatively to each other within utterances (p. 5).

Earlier, Jespersen (1965) had invoked human language processing for defining formulas and free expressions—concepts that were linked to the classes of regular and irregular.

> While in handling formulas memory, or the repetition of what one has once learned, is everything, free expressions involve another kind of mental activity; they have to be created in each case anew by the speaker, who inserts the words that fit the particular situation (p. 19).

Formulas are whole, petrified units such as *How do you do?*, retrieved intact from memory rather than being generated by productive rules or habits from their components, whereas free expressions are the result of applying a rule or series of rules, and, according to Jespersen, "always show a regular formation" (p. 24). That this dichotomy might engender some difficulty for the analyst was admitted by Jespersen, but somehow he felt that careful scrutiny would solve all: "[I]t follows that the distinction between them [free expressions] and formulas cannot always be discovered except through a fairly close analysis" (p. 20). But if we accept the definition that free expressions are "created in each case anew by the speaker . . ." then it is not analysis that is required, but experimentation—somehow we must lift the cranial carapace, expose the mental activities to view, and observe whether units are being switched directly from memory to output channels or whether there is a more complex shuffling and joining of separate building blocks into wholes.[1] Analysis can lead to hypotheses about which utterances could be free expressions, but direct observation of production itself is necessary to be strictly in line with Jespersen's classification. Even Bloomfield (1933), the archantagonist of neuronal explication, brushed dangerously close to the cerebral cortex in defining regular and irregular forms.

> [W]e may say that any form which a speaker can utter without having heard it, is regular in its immediate constitution and embodies regular functions of its constituents, and any form which a speaker can utter only after he has heard it from other speakers, is irregular (p. 274).

As examples of the application of this definition, Bloomfield cites the formations of the regular plural *foxes* and the irregular plural *oxen*. Bloomfield no doubt meant by *can utter* the phrase 'has the capability to utter', but even this is an extension of the linguist's analysis to the mind of the speaker (an accusation that no doubt would have rapidly elevated Bloomfield's blood pressure). In reality, the mature native speaker cannot utter (or, 'does not have the capability to utter') the plural of any noun until he has heard some other speaker produce the plural, assuming that *utter* implies 'produce with certainty of correctness' and not just 'produce'. Given that the speaker knows one irregular noun plural, then he can never be certain that another irregular noun plural will not occur, hence, though we may assume that the native speaker will tend to respond in accord with the regular forms, we cannot assert

---

[1] Experiments such as those devised by J. Berko (1958) for exploring the child's morphological patterns could not be applied here. Assume that the noun /wʌg/ was input to a speaking mechanism (human or not), the "plural" button pushed, and out came /wʌgz/. What does this show? If the mechanism had never heard /wʌg/ before, we might claim (especially if we had positive results for a large corpus of synthetic nouns) that the mechanism possessed a rule for forming the so-called regular noun plural—and that the mechanism applied this rule to all unfamiliar nouns. But we could not assume that the production of a familiar plural noun such as /bʌgz/ was a result of the rule application rather than memory. At some point, the mechanism will encounter irregular nouns, which implies that memory of particular words must play some part in pluralization because now the plural rule can be applied only to a nonexhaustive and unpredictable list of nouns.

that he will respond this way without making inferences about his language-processing strategies.[2]

If we insist that *can utter* means only 'possesses a rule for uttering', then we face the dilemma of deciding what rules a native speaker possesses. To claim that the native speaker possesses all rules that the linguist can describe as regular vitiates the original definition in that now regular forms are those that the analyst calls regular, and the speaker is removed from the loop. On the other hand, claiming that the only forms that a speaker can't utter are those that he has no previous experience for basing his utterance on, such as the plural of *ox*, leads to contradictions, at least for Bloomfield. The alternation of /f/ to /v/ in the plurals of *knife, wife,* and the like would become regular because the speaker could (conceivably) possess a rule for this alternation, assuming that he were told when to apply it (just as he must be told when to apply the noun plural rule, because exceptions exist). But Bloomfield calls this specific alternation "irregular" (1933, p. 214).

Hockett (1958, p. 280), like most other present-day linguists, appeals to linguistic description in the person of frequency: "[A]n alternation is regular if it is what occurs most frequently under stated conditions, any other alternation which occasionally occurs under the same conditions then being irregular." There are two problems in attempting to apply this definition. First, what constitutes a legitimate "stated condition"?—a problem to be discussed shortly. And second, what does one count to arrive at "frequency"? On this latter problem, observe the Modern English pronunciations of the words *hideous, idiot, Indian, median, palladium,* and *perfidious* in which there is no palatalization of [dj] or [di] to [ǰ], as there generally is in *cordial* and *soldier.* This palatalization has taken place almost invariably, however, before unstressed [ju] and [iu], as, for example, in *individual* and *residual.*[3] The simplest rule to cover these words, assuming they are representative of [di] and [dj] sequences, would be to assign the *hideous, idiot,* and

---

[2] Everywhere else in Bloomfield's writings regularity is defined in relation to the analyst's description, for example, "a set of forms that is not covered by a general statement, but has to be presented in the shape of a list, is said to be irregular" (1933, p. 213) and "since the distribution of the three alternates [noun plural, *-s, -z, -Iz*] is regulated according to a linguistically recognizable characteristic of the accompanying forms, we say that the alternation is regular" (1933, p. 211).

[3] Exceptions are *produce* (N), which probably has been influenced by *produce* (V), where the stress on [u] prevents palatalization, and *mature,* which has shifted stress after palatalization.

so forth and the *arduous, educate,* and so forth groups to the regular class and label *cordial* and *soldier* as irregular, that is, to assume that palatalization of [d] defore unstressed [iu] and [ju] is regular and any other [d] palatalization is irregular. This is justified on the basis of frequency: two irregular forms—*cordial* and *soldier*—and several handfuls of regular forms.

If, on the other hand, the entire series of palatalizations that occur in English are included in the tally, a different separation of regular and irregular results. Consider the word lists below in which [sj] → [š], [zj] → [ž], and [tj] → [č] have taken place.

[š]	[ž]	[č]
atrocious	abrasion	bastion
controversial	ambrosia	celestial
cynosure	aphasia	creature
issue	measure	fatuous
nation	pleasure	mutual
nauseous	usual	question

In the company of these forms, *cordial* and *soldier* represent the regular result, whereas *hideous, idiot,* and so on represent the irregular. Even if the connection between the [s,z] and the [t,d] palatalizations is rejected, the combined frequencies of [t,d] palatalizations would still leave *cordial* and *soldier* as regular forms.

From the linguist's vantage point, the more general solution is preferred, assuming that such blanket coverage can be justified by more than aesthetic appeals. This appears to be the situation here where an articulatory link between the [s,z] and [t,d] palatalizations exists.

If defining regularity has been difficult for linguists, it has been impossible for educators, even though many prescriptions for inducing proper reading behavior in the young depend upon a precise division of the regular and the irregular words in terms of their spellings. Clarence L. Barnhart (1967) summarized the need for regularity in what he and Bloomfield advanced as the "linguistic" approach to reading instruction:

> Advocates of a linguistic method, then, assume that the first task is to break the alphabetical code and grade words according to their phonetic difficulty, not their semantic difficulty. They control spelling patterns so that only regular patterns are presented in lists and in reading; after the regular patterns are learned, the irregular spellings are grouped and introduced in patterns (p. 117).

Affording primary attention to regularly spelled words, however, did not originate with twentieth-century linguistics. In a recent survey of the history of reading instruction, M. M. Mathews (1966) points out several nineteenth-century regularists, starting with the Alsatian Joseph Neef in 1813. Exactly what a "regular" word is seldom finds discussion in educational tracts, yet educators have had no reluctance in making rather exact estimates of the number of regularly spelled words in the English language.[4] The purpose of the remainder of this section is to present some of the problems that occur in applying the labels "regular" and "irregular" to English words. Both reading and spelling will be considered here. Later, a classification scheme more befitting the nature of English orthography is produced.

The first problem is to decide regularity for what: reading or spelling—or both? Geminate consonant clusters in *ebb, add, odd, inn, boycott, butt, mitt, putt,* and *watt* are regular for reading; they are pronounced the same as single consonants in these positions. Yet for spelling they are irregular, because *b, d, n,* and *t* typically do not double at the end of words. (The appeal here is to frequency: *b, d, n,* and *t* do not double at the end of any other nonproper nouns in the Thorndike-Lorge 20,000 word list.) *Dove, glove, love, shove* and *cove, rove,* and so on are irregular for reading because the pronunciation of *o* before *v* cannot be predicted. At best, the irregular group can be reduced to *dove, glove, love, shove,* and a few others because these words disobey the final *-e* pattern (Venezky, 1967). Yet, for spelling, there are invokable and not entirely ad hoc rules for these spellings:

1. Stressed [ə] before [v] is most often spelled *o*; [o] before /v/ is spelled *o*.

2. *v* (which spells [v], making *of* irregular) does not double (thereby making *navvy, flivver,* and *divvy* irregular).

3. Where *v* would otherwise occur in final position in a word, place an *e* after it.

Oyster is another example in reading regularity, but spelling disaster.

---

[4] The percentage of regularly spelled words in English, like the price of beer, has been creeping upward for years, although no perceptible change in English orthography has occurred during this same period. Jean S. and Paul R. Hanna started with 80 per cent regularity (1959), then upped the ante to 90 per cent (1965). Recently, Axel Wijk (1966) bumped the Hannas by five percentage points, claiming that "the vast majority of English words, about 90–95 per cent of the total vocabulary, do in fact follow regular patterns in regard to their spelling and pronunciation" (p. 8). Spelling reformers, no doubt, view this educational cabalism with increasing alarm.

Oi and *oy* are both pronounced /oi/ so that in reading no irregularity is aroused by the *oy* in *oyster;* for spelling, *oy* is irregular, because *oi* almost invariably occurs before consonants, *oy* in all other positions.

Second on the problem list is the criterion for regularity. Is frequency alone sufficient—and if so, what is to be counted? Or should predictability be considered—and if so, what constitutes legitimate predictability? Assume first that frequency of occurrence is a primary factor. *Ch* has three pronunciations in English: [č] as in *chief,* [š] as in *chef,* and [k] in *echo.* In the Thorndike-Lorge 20,000 word list, approximately 62 per cent of the *ch* spellings are pronounced [č], 26 per cent [k], and 12 per cent [š]. Does this imply that 62 per cent of the *ch* spellings are regular and 38 per cent are irregular? How does a reader know when he looks at a word with a *ch* spelling that the word is regular or irregular? Furthermore, shouldn't a [š] pronunciation at only 12 per cent be more irregular than a [k] pronunciation at 26 per cent? Furthermore—and more crucial to the regularity decision—should types or tokens be considered in evaluating regularity? The figures cited above are obtained by assigning equal weight to every word that contains *ch,* regardless of that word's popularity in present-day English. Should special weight be given to the more frequently occurring words?

This argument could be crucial in some instances, as, for example, in the pronunciations of medial *ch,* assuming that frequency could share equal importance with position. [č], although the most frequent pronunciation for *ch* in total occurrences, actually trails the [š] pronunciation in medial position by many percentage points. However, the medial *ch* → [š] words are considerably rarer than the medial *ch* → [č] words (*cliché, crochet, sachet,* and so on vs. *achieve, archer, merchant,* and the like).

If, on the other hand, regularity is to be judged by predictability, the basis of prediction—Hockett's "stated conditions"—then becomes the stumbling block. In the *ch* words, for example, a familiar orthographic bromide assigns the French words to [š], the Greek words to [k] and the unadulterated American forms to [č].[5] But how is the child to know, faced for the first time by one of these formidable letter strings, whence the word's original citizenship? For the trained etymologist, this may be a basis for predicting pronunciation, but for the reader it is not.

---

[5] This is not strictly true. Most words borrowed from French before the French sound shift of [č] to [š] retain the ch → [č] pattern. *Chief* and *chef,* for example, are derived from the same French root, *chief* being borrowed into English before the [č] → [š] shift and *chef* after. In addition, *arch-,* ultimately from Greek, has [k] in *archangel,* but [č] elsewhere (for example, *arch, archbishop, archenemy*).

Language origin, therefore, is inadmissable evidence for operational predictability. What about syllable divisions? One of America's best dictionaries (Webster, 1956) gives as a guide to the perplexed reader the following advice: "*b* is usually silent after *m* in the same syllable, as in *bomb, climb, thumb,* etc." How is one who has not seen or heard such words as *bomber, bombard, thimble,* and *amber* going to syllabify these forms correctly from their spellings? There is no rule in his speaker's intuition that would select [bám ó] over [bám bó], but [æ mbó] over [ǽ m ó]. In other words, the "same syllable" is not a rule for correlating spelling to sound, but rather a statement of English phonotactics. Furthermore, English phonology is notorious for its ambulatory syllable boundaries. In *keeper,* for example, the syllable break, if it occurs, can be before the [p] or after it. (Most often in fast speech [p] in *keeper* is an interlude linking the nucleus of the first syllable with nucleus of the second—*sans* break.)

Prediction rules based on syllable breaks simply cannot be applied to many English words. (This is not to say that some syllable boundaries cannot be predicted from spelling. Intervocalic consonant clusters that cannot be word initial or word final, for example, obviously must be split between the preceding and succeeding syllables, as in *grandpa.*)

Stress, another candidate for predictor, is an extremely complex factor to assess. There are certain preferred stress patterns in English, so that by frequency alone stress could be predicted with some calculable (and high) probability of success. To predict stress exactly, however, where no stress-fixing prefixes or suffixes occur (such as *-ity*) requires in many situations a knowledge of word origin, and this has already been rejected as a predictor.

This does not leave a whole lot, assuming that the ground rules require, at least for reading, that sound be predicted from the graphemic form of the word, in the absence of any knowledge based on that particular word as a whole. This means that rules for prediction must not include lists of words to which the particular rules apply (or do not apply). Such rules might state that a letter in a particular word position has a particular pronunciation or that a letter has one pronunciation before certain letters and another before all others, but not that letter *x* in word *y* is to be pronounced as *z*. There is a dilemma even here, however. Consider the rules for the letter *f*. In all its occurrences in English words, except for one (*of*), *f* is pronounced [f]. (*ff* can be handled by a general rule for leveling geminate clusters.) The rule for pronouncing *f*, therefore, is (in appropriate shorthand) "*f*→[f] except in *of* and its compounds, where $f\to$[v]." But now a word list is included and we no longer have, by the arguments adduced above, a legitimate predictor of pronunciation. One cannot predict the pronunciation of f until he checks whether or not he is dealing with *of* or one of its compounds. The path out of this entanglement is to have two ordered rules, the first stating that f in *of* is [v], the second covering everything else. Reality is not altered, but by assuming prior elimination of exceptions, all sorts of things can be made to appear regular.

In the next section, differences within the so-called regular and irregular patterns are discussed, and finally a new classification scheme for spelling-to-sound and sound-to-spelling patterns is introduced.

REGULAR PATTERNS

Invariant Correspondences

An invariant correspondence is one that holds regardless of its position in a word (spelling or sound), the position of word stress, or any other modifying feature. A few such correspondences exist for both reading and spelling. For reading, v always corresponds to /v/, and for spelling, with the exception of *of*, /v/ is always spelled v. For reading, the correspondences $j \to$ /j/, $q \to$ /k/, $ck \to$ /k/, and $tch \to$ /č/ are invariant. In the reverse direction, however, no such regularity holds. /ǰ/ can be spelled g, j, dg, or d as in *gem, jam, ridge,* and *cordial;* /k/ can be spelled q, k, ck, c as in *queen, kin, luck,* and *can;* and /č/ can be spelled *tch, ch, t,* and c as in *match, chin, bastion,* and *cello.* On the other hand, /ð/ and /θ/ are always spelled *th,* yet the pronunciation of *th* from a reading standpoint is not invariant (but still not entirely irregular).

Few other sound-spelling or spelling-sound correspondences are invariant. (/h/ is always spelled h, yet the existence of silent h's as in *vehement* and *philharmonic* could be interpreted as irregularities for the /h/ $\to h$ pattern.)

Regular, Variant Correspondences

Many letter-sound and sound-letter correspondences are not invariant, yet are still regular in that their occurrences can be predicted by graphemic, morphemic, or phonemic features (assuming that these features are admissable predictors). The simplest variant patterns are those that depend on position within a word. Initial t, for example, always corresponds to /t/, and initial /t/ corresponds to t, except in *thyme.* Final c always corresponds to k, but the reverse pattern, that of /k/ and its various spellings, cannot be predicted on the basis of position alone.

Some other regular variant correspondences for reading and spelling are tabulated below (these are not exhaustive listings).

Reading

1. Initial *c* before *a, o, u,* or a consonant corresponds to /k/; otherwise, to /s/.[6]

2. Initial *th* corresponds to /ð/ in functors, that is, in adverbs, conjunctions, prepositions, and articles; otherwise, initial *th* corresponds to /θ/.

3. Initial *k* before *n* is silent; in all other environments it corresponds to /k/.

4. Initial *x* corresponds to *z;* final *x* corresponds to /ks/.

5. Initial or medial *e* in monosyllables, when not followed by a consonant plus final *e,* corresponds to /ɛ/.

Spelling

1. Final /ks/, in a single morpheme, corresponds to *x.*

2. Initial /k/ before front vowels corresponds to *k.*

3. /s, z, iz/ as plural morphemes, correspond to *es* after /č, ǰ, š, ž/ and to *s* otherwise.

4. Initial /w/ corresponds to *w.*

5. /ŋ/ is always spelled *n.* (In final position, however, a silent *g* always occurs after this *n.*)[7]

6. In monosyllables, /I/ is spelled *i,* with a few exceptions, for example, *creek* (dialectal), *been.*

All these patterns are regular in the sense that they can be predicted. Yet they are not invariant, that is, the spellings (for reading) always have other pronunciations and the sounds (for spelling) always have other spellings. What is important here is that various types of regularity

---

[6] Italian borrowings, such as *cello,* are exceptions to this pattern.

[7] Whether to teach the spelling of /ŋ/ in such words as *strong* as *n* plus silent *g,* or as *ng* is a matter of practice and not of theory. Though I doubt if any spelling series at present even points out that the *g* in *strong,* like the *b* in *bomb,* is silent, I see many reasons to do so. Consider, for example, the relationship of *strong* to *stronger* and *bomb* to *bombard,* where the *g* and the *b* are silent in one and pronounced in the other. Though *ng* and *mb* are parallel spellings, both having a final silent letter, most spellers and dictionaries claim that *ng* spells /ŋ/, but that *m* spells /m/, the *b* being silent. The one exception that I am aware of is the *Century Dictionary and Cyclopedia* (1911, p. 2423): "and the combination *ng* representing it [/ŋ/] is simply one in which the *g,* formerly pronounced, has become silent, like the *b* of *mb* in *lamb, climb, tomb,* etc."

exist, and each requires different skills for the child who is attempting to master them. The invariant correspondences require simply a consistent connection of a spelling with a sound, or a sound with a spelling. But the variant correspondences require considerably more complex concepts. Positions within words must be recognized, stress patterns and morpheme boundaries must be observed, and such concepts as *plural, front vowel,* and *monosyllable* must be mastered.[8]

IRREGULAR PATTERNS

Even the irregular patterns show important differences. For reading, the correspondence of *o* to /I/ in *women* is irregular and occurs in this word only. The correspondences of *ea* to /i/ and /ɛ/, however, are much more frequent and pose, therefore, a different reading problem. Because *o* → /I/ occurs only in *women,* this word should be presented as a sight word for reading to minimize the chances of transferring the *o* → /I/ correspondence to other *o* words. For *ea,* large groups of words exist for both /i/ and /ɛ/. Therefore, presenting each *ea* word as a separate, exceptional reading word will be less efficient than presenting groups of *ea* → /i/ words and groups of *ea* → /ɛ/ words so that the child can attempt to use intragroup association to aid in retaining the correct *ea* correspondence.

Another type of irregularity is contained in *damn.* Although for spelling there is no clue within this word for indicating the final, silent *n,* there is a clue for it in *damnation.* Similarly, *autumnal* and *hymnal* provide clues for the final, silent *n*'s in *autumn* and *hymn.* Whether or not these patterns are considered predictable is not important. What is important is that both the association of the final *-mn* words with each other and the association of each with a suffixed form in which the *n* is pronounced can be used to teach their spellings.

---

[8] Two sets of regular patterns are not discussed here. The first includes those letter-sound or sound-letter patterns that are based not on particular letters or sounds, but on classes of these entities. For example, the correspondences for a geminate consonant cluster can be predicted by a general rule based on the presence or absence of a morpheme boundary between the two elements of the cluster. Many of these patterns are discussed in Richard Venezky (1967). The second set includes those patterns based solely on letters, or solely on sounds (generally termed "graphotactical" or "phonotactical"). The alternations of *i* and *y* (*candy, candied*), and the dropping of final *e* (*change, changing, changeable*) fit into this class as do the rules for stress shift with suffixation (áthlete, athlétic). For graphemic rules in the class, see Venezky (forthcoming).

RECLASSIFICATION OF PATTERNS

On the basis of the foregoing discussion, the following classifications are offered for sound-spelling and spelling-sound patterns:

I. Predictable: patterns that can be predicted on the basis of regular graphemic, morphemic, or phonemic features of the words or sentences in which they occur.
   A. Invariant: patterns that admit no (or very few) variations or exceptions.
   B. Variant: patterns that have predictable variations or exceptions. (Variant patterns could be divided further on the basis of the features needed to predict each pattern.)
II. Unpredictable: all patterns that do not fit into category I above.
   A. Affix aided: patterns that could be derived by relating the word to one of its prefixed or suffixed forms, for example, *sign, signal.*
   B. High frequency: occurs frequently (frequently enough to allow an association group to be profitably employed in teaching).
   C. Low frequency: occurs too infrequently to merit the formation of an association group.

The importance of this classification is that it separates patterns according to the pedagogy that can be employed to teach them. All predictable patterns could be taught by rules, that is, through reasoning, although this may not be the best technique for some of them.

Furthermore, the difference between the invariant and variant predictable patterns can be related to the teaching of a set for invariance as against teaching a set for variance. Presenting all the invariant patterns before the variant ones may interfere with the teaching of the latter through the reinforcement of a set for invariance.

In the unpredictable class, the low-frequency patterns should not be presented as letter-sound or sound-letter patterns, because this may encourage transfer to inappropriate situations. The high-frequency patterns cannot, in a strict sense, be transferred either, because there is no way to predict where they apply. However, by associating the words in which a particular pattern occurs, an extra measure of learning efficiency might be gained. With the affix-aided patterns, further associations are possible.

From this classification for letter-sound and sound-letter patterns, the following threefold classification for reading and spelling words has been derived. (The word groups for reading will rarely be the same as those for spelling.)

1. Transfer words: words that contain predictable patterns. The patterns in these words can be transferred to the pronunciation (or spelling) of other words in which the same spellings (or pronunciations) occur.

2. Association words: words grouped according to frequently occurring, but unpredictable patterns.

3. Isolated words: words that should be handled as whole words to inhibit transfer of irregular or low-frequency patterns.

The problems in defining "regular" and "irregular" are solved by simply throwing out these terms and adopting the more precise labels "predictable" and "unpredictable," along with their various subclasses. For the educator, the task then becomes one of deciding at any level of reading or spelling instruction which words contain patterns that can be transferred to other words, which contain frequently occurring but nontransferable patterns, and which words should be taught as isolated whole units. The further question of the best sequence (or sequences) of patterns for optimum learning efficiency is left for future consideration.

REFERENCES

Barnhart, C. L. A reaction to Sister Mary Edward Dolan's linguistics in teaching reading. *Reading Research Quarterly,* 1967, *2,* 117–122.

Berko, J. The child's learning of English morphology. *Word,* 1958, *14,* 150–177.

Bloomfield, L. *Language.* New York: Holt, Rinehart & Winston, 1933.

Century Dictionary and Cyclopedia. Vol. 4. New York: Century, 1911.

Hanna, J. S., & Hanna, P. R. Spelling as a school subject: a brief history. *National Elementary Principal,* 1959, *38,* 8–23.

Hanna, J. S., & Hanna, P. R. The teaching of spelling. *National Elementary Principal,* 1965, *45,* 19–28.

Harris, Z. S. *Structural Linguistics.* Chicago: University of Chicago Press, 1951.

Hockett, C. F. *A Course in Modern Linguistics.* New York: Macmillan, 1958.

Jespersen, O. *The Philosophy of Grammar* (1924). New York: Norton, 1965.

Liberman, A. M. Some results of research on speech perception. *Journal of the Acoustical Society of America,* 1957, *29,* 117–123.

Mathews, M. M. *Teaching to Read: Historically Considered.* Chicago: University of Chicago Press, 1966.

Venezky, R. L. English orthography: its graphical structure and its relation to sound. *Reading Research Quarterly,* 1967, *2,* 75–106.

Venezky, R. L. The basis of English orthography. *Acta Linguistica,* forthcoming.

Webster's New Collegiate Dictionary. Springfield, Mass.: Merriam-Webster, 1956.

Wijk, A. *Rules of Pronunciation for the English Language.* London: Oxford University Press, 1966.

4 W. NELSON FRANCIS

Linguistics and Reading:
A Commentary on
Chapters 1 to 3

These three chapters deal, from different points of view, with the most important theoretical question underlying the practical problem of teaching children to read their native language: What is the nature of the writing system and what is its relationship to the other subsystems of language, specifically of English? As a theoretical question, this definitely belongs within the field of linguistics, although linguists were not much concerned with it before the last decade or so. This question also raises issues about the nature of the speaker's knowledge of his language. These concerns fall equally and perhaps primarily within the province of psychologists, although Chomsky, for one, does not refrain from making assertions in this domain about which psychologists would be more cautious, if they did not dismiss them entirely. Moreover, these chapters are of ultimate concern to the pedagogue, because any attempts to improve on existing methods of teaching the native speaker to read, if they are to be any more than undirected or misdirected trial-and-error innovations, must be built on linguistic and psychological theory. It is thus quite appropriate that this collection of studies about the teaching of reading should begin with these primarily theoretical chapters.

The chapters are presented in decreasing order of theoretical complexity and abstraction, if not profundity. Chomsky presents in brief compass and in popular form the gist of a new and in some ways revolutionary approach to phonology in general and English phonology in particular. This approach is given its full exposition in a book of more than 400 pages that he has recently published in collaboration with Morris Halle (Chomsky & Halle, 1968). Reed is more immediately concerned with the problems of the beginning reader, but he, too, comes in his final few pages to deal with the same basic questions, and he suggests that his theoretical foundation has much in common with that of Chomsky. Venezky's chapter is more superficial (in a nonpejorative sense of the word); in one sense it can be considered a long commentary on Chomsky's frequently repeated assertion that "conventional orthography . . . is near optimal for the spoken language. . . ." Certainly the question of regularity, or predictability, as Venezky prefers to call it, is a central one in evaluating the efficiency of the writing system.

In spite of sometimes important differences in theory, method, and preoccupation, these three writers, together with others working in the same area (most recently, Smith, 1968), reveal a consensus on certain matters that are of fundamental importance to those interested in the teaching of reading to native speakers of English. Some of these matters of consensus are the following:

1. The abandoning of the notion that writing is "simply a way of representing speech" (Hall, 1961), in which the aim, imperfectly realized in virtually all standard orthographies, is to give an accurate representation of the string of phonemes underlying the phonetic continuum of speech. This notion is often forcefully stated as a counter to the widespread popular faith in written language as somehow more authentic and trustworthy than speech, and it is responsible for the relative neglect by linguists of the theoretical study of writing systems. After all, if writing is considered nothing more nor less than a crude and perhaps misleading picture of speech, which is "real language," it is not an object worthy of serious study. Even spelling reform, which gave rise in the sixteenth century to the characteristically English school of phoneticians, has more recently been chiefly the province of cranks and amateurs, who have focused almost entirely on the most superficial aspects of English spelling with no overt understanding of the underlying system (though many of their proposals, such as replacing *night* by *nite*, show an unconscious acceptance of the system).[1]

In contrast to this view, the three writers represented here start from

---

[1] For noteworthy exceptions, see Wijk (1959) and especially the review of Wijk by Martin Joos (1960).

the premise that writing is systematic in its own right and that standard orthographies are not phonemic transcriptions *manqué* but representations of linguistic structures at a somewhat deeper level, bearing a rather complicated relationship to any given acoustic-auditory phenomenon, which must in turn be considered merely an alternative representation of the same underlying structures. Orthographies are thus of a different nature from the kind of trivial isomorphic representation of writing found in Morse code or holes punched in a Hollerith card. Just what they do represent and how systematic and predictable the representation is are still open questions.

2. As a corollary to this, recognition that the concern with sound-spelling (grapheme-phoneme) correspondences that characterizes a good deal of the more recent "linguistically oriented" discussion of reading, as well as the older and more naïve "phonics" school,[2] is overly preoccupied with superficial phenomena and does not focus on the real controlling system. It is true that these correspondences must be learned by the prospective reader, and if we are to attain deeper understanding of the reading process—not to mention the learning-to-read process—they must be analyzed and tabulated somewhat in the way Venezky has done. But we cannot rest content with the position that the whole problem lies there. We must get at the underlying system that makes both processes possible. It is in this sense that both Chomsky and Reed can be said to deal more profoundly (and hence probably less satisfactorily) with the linguistic issues involved.

3. Another corollary of 1 above (for Chomsky and Reed at least) is the positing of a deeper level than the phonemic one, at which the utterance is conceived as neutral with regard to its ultimate fate: whether it is to issue as speech or as writing or is to die, as it were, stillborn as a linguistically formulated but unexpressed "thought," perhaps accompanied by suppressed articulatory movements (or at least neural gestures), or mental images of writing, or both. It is the nature of that level that is the major issue here and that will be the recurrent theme of the following discussion. It is a hypothesis that raises many questions, both linguistic and psychological. Some of these questions seem to be beyond our power to answer at present, except by the kind of unsupported assertion that is the weakest aspect of Chomsky's demonstration. Having only a layman's knowledge of psychology, I shall per-

---

[2] A good discussion, historical and analytic, of phonics is that of C. C. Fries (1963, pp. 133–146).

force emphasize the linguistic side, although with due apologies to the psychologists who are contributors and readers of this book I shall occasionally venture into their territory.

CHOMSKY: PHONOLOGY AND READING

It would be well to remind ourselves of some facts that are, I believe, accepted universally as facts by linguists. First, language in all its aspects except for the existence of writing systems is a universal human possession, in the sense that all humans except hopeless mental defectives and those accidentally deprived of access to a language by isolation, deafness, and the like learn a language (sometimes more than one) in early childhood. Second, this has been the case for a very long time, perhaps as much as half the time that *Homo sapiens* has been a species. Indeed, the use of a fully developed language, or at least the innate ability and compulsion to learn one, may be the most distinguishing characteristic of *Homo sapiens*. Third, writing is a fairly recent invention, apparently inspired by the growth of complex societies that could no longer carry on their business by word of mouth efficiently or preserve their archives in the memories of living men. Fourth, it is possible—in fact, in many societies it has been and is the norm—for intelligent persons to live in daily contact with written samples of their native language without ever learning to read and write. Except in a relatively few individuals, who are probably highly motivated by an intensely literate environment, there is no innate compulsion to incorporate literacy into one's linguistic equipment comparable to the basic compulsion to learn to talk.

In consequence of these facts, we are led to conclude, perhaps, that the integration of writing into the polysystemic structure of language is incomplete and its position marginal. Or we might conclude that those languages that have writing systems are different in important ways from those that do not and, hence, that the linguistic knowledge of a literate speaker of such a language is different in kind from that of an illiterate speaker of the same language, as well as from that of a speaker of a language without a writing system. Rather than being forced to choose between these alternatives, I believe we can reconcile the two by taking account of the fact that the role of writing—socially and hence linguistically—may cover a wide range, from the almost completely peripheral position held by runic writing in early Germanic to the overwhelming importance of print in a modern industrial society.

For the former, our first alternative—that writing is marginal—applies; for the latter, the second—that the literate speaker's knowledge of his language is different in kind.

Turning more specifically to English, a few more generally accepted facts must be noted. First, except for some marginal use of the runic system, English acquired writing only after it was settled in England and its speakers had been converted to Christianity. Second, though it was derived from the Latin system, the system adopted for English was rather closely isomorphic with the surface phonology (phonemics) of the language, with the usual omission of indications of prosodic features and, in most cases, vowel length. Third, during the period from the seventh to the fifteenth century, when extensive changes in the phonological system were taking place, the writing system was from time to time readjusted to represent the results of these changes, but its isomorphic relationship to the phonology was compromised in many ways[3] Fourth, partly as a consequence of the establishment of printing in England, the writing system became frozen in the latter part of the fifteenth century, so that there has been little substantive change during the last 500 years. Fifth, there have, however, been further extensive changes in the phonology of both Standard (London) English and of all regional varieties during that 500 years. Sixth, from the thirteenth century to the present, there has been extensive borrowing of lexical items, together with their orthography or a rationalized adaptation thereof, from Latin, French, and Greek, with the result that more than half (at a modest guess) of the vocabulary of educated modern written English is non-Germanic in origin.

The relevance of these facts will become apparent below, when we come to the discussion of Chomsky's claim that "conventional English orthography in its essentials appears to be a near-optimal system for representing the spoken language." But first it must be emphasized that Chomsky does not mean by this statement that the conventional orthography is isomorphic with the surface phonology, that is, that it has a one-to-one relationship with the string of phonemes (or bundles of phonetic features) that underlies spoken discourse. Instead, he claims that the conventional orthography "is to a large extent merely a direct point-by-point transcription of a system that the speaker of English has internalized and uses freely, a system that I will refer to as 'lexical

---

[3] For a review of the changes in the English writing system, see Francis (1965, pp. 199–217).

representation.' " As he demonstrates later in his chapter, this hypothesized underlying system must go through a process of modification by a rather complex series of "perfectly automatic" rules that indicate the "phonetic representation" appropriate to the dialect of the speaker. It is apparent, though not specifically claimed, that many of these rules recapitulate phonological changes that have taken place over the last 600 to 800 years.

There are in essence three parts to Chomsky's claim: (1) that the prephonetic level of surface structure, the level of lexical representation, is linguistically meaningful; (2) that this level and the lexical representations that it includes are psychologically real, though below the level of conscious knowledge; and (3) that the standard orthography is, with minor exceptions, isomorphic with that level. These claims must be taken up separately before we can evaluate this concept as a whole.

With the constraint of psychological reality removed, the notion of a level of linguistic structure between the output of the syntax (however that is conceived of) and the phonetic realization has much to recommend it. In general terms it is not a new idea; it has variously been considered a morphophonemic level, a level of interstratal anataxis between the morphemic and phonemic strata (Lamb, 1966), the morphophonic level (Smith, 1968), and the "linguon" level (Reed, 1965 and in this volume). What is new here, and especially in *Sound Pattern of English* (Chomsky and Halle, 1968), is the thorough and insightful way the authors have specified the cyclical rules that are needed to convert automatically their hypothesized lexical representations into phonetic representations, with a very small residue of irreducible exceptions. This is not the place to review the longer work, but it should be at least mentioned that it presents, among other things, the most complete rule yet formulated for predicting English stress (the "main stress rule"). The principal value of the lexical representation level, at least to descriptive linguistics, is that it provides a uniform transcription for derivationally related lexical items that are phonologically different, and it provides by means of the phonological rules a systematic way of accounting for the difference. Chomsky illustrates this with *courage, courageous;* he could have used even more striking examples such as *artifice, artifact, artificer,* or *prodúce, próduce, product, production.* The assumption of a uniform lexical level underlying dialectal variants, with the consequent location of dialect variation in the rules for phonetic realization (as Reed suggests also), provides a much needed rationale for making a fairly clear-cut distinction between language and dialect.

Some problems of a linguistic nature, however, suggest themselves. How far should we carry the effort to bring related lexical items under a single representation? This becomes crucial in the case of cognates such as *reason, rational* or even *fisherman, piscatorial.* Rules could presumably be written to account for the first of these pairs, but they would have to be specific to this pair to avoid *season, sational* and *treason, trational.* The answer is, of course, that the rules must be of maximum generality and that only those items that respond to the rules (with a few inescapable exceptions) are to be considered as having common underlying forms. The danger of circularity here is obvious. More important, however, is the fact that the assumption of the psychological reality of the lexical representation level would require that for the educated speaker who naturally uses *rational* as the adjectival form of *reason,* these two words have presumably the same sort of psychological links as do *season, seasonal* or *reason, reasonable.*

This brings us to the second of Chomsky's claims—that the speaker has internalized and uses freely a system of lexical representations in precisely the form in which Chomsky presents them: a sequence of segments that "contain all information not predictable by the phonological rules." The claim is made that "the psychological reality of lexical representation, in this sense, is hardly open to question." It is thus asserted that the speaker stores the lexicon as a collection of formatives, each in the shape of an unvarying string of "segments," which are themselves bundles of binary features, though for notational convenience they may be represented by unitary symbols such as k and g. Presumably, when lexical items are to be incorporated in discourse, the formatives are brought out of storage and fitted into the surface structure string that is the product of the transformational component of the grammar. Then they are either put through the elaborate cyclical rules that convert them into phonetic matrices or their segments are transcribed in virtually point-to-point fashion into graphic symbols. In turn, the phonetic matrices somehow trigger the proper articulatory motions that result in speech, or the graphic symbols trigger the muscular actions that produce writing or typing.

Though, as I said above, my knowledge of psychology is that of the layman, I cannot find this claim "hardly open to question." I leave it to the psychologists to bring their professional competence to bear on it; I shall simply instance a few commonsense objections. In the first place, the assumption that all speakers store the same lexical items in the same way seems to run counter to the great individual diversity that obtains in other forms of memory. The way in which particular parts of other systems are stored may be highly idiosyncratic, probably as a result of the way in which they were learned. In the case of the multiplication table, for example, why do I have trouble remembering that $8 \times 7 = 56$, alone among the products of single digits? Or why do I seem to scan a spatial image of the year or the week in order to locate a given month or day? I am assured that others seem to operate quite differently. One could cite myriad actions—tying one's shoelaces, as a simple example—in which the same output is reached by different individuals along different routes. Yet Chomsky claims that "it seems to be the case not only that lexical representation is a basic element in the system freely used by the speaker-hearer, but also that it varies very little from speaker to speaker, even across major dialect boundaries." Why should this kind of uniformity prevail in language and not in other kinds of learned behavior?

A second commonsense objection is to some degree forestalled by Chomsky's concession that the speaker "may not be able to give conscious expression" to his knowledge of lexical representation. But it still seems to the layman that if lexical representations of the form here posited are indeed psychological realities, there should be some way of getting at them by some other route than the highly ingenious analysis that Chomsky and Halle have used and that has taken them a good many years to work out. Granted that the lexical representations may not be accessible to ordinary recall, but certainly under drugs or hypnosis, in deep analysis, or in dreams they should be subject to recovery. Or at least there should be some kind of intuitive shock of recognition when one is faced with them. Yet my first reaction to being told that "the underlying lexical representation for the form *courage* is, in fact, /koræge/" and that "it is this form that is internalized, as part of his knowledge of English, by the speaker-hearer who is acquainted with this word" was one of extreme skepticism. The response of other native speakers of English whom I have asked has been the same. It was not until I had studied the full exposition of the Chomsky-Halle system, as set forth in *Sound Pattern of English*, that I was prepared to recognize this form as an ingenious construct that, given an equally ingenious set of rules, could be set up as an underlying element of *courage* and *courageous*. This reaction is, of course, no more a refutation of the psychological reality of uniform lexical representations than Chomsky's unsupported assertions are proof thereof. It is only meant to suggest that the question is still open and cannot be claimed to be a fact until psychologists devise and employ adequate measures to test it. Meanwhile, it is unfortunate that a brilliant linguistic demonstration is weakened by extravagant and unsupported psychological claims.

The third part of Chomsky's claim is that conventional orthography, not only in the case of English but in that of "any other language of which I have any knowledge," is a near-optimal transcription for the spoken language. Presumably he either has no knowledge of Chinese, or he does not consider its writing system to be a conventional orthography. But that is by the way; we are here concerned with English. In the light of the facts about the history of English cited above, it would be indeed remarkable if his claims were true. As these facts suggest, English orthography is not a single consistent system but a conflation of modified forms of at least four systems: the Old English, the Latin, the French, and the Greek. It is true that for the educated speaker, especially if he has some acquaintance with Latin, French, and Greek, it is an excellent, though complicated, system. The sophisticated speaker is likely to be intrigued rather than bothered by the fact that a straight line subtending an arc is a *chord,* whereas a piece of string is a *cord.* Furthermore, it is probable that for him, unlike the etymologically less sophisticated speaker, these two items are stored in different form. It would seem likely that, for the highly literate person, there is a good deal of this kind of feedback from the written language on the storage system, resulting in such connections as *isolate, solitary* and *insulate, peninsula,* which illiterate speakers might never see. By the same token, the literate speaker is not led to see any connection between *physic* and *fizzing,* though the illiterate, especially if he is given to dosing himself with citrate of magnesia, might do so.

Trivialities aside, the principal objection to Chomsky's claim is that it is rather strongly overstated. The English orthographic system is undoubtedly far superior to a straight phonemic system, and I like it better than any reformed system that has so far been put forward. But the claim is too sweeping that "disregarding a class of true exceptions and a set of oddities" it is in virtual one-to-one correspondence with the segments of the internalized lexical representations. If this were so, why would people have so much trouble with English spelling? Or why is it necessary to represent the underlying form of *courage* as /korœge/, in which only half of the segments correspond to the orthography? Or is this one of the oddities?

In sum, I find Chomsky's chapter, especially when read in the light of the full exposition in *Sound Pattern of English,* to be a brilliant and provocative phonological theory, marred by unsupported assertions in the field of psychology and rather intemperate claims about orthography. I should like especially to give complete and hearty endorsement to the wisdom and good sense of his opening paragraph and to conclude that I expect more of use in the teaching of reading to come from studies of this sort than the modest disclaimer in his final paragraph predicts.

REED: LINGUISTIC FORMS
AND THE PROCESS OF READING

Reed's chapter makes three main points, the third of which is basically a more tentative and less extensively developed version of Chomsky's main point. The other two points are (1) there is a sharp distinction between the process of reading and the use of reading, and (2) a demonstration of the fact that linguistic forms other than the word must be identified by the reader. Both points are clearly put and largely unexceptionable; discussion of them here can be limited to a few rather trivial comments and some suggestions of their implications for research.

The distinction between process and use is in effect a necessary disambiguating of the English word *reading* (note that *writing* is ambiguous in much the same way). Normally, this ambiguity does not cause much trouble, because context usually indicates which meaning is applicable (compare *I can't read your handwriting* with *I can't read Hart Crane's poetry*). But in the context of early instruction the ambiguity has caused confusion sometimes even to the point where the teacher assumes that in teaching reading she is actually teaching the child his language. Presumably enough has been said on this point so that it need not be belabored. But once process and use have been separated, the question arises as to how much they can or should be kept separate in instruction. The answer, it seems to me, is dependent on the previous linguistic experience of the learner. At one end of the scale would be the congenitally deaf child, whose first contact with language may be visual. At the other end would be an adult with full command of the spoken language and considerable oral exposure to literature, who simply didn't happen to learn to read as a child. Both of these are rare, and most learners fall somewhere between. Even so, however, there is a wide range, from the linguistically deprived child, whose exposure to language (especially of the kind that usually gets written down) is meager, to the child from a highly verbal, intellectual background, who has heard a great deal of adult conversation and has been read to from various kinds of literature. It is obvious that the deprived child needs attention to "the enlargement of [his] knowledge of the universe, of himself, and of the language in which these kinds of knowledge are embodied and communicated," whereas the latter needs only to be given the clues to the coding system.

It is also true, of course, that very early in the process of learning to read one encounters a kind of language that is never (or very seldom) spoken. For example, *Had I but known the danger, I would never have entered the cave*, is certainly an allowable written sentence, even in relatively juvenile literature. By all the signals the child is likely to know, as they are set out in Reed's chapter, this should be a question, and the child will probably have to be told that it is not. The point is, of course, that even if the Dick-and-Jane type of basal readers, with their very artificial grammar, are discarded, the child will encounter quite early new linguistic forms that are characteristic only of written discourse. Thus, the reading teacher must also become something of a language teacher. But it remains important for the teacher to know at any given juncture whether she is teaching reading process or reading use. There must also continue to be research into the differences (other than lexical ones, which have already been extensively studied) between various modes and styles of language, including the spoken language of preliterate children, so that these two aspects of the reading teacher's role can be more accurately distinguished.

The second part of Reed's chapter is a demonstration of the clues, other than punctuation, that the reader can use to determine whether or not a written sentence is a question. Reed shows that this can be determined from the first few words of the sentence, except for a few omissions, such as the tag question (*He's coming, isn't he?*) and the question sentence beginning with a subordinate clause (*If it rains, will you still go to the picnic?*). The obvious moral is that it is not enough to teach reading word by word; the child's attention must also be directed to the sentence structure. An implied question, which must be answered by experts in pedagogy, is whether it would be advantageous to pursue this kind of analysis to the point of identifying the graphic clues to all kinds of linguistic forms larger than the word. Should we teach them overtly or devise reading materials that present them systematically, rather than more or less at random?

In the last part of his chapter, Reed puts forward the idea of a level on which linguistic forms are represented by "linguons," segments that "are more abstract than phonemes, being at one and the same time morphophonemic and diaphonemic." The resemblance to Chomsky's "segments" is obvious, but a few differences may be pointed out. In the first place, Reed makes no explicit claim to psychological reality for these units—they are presumably not entities that exist in the brain, but rather abstractions that are to be postulated. Actually, Reed leaves open the question of their "reality"; to revert to an opposition once suggested by Fred Householder, he does not commit himself on either the "God's truth" or the "hocus pocus" side. Second, though he speaks of rules for deriving both orthography and various kinds of spoken English, he gives no illustrations of what these rules are like. Finally, he is more optimistic about the potential usefulness for research and teaching in reading than Chomsky allows himself to be. In any case, it is a good sign, as I pointed out at the beginning of this chapter, that various linguists, moving from their own particular starting points, are converging on notions about the relation of writing, speech, and language that are more meaningful than previous notions, which involved mere tabulation of the surface configurations. Many practical matters, such as the reform of English spelling and the use of special quasi-phonemic "teaching alphabets," will be affected by further research in this area.

VENEZKY: REGULARITY IN READING AND SPELLING

Venezky's chapter, as I have said above, can from one point of view be considered a long and detailed comment on Chomsky's claims for the near-optimal state of English orthography. Certainly, no one who reads it can avoid the conclusion that Chomsky's assertion must be taken with more than a grain of salt. On the other hand, by demonstrating the types and limits of regularity in the algorithms for converting language to writing and vice versa, Venezky strikes a balance between Chomsky's position and that of those who condemn English orthography as merely chaotic (usually as a preface to introducing some superficial reform in the direction of making it more "phonetic"). Nor, in an age of nearly universal literacy, is the question of pedagogical expediency an unimportant one. It is not enough to conclude that because the system works it is adequate. The Chinese system works, but at great cost of the learner's time at a crucial period in schooling. When time is short and there is so much to learn, much of it depending on the ability to read, the efficiency of the writing system, measured by the amount of time and energy that the child must invest in mastering it, is vital.

Presumably, one of the variables determining that efficiency, given the natural human inclination to generalization, is the amount of regularity that the system possesses.

The heart of Venezky's presentation is his framework for classifying graphic representations on grounds of their predictability, that is, their amenability to rule (see page 41). It is a useful starting point, although I should be inclined to assign his "unpredictable affix-aided" category to the predictable class. One of the facts about English pronunciation that is clearly brought out in *Sound Pattern of English* is the importance of morpheme (or, in Chomsky-Halle terms, formative) boundaries, especially those between stem and affix. Even such apparent irregularities as the contrast between *finger* and *singer* are seen to be regular, and the placing of stress is dependent on both the syllable structure and the morphemic constituency of words.

Venezky's classification will be most useful, it seems to me, if it is used not as a static framework into which all the words of the language are fitted once and for all, but rather one that can be used to classify the rules used by a given speaker at a given point in his linguistic development. In general (as Chomsky suggests), as the command of educated English increases, more and more items will be moved from the unpredictable to the predictable categories. This will often take the form, as I have suggested, of feedback from the orthography resulting in the creation of associations that may be missing for the nonliterate speaker. This will be true of pairs in which vowel gradations and stress shifts in the phonology may obscure morphological and etymological connections, which are more apparent in the graphic forms, as in Venezky's illustration *sign, signal,* or such pairs as *column, columnar* and *solemn, solemnity.* Even language of origin, which Venezky dismisses, may at a certain level become relevant, by locating a word within one of the special subsystems of the English graphic system. One does not need to know Greek to recognize that the presence of an initial cluster such as *ps-* or *pn-* puts a word into a system in which *ch* will spell /k/ and final /k/ will be spelled *c* rather than *ck*.

In conclusion, a linguist must be encouraged by these essays, not so much for their direct contributions (though these are by no means negligible), as for what they reveal about the state of research into the areas of linguistics most directly applicable to the problem of the teaching of reading. There is more for linguists to do, but the big task now seems to be that of the psychologist and psycholinguist. Some of the questions that I should like to see answered are: How does the speaker actually store his knowledge of language? What are the mechanisms of access and retrieval? Are these uniform for all speakers, or are there differences resulting from accidents of learning? Does the acquisition of literacy simply add a new dimension to this knowledge? Or does it bring about a major restructuring? What, if anything, can be done with the writing system—the only part of language readily open to manipulation—that will make it easier to learn and remember? Will we ever, to use Venezky's metaphor, "lift the cranial carapace, expose the mental activities to view, and observe whether units are being switched directly from memory to output channels or whether there is a more complex shuffling and joining of separate building blocks into wholes"? These are large questions, so large that perhaps only a layman would dare to ask them. But even some hints toward answers may revolutionize our views of the reading process and how it is to be taught.

REFERENCES

Chomsky, N., & Halle, M. *Sound Pattern of English*. New York: Harper & Row, 1968.

Francis, W. N. *The English Language: An Introduction*. New York: Norton, 1965.

Fries, C. C. *Linguistics and Reading*. New York: Holt, Rinehart & Winston, 1963.

Hall, R. A. J. *Sound and Spelling in English*. New York: Chilton, 1961.

Joos, M. Review of Axel Wijk, *Regularized English. Language*, 1960, *36*, 250–262.

Lamb, S. Prolegomena to a theory of phonology. *Language*, 1966, *42*, 536–574.

Reed, D. W. A theory of language, speech, and writing. *Elementary English*, 1965, *42*, 845–851.

Smith, H. L., Jr. English morphophonics: implications for teaching of literacy. Monograph No. 10, New York State English Council, 1968.

Wijk, A. *Regularized English*. Stockholm: Almqvist & Wiksell, 1959.

ELEANOR J. GIBSON

ARTHUR SHURCLIFF

ALBERT YONAS

Utilization of Spelling Patterns by Deaf and Hearing Subjects

For more than half a century, we have known that a good reader does not read sequentially, letter by letter, but takes in and processes larger graphic units (Cattell, 1885). Yet, except for the obvious surmise that a familiar word constitutes a unit, there has been little research or even speculation on the relevant grouping principles. How are larger graphic units constituted? By meaning? By frequency? By rules? If rules, what kind of rules? A large number of experiments on the perception of words[1] has shown that word frequency is correlated with speed and accuracy of perception. But more recent experiments have shown that other principles than frequency play a role in the formation of graphic units. Among these are degree of approximation to English (Miller, Bruner, and Postman, 1954; Wallach, 1963) and internal structure of letter strings—redundant strings as opposed to random ones, as defined by a grammar or set of rules (Miller, 1958). In general, any property that increases redundancy is a good possibility for facilitation of perception, recognition, or retention. One of the major psycholinguistic generalizations, according to Diebold (1965) in a review of recent psycholinguistic research, is that speech recognition increases directly with the increase in redundancy for all sizes of message units. Surely we can expect this principle to apply to written as well as spoken messages.

---

[1] See Gibson, Pick, Osser, and Hammond (1962) for a review of these experiments.

57

One property that one might think of as contributing redundancy, so as to reduce information and facilitate reading a string of letters as a unit, is invariance of spelling-to-sound correspondence. Hockett (1963), Venezky (1963), and Venezky and Weir (1966) have all worked on the problem of how English spelling patterns are mapped to sound. One often hears the assertion that spelling-to-sound correspondences in English are irregular and unpredictable, but the work of these linguists demonstrates that the mapping rules and constraints are there, if graphic units larger than the single letter are considered. The hypothesis was proposed, therefore (Gibson et al., 1962), that units for reading are formed by a relatively invariant mapping to speech sounds. For English spellings this would mean that letter clusters in a given position in a word and in a given environment, when they map with regularity to pronunciation, will operate as units and that grouping is functionally determined by the relationship to speech sounds. A stimulus property that is invariant over a set of items constitutes a constraint or rule that is a good bet for creating a unit or "chunk" of otherwise randomly organized parts.

A letter string that has high internal transitional probabilities is not the same thing as one that maps with invariance to speech; *ati*, for instance, is a high frequency trigram, but it is not a unit for reading, because it is pronounced differently, depending on context (for example, *relation* vs. *relative*). Certain clusters are always pronounced the same way, wherever they appear (for example, *sh*). But some are pronounced differently depending on their location in the word (for example, *gh*, in *ghost* vs. *enough*). This condition is rule-like, however, and constitutes a higher-order constraint; *gh* is always pronounced in one way at the beginning of a word, but never this way at the end.

That the reader is not always aware of mapping rules from spelling to speech need not mean that order and regularity are not abstracted and used in the course of learning to read. As Venezky and Weir (1966) have shown, the rules are indeed high-level ones, and a long program of computer-aided research was required to formulate them. The question is whether the skilled reader, knowingly or not, actually uses them in perceiving written language.

We tried to answer this question with an experiment in which pseudo-words—that is, letter strings that were not real words, but that in some cases might have been—were presented tachistoscopically to skilled readers of English. The words were all monosyllables, consisting of an initial consonant cluster, a vowel cluster, and a final consonant cluster. Half were constructed so that the initial consonant cluster had a single regular pronunciation in that position, the final cluster in its position, and the vowel cluster a regular pronunciation when preceded and followed by the selected consonant clusters. These were called pronounceable words, because the clusters had an invariant mapping from spelling to sound in this arrangement. A control set of words was constructed from the same letters, but with the initial and final consonant clusters reversed, rendering them unpredictably pronounceable. These were called the unpronounceable words. For instance, a pronounceable pseudoword was *glurck;* its unpronounceable counterpart was *ckurgl.*

The experiment was run and replicated several times (Gibson et al., 1962) and very consistently gave significant results in the predicted direction. In the meantime, several theoretical questions were brought up by members of the research group as to the exact interpretation of the results. What did pronounceability really mean? Was it actually the invariance-to-sound mapping that was crucial? Partial answers to these questions were sought in the two following experiments. All the words were rated for pronounceability on a nine-point scale (following the method of Underwood and Schulz, 1960). The words constructed to be pronounceable were indeed rated high in pronounceability, their counterparts low. Second, sixteen subjects were asked to read aloud all the words, and their pronunciations were recorded on tape. The pronunciations were analyzed by two linguistics and the variability of pronunciation was determined for each word. Variability was very high for the unpronounceable words, but low for the pronounceable ones. The variability score correlated .83 with the pronounceability rating.

The results were published at this point, and soon afterward several alternative interpretations were suggested. In all, five different interpretations appeared to warrant consideration or test. They are as follows:

1. Rules of spelling-to-sound mapping suggest that mapping invariance creates larger units for reading and therefore faster processing. This is the original hypothesis described above.

2. Transitional probabilities in written English, without regard to sound, account for the superiority of the so-called pronounceable words. It was suggested (Anisfeld, 1964) that summed bigram or summed trigram counts would predict the results obtained in the experiments. The counts were made and correlated with number of correct perceptions (Gibson, 1964). The count did not predict success in reading the pseudowords when pronounceability was partialed out and length held constant.

3. Pronounceable words are more readily perceived because they match an acoustic representation. When a word (or letter string) is exposed, it is silently rehearsed and matched with a stored auditory representation (Levin and Biemiller, 1965). This hypothesis implies auditory encoding before successful reading of a pseudoword.

4. Processing of letter strings in reading involves encoding and matching to an articulatory representation, or plan. (See Liberman, Cooper, Harris, and MacNeilage, 1963.)

5. Complex orthographic rules cover structural patterns of letters permissible in English words. Such rules are not merely transitional probabilities but are a kind of syntax, analogous to grammar. Such rules could be learned, as one learns to read, with or without relating them to speech sounds. An obvious example is the case of consonants or consonant clusters that cannot be used initially but can be used finally, and vice versa, such as *ck* and *qu*. The principle was used in construction of words in the present experiment. Mapping to speech, when invariant, would be an added, redundant constraint.

THE EXPERIMENT

Because a resolution among these alternatives would have important implications for teaching reading, experiments were sought that might decide among them. A comparison of deaf and hearing subjects, it was thought, should be instructive, especially when various potential predictor variables were weighed against performance with pronounceable vs. unpronounceable words. Accordingly, the original experiment was modified slightly for replication with deaf subjects.

Method

The method followed closely that of the original experiment except that all instructions were presented in writing and a red light was used as a ready signal. The words used were the same as those used by Gibson et al. (1962), except that two pairs were dropped because the difference in their pronounceability ratings was slight. The words varied in length from four to eight letters.

The words were projected tachistoscopically one at a time on a screen for 100 milliseconds. Contrast between letters and background was high enough so that some letters could always be read. The pronounceable and unpronounceable items were projected in a random order. After the series had been shown, it was repeated, this time in a reverse order, with the same exposure time. The subjects were seated ten feet from the screen. They wrote what they saw after each presentation on numbered lines, four lines on each page of a scoring sheet, and turned to a new page after one was filled. This procedure was followed to assist them in keeping to the order. The subjects were run in small squads of three or four to permit equivalent viewing angles. The height of the letters projected on the screen was three and three-quarter inches, the width about two and one-half inches. Exact instructions were as follows:

This is an experiment on reading sets of letters when they are flashed on the screen in front of you for a very short time. The letters do not form real words, but try to read them and write down what you see. We will call them nonsense words. Write all the letters of the nonsense word in the order that you saw them, if you possibly can. *If you are not quite sure, write them down anyway, as you think you saw them.*

I will show you some practice nonsense words, before we begin the experiment. A red light will flash, so you can be ready. When the light flashes, look at the center of the screen. The nonsense word will be flashed on the screen just one second after the ready signal. After the nonsense word is flashed, write down what you saw at once. Here is a practice word. Watch for the red light, and then for the word.

Subjects

Thirty-four subjects were secured at Gallaudet College for the Deaf in Washington, where both staff and students cooperated in every possible way. An interpreter was present in case the subjects had any questions. We requested subjects who were congenitally deaf, or nearly so, and who had maximal hearing losses. Afterward, the staff furnished for subjects hearing ratings, speech ratings, age of onset of deafness, and scores on various tests such as reading and verbal aptitude. At the close of the experiment, the subjects themselves answered questionnaires regarding the way they were taught to read.

A new control group of thirty-four subjects was run with the same procedure as that used with the deaf subjects. They were Cornell students drawn from an introductory psychology class. The native language of all subjects was English.

Results

Comparison of Deaf and Hearing Subjects

The deaf subjects, not surprisingly, made more errors than hearing subjects for both pronounceable and unpronounceable words. But the difference between the two sets of words is just as significant and just as striking for the deaf as for the hearing. Whatever it is that facilitates reading the words in the pronounceable list seems to be operating equally well for them. Labeling the difference between the two lists "pronounce-ability" evidently served only to pull the wool over our eyes, for the deaf students had never heard the words pronounced. Another experiment with similar results, though on a smaller scale, recently came to our attention (Doehring and Rosenstein, 1960). In that experiment, lists of trigrams were shown tachistoscopically to deaf and hearing children. The lists were roughly equivalent in frequency, but one list was all CVC, such as *zif*, whereas the other was CCC, such as *rch*. The authors referred to the first list as pronounceable and the other as unpronounce-able. Both groups of children made fewer errors on the CVC trigrams,

Table 5–1.

	MEAN ERRORS	
	PRONOUNCEABLE WORDS	UNPRONOUNCEABLE WORDS
Deaf	21.27	36.36
Hearing	15.86	25.68

the deaf being relatively at least as much better on these as the hearing.

Error data, by words, for both our groups of subjects were correlated with data from the earlier experiment, as a check on reliability, The coefficients were very high, .91 and .96 respectively, indicating excellent replicability and similar performance on individual words by the deaf and earlier hearing subjects.

It seemed possible that an examination of the errors might reveal something more, because the scoring used to obtain the criterion for the measures in Table 5–1 was simply "right" or "wrong." We were fortunate in having available a computer program for the analysis of graphic errors in reading that would allow us to compare part scores of several types, using as data the actual errors—the wrong spellings recorded by the subjects. These errors were all punched on cards, along with the correct spelling of the word, and the error compared with the word exposed. The spellings were compared for the number of same letters in the two (regardless of position), the length of a correct string reading in a forward direction (starting in any position), the length of a correct string reading in reverse, the number of letters same at the beginning of a word, and the number same at the end.

Means are given for these counts in Table 5–2, separated for deaf and hearing subjects and for pronounceable and unpronounceable words. When the five measures are compared for pronounceable and unpronounceable words, there are some slight differences in the expected direction. The length of a correct letter sequence in the forward direction

Table 5–2. *Analysis of Graphic Errors.*

	DEAF		HEARING	
	PRO-NOUNCEABLE	UNPRO-NOUNCEABLE	PRO-NOUNCEABLE	UNPRO-NOUNCEABLE
M no. same in any order	4.58	4.64	4.45	4.70
Length of correct sequence forward	3.77	3.09	3.52	3.08
Length of correct sequence reverse	.52	.73	.60	.74
M no. same in sequence, beginning of word	2.58	2.50	2.64	2.44
M no. same in sequence, ending of word	1.68	1.00	1.14	1.18

is longer for the pronounceable pseudowords. The mean number "same" in sequence at the beginning is somewhat longer for pronounceable words. The number of letters same without regard to order, and the length of span correct in reverse order, go to a small extent, in the other direction, which is reasonable, because length in these cases is symptomatic of error rather than of accurate reading. There is no other significant difference here. The slightly longer mean number correct at the end for pronounceable words for the deaf subjects may simply have to do with the fact that they made more errors. This is certainly the explanation of the slightly larger means in several other cases of the deaf subjects, compared with the hearing, because it was not feasible to correct

Table 5-3. *Correlations between Errors for Pseudowords and Various Predictor Variables (Hearing and Deaf Subjects).*

	LENGTH	B.F.	T.F.	PRON. RATING	HEARING ERRORS	DEAF ERRORS	M.B.F.	M.T.F.	COMBINED ERRORS
Length	1.0	.64	.21	.35	.85	.82	− .02	.07	.84
Bigram frequency		1.0	.73	− .03	.41	.41	.31	.55	.42
Trigram frequency			1.0	− .14	.02	.06	.28	.75	.05
Pronounceability rating				1.0	.61	.68	− .63	− .45	.66
Hearing errors					1.0	.93	− .29	− .16	.98
Deaf errors						1.0	− .37	− .21	.98
Mayzner bigram frequency							1.0	.65	− .33
Mayzner trigram frequency								1.0	− .19
Combined errors									1.0

for total number of errors. A deaf subject might get four letters correct in forward order in a five-letter word, whereas hearing subjects made no errors. At any rate, there is no indication of an interaction here that we might have missed in our original method of scoring by number of words wholly correct.

Prediction of Errors

In an attempt to analyze what accounts for the facilitation of the pronounceable words, we examined the effect of a number of potential predictor variables in several multiple regression analyses. The data used in these analyses are presented in a correlation matrix in Table 5–3. Errors for hearing and deaf subjects were correlated separately and in combination with word length, pronounceability rating, summed bigram frequency, summed trigram frequency (the two latter measures taken from Underwood and Schulz, 1960, combined count), and two recent measures of summed bigram and trigram frequency compiled by Mayzner and Tresselt (1965) and Mayzner, Tresselt, and Wolin (1965). These last two measures take into account letter position in the word and word length.

Table 5–4 presents the results of these analyses. Errors were, in every analysis, the dependent variable. Each row across the table presents one analysis. Because the analysis was in steps, the variable tested first is presented in the first column, the next second, and so on, until variables significant at the .05 level or better are exhausted. Under the first variable is listed the per cent of variance that it accounts for, and under the following the cumulative variance accounted for when another significant predictor variable is added. When variables were omitted from an analysis, it is so indicated.

In the first three rows, all variables were included, with hearing errors as dependent variable in row 1, deaf errors in row 2, and hearing and deaf combined in row 3. The variable tested first (with highest predictability) was length of word. It accounts for 67 to 73 per cent of the variance, a reasonable finding, for the longest words were always perceived erroneously and the shortest most successfully. Pronounceability is the second significant predictor variable in all three rows, and, when added to length, 84 to 87 per cent of the variance is accounted for. The only frequency count reaching significance is the Mayzner bigram count, and it adds only one percentage point for the deaf subjects and none for the hearing ones.

These findings are very convincing in themselves. Pronounceability

Table 5–4. *Stepwise Regression Analyses for Predictor Variables.*

DEPENDENT VARIABLE	PREDICTOR VARIABLES SIGNIFICANT AT .05 LEVEL OR BETTER AND PER CENT OF VARIANCE ACCOUNTED FOR (CUMULATIVE)			
Hearing errors	length 73%	pronounceability 84%	all others NS	
Deaf errors	length 67%	pronounceability 84%	Mayzner bigram 85%	all others NS
Hearing and deaf errors combined	length 72%	pronounceability 87%	Mayzner bigram 88%	all others NS
Hearing and deaf errors combined	length 72%	Mayzner bigram 83% pronounceability omitted	all others NS	
Hearing and deaf errors combined	bigram F 17%	Mayzner bigram 48% pronounceability and length omitted	trigram F 53%	others NS
Hearing and deaf errors combined	pronounceability 43%	bigram F 63% length omitted	trigram F 69%	others NS

rating is a significant predictor of error, and the frequency counts add nothing for the hearing subjects given the first two variables. The finding is as strong for the deaf as for the hearing subjects. The fact that the Mayzner count adds to the prediction slightly for the deaf subjects may mean that their attention is drawn more to regularities in the purely visible orthography, but the effect is too small to warrant much speculation.

Pronounceability is obviously a better predictor than any of the frequency counts. A proponent of frequency might ask, however, what would happen if pronounceability were left out. Would the counts then have any predictive value? Row 4 in Table 5–3 shows the results of such an analysis. Length, of course, is still significant, and in this case one of the frequency counts, the Mayzner bigram count, adds significantly to the prediction of errors. It correlates better with pronounceability than the Mayzner trigram count, and the latter does not add significantly to the prediction. This count is a more plausible predictor than sheer bigram frequency, because it takes letter position and word length into account. It is not so good a predictor as pronounceability, however, as the previous analyses show. This is not unreasonable, when one considers the sample used in making the count. Tokens, rather than types, were the sample—all the words three to seven letters in length in a text of 20,000 English words. Because the sample was running text rather than dictionary entries, a trigram such as *the* occurred very often (2,401 times in the first three positions), whereas *qui*, an acceptable and highly constrained pattern for beginning an English word, had a total count of only twenty-three in the first three positions—little more than *cki*, which did not occur, but in fact cannot occur. Thus, even this frequency count, though it reflects the rules to some degree, does not do so perfectly. This suggests that the pronounceability measure accounts for most of the variance predicted by the one significant frequency count, and something more.

When both pronounceability and length are omitted, the frequency counts in some combination account for 53 per cent of the variance. The significance of bigram frequency as a predictor, in this case, is owing to its correlation with length. It does not do so well as length, but is clearly taking up some of the variance which that variable would, if present. The Mayzner bigram count again increases the prediction fairly effectively.

When length alone is omitted, pronounceability is the lead predictor, with 43 per cent of the variance. The two sheer frequency counts add to the prediction, again because they are contributing what length would have, had it been there. The Mayzner counts do not appear. Their potential contribution to the prediction is absorbed by the pronounceability rating.

These analyses seem to indicate that the pronounceability rating is actually measuring something more than sheer pronounceability, something that is reflected, but to a lesser degree, in the Mayzner bigram count, and something that is potentially present in orthography alone, in that it facilitates the deaf at least as much as the hearing. It is our opinion that the rules in the spelling account for the variance in these cases. The two ordinary frequency counts, on the other hand, are not predicting (when they predict anything) the same thing, as their low correlation with pronounceability shows us.

Prediction of Deaf Errors by Linguistic Variables

Scores and ratings on a number of variables having to do with aspects of speech, hearing, or reading were furnished us for the deaf subjects. They were rating for degree of residual hearing; rating for comprehensibility of speech; age of onset of deafness; and scores on a reading test, two verbal aptitude tests, a vocabulary test, and a nonverbal aptitude test. These measures were all correlated with errors and with one another. The correlation matrix is presented in Table 5–5. The matrix was subjected to stepwise multiple regression analysis with errors as the dependent variable. The analysis revealed that only the hearing rating was a significant predictor of errors and that only at about the 5 per cent level of significance. The fact that hearing level, even very low (and they all were quite low, with loss of high frequencies in the speech range), has any predictive value may seem odd in view of the similar correlations between pronounceability and errors for deaf and hearing subjects. It probably reflects the fact that exposure to education in general is facilitated by even a little hearing, a point reflected by the overall higher scores for the hearing subjects.

Answers to Questionnaires

The answers to questions regarding methods of training in early reading proved to be of little value. Most of the subjects reported that some attempts had been made to give them speech training before or during early reading instruction, but there is no way of knowing how successful this was, or to what extent, if any, it was related to reading instruction. Many subjects simply said they did not remember. Pictures with words or words lettered on objects were mentioned in some cases.

An interesting point does come out of the answers to the final, open-ended question, however. The question asked was "Describe as well as you can how you were taught to read." Most of the subjects wrote a short paragraph in answer. In examining these paragraphs, we were struck by the fact that there were practically no spelling errors, but by contrast there were numerous grammatical or morphological peculiarities. Wrong tenses, confusion of singular and plural, and elliptical statements were frequent. Here are some examples:

> After I come back from school, my mother taught me how to read the words in the school books. She used both loud voice and clear lip movement to help me to learn how to read. I was taught to form letter when read. Learn to read comes from oraling.

Table 5–5. *Correlations between Errors for Pseudowords and Various Predictor Variables (Deaf Subjects Only).*

	ERRORS	HEARING	SPEECH	ONSET	SCAT VERBAL	STEP READING	SRA VERBAL	VOCABULARY	SRA NONVERBAL
Errors	1.00	.44	.32	− .24	− .04	− .31	− .37	− .25	.23
Hearing rating		1.00	.53	− .31	.09	− .16	− .23	.04	.04
Speech rating			1.00	− .43	− .22	− .54	− .23	− .23	− .01
Age of onset				1.00	.05	.21	.05	− .10	− .17
SCAT verbal					1.00	.32	.27	.54	.08
STEP reading						1.00	.39	.70	.15
SRA verbal							1.00	.54	− .24
Vocabulary								1.00	.04
SRA nonverbal									1.00

I was learning to read through writing alphabets on notebook. . . . Later my teacher display several cards with pictures on a board.

It is not our aim here to interpret these errors, but it is notable that they are not similar to telegraphic statements or misusages of a young hearing child. Morphological conventions easily picked up by a hearing child seem often to be lacking. Evidently, it is very important to hear speech to learn to use these conventions consistently. But this does not seem to be the case for spelling patterns; they have become effective in the deaf group without their hearing the sounds they map to.

DISCUSSION

In the light of these data, let us reconsider now the five hypotheses presented earlier. Are any of them confirmed or weakened? Consider first the ones that can reasonably be eliminated.

The hypothesis that a word is matched to an acoustic representation before it is read and that a familiar sound is facilitating cannot be right. It is obviously impossible for the deaf subjects. Even those with the highest ratings for hearing were unable to discriminate speech sounds.

It is equally unlikely that matching to an articulatory plan can adequately explain the difference between the pronounceable and unpronounceable words. Most of the deaf subjects spoke very little and furthermore the speech rating (its comprehensibility and therefore its differentiation) did not predict errors.

What about sequential dependencies? Ordinary summed bigram and trigram frequencies were poor predictors of errors, so sequential probability as such, taking no account of beginnings and endings of words, is inadequate. The Mayzner bigram count, which considers structural features of words such as letter position and length, was better, however, and thus indicates the importance of these features.

We come now to the hypothesis that inspired our first experiment— that spellings that map with invariance to sound become chunks or larger units because of the one-to-one mapping rule. With great reluctance, we conclude that this hypothesis is seriously weakened. The fact that the deaf subjects were equally or indeed more facilitated in reading pronounceable spellings must mean that the mapping relation to sound is not essential—or, rather, that it is not essential that the reader experience the cross-modal invariance.

In another sense, however, the cross-modal invariance is essential.

It is essential in the evolution of written language. Our fifth hypothesis was that pronounceability ratings are measuring orthographic regularity (rules governing the internal structure of English words) and that it is this kind of structure in the pronounceable words that facilitates perception. The words are rated pronounceable, because the writing system—and therefore rules for spelling—evolved in relation to sound. Therefore, pseudowords that follow the rules must map to sound with regularity and must be rated pronounceable by hearing subjects.

Writing is a surrogate for speech; but orthographic rules are rules in their own right and apparently can be learned as such, quite aside from the fact that any word they produce maps predictably to speech sounds. Sound would seem thus to be not necessarily a part of the individual's processing in forming higher units of reading, although historically it formed them in the spelling patterns of the written language. An intelligent deaf reader does master and use the regular spelling patterns of the language in processing graphic material and is facilitated by their presence. The redundancy contributed by invariant mapping to speech sounds may well make it easier for the hearing child to pick up the common spelling patterns and regularities as he learns to read, but clearly it can be done without this.

We need now to know more about the structural constraints within the words that contribute order and reduce the amount of information to be processed. We need also to find out the best way of learning them. Given a hearing child, will he abstract the common patterns in different words more easily if the redundant common (invariant) sound patterns always accompany them? Or will this added information serve at first to distract him, divide his attention, and lengthen the time required for abstracting the spelling patterns and rules?

Probably only research with the child as he is actually learning will help us to answer these questions. In a first onslaught on the problem, we are studying the abstraction of very simple spelling patterns by five- and six-year-old children just prior to their entering first grade. A learning set procedure has been adopted, with a task that combines discrimination and classification. A set of cards each containing a word is given the child, who proceeds to sort them into two piles. In one pile go all the words that contain the "concept," a common cluster such as *st* at the beginning of the words. In another go all the "negative instances." As the child proceeds from problem to problem, the abstraction of a new pattern may become easier. In pilot data, we found that in a few children the set built up quickly and led to 100 per cent success after a few days of practice. In others, success came hard, if at all. Would these children profit by adding the spoken counterparts, so that they can abstract the common auditory feature? Little is known about the effect of cross-modal redundancy in concept formation, especially in children, but the issue seems to us a critical one.

It is possible that beginning with morphological rules already known to the child, such as formation of plurals, and linking them with the appropriate spelling pattern would lead easily into the set to abstract order within words. How much verbal instruction helps is another question. That it does help in a specific instance of a pattern is true, we have found, but it seems also to hinder transfer in some cases. The question is how to build a general set to abstract the rules, and thereby gain the most powerful aid to transfer in reading new words that follow rules, if we are concerned with building skill in reading by larger units and thus reducing the information load.

SUMMARY

As experiment was reported in which deaf and hearing subjects were compared for the ability to read, under tachistoscopic presentation, letter strings (pseudowords) that did, or did not, follow rules of orthography that rendered them pronounceable or relatively unpronounceable. Deaf as well as hearing readers were more successful in reading the pronounceable ones. This finding must mean that orthographic rules were used by these subjects even though the invariant sound mapping was not available to them. Research is needed to show the best way to teach or promote induction of spelling patterns in order to promote skill in processing written language in units that reduce the information load.

REFERENCES

Anisfeld, M. A comment on "The role of grapheme-phoneme correspondence in the perception of words." *American Journal of Psychology*, 1964, *77*, 320–326.

Cattell, J. McK. Uber der Zeit der Erkennung und Benennung von Schriftzeichen, Bildern, und Farben. *Philosophische Studien*, 1885, *2*, 635–650.

Diebold, A. R. A survey of psycholinguistic research, 1954–1964. In C. E. Osgood and T. A. Sebeok (eds.), *Psycholinguistics: A Survey of Theory and Research Problems*. Bloomington, Ind.: Indiana University Press, 1965.

Doehring, D. G., & Rosentein, J. Visual word recognition by deaf and hearing children. *Journal of Speech and Hearing Research*, 1960, *3*, 320–326.

Gibson, E. J. On the perception of words. *American Journal of Psychology*, 1964, *77*, 668–669.

Gibson, E. J., Pick, A., Osser, H., & Hammond, M. The role of grapheme-phoneme correspondence in the perception of words. *American Journal of Psychology*, 1962, *75*, 554–570.

Hockett, C. F. Analysis of English spelling. In *A Basic Research Program on Reading*, Cooperative Research Project No. 639, Final Report to U.S. Office of Education, 1963.

Levin, H., & Biemiller, A. J. Studies of oral reading: I. Words vs. pseudo-words. In H. Levin, E. S. Gibson, and J. J. Gibson, *The Analysis of Reading Skill*, Cooperative Research Project No. 5-1213, Final Report to U.S. Office of Education, 1968.

Liberman, A. M., Cooper, F. S., Harris, K. S., & MacNeilage, P. F. A motor theory of speech perception. In *Proceedings of the Speech Community Seminar*. Stockholm: Royal Institute of Technology, 1963.

Mayzner, M. S., & Tresselt, M. E. Tables of single-letter and digram frequency counts for various word-length and letter-position combinations. *Psychonomic Monograph Supplement*, 1965, *1*, 13–22.

Mayzner, M. S., Tresselt, M. E., & Wolin, B. R. Tables of trigram frequency counts for various word-length and letter-position combinations. *Psychonomic Monograph Supplement*, 1965, *1*, 33–78.

Miller, G. A., Bruner, J., & Postman, L. Familiarity of letter sequences and tachistopscopic identification. *Journal of General Psychology*, 1954, *50*, 129–139.

Miller, G. A. Free recall of redundant strings of letters. *Journal of Experimental Psychology*, 1958, *56*, 484–491.

Underwood, B. J., & Schulz, R. W. *Meaningfulness and Verbal Learning*. New York: Lippincott, 1960.

Venezky, R. L. A computer program for deriving spelling-to-sound correlations. In *A Basic Research Program on Reading*, Cooperative Research Project No. 639, Final Report to U.S. Office of Education, 1963.

Venezky, R. L., & Weir, R. H. *A Study of Selected Spelling-to-Sound Correspondence Patterns*, Cooperative Research Project No. 3090, Final Report to U.S. Office of Education, 1966.

Wallach, M. A. Perceptual recognition of approximations to English in relation to spelling achievement. *Journal of Educational Psychology*, 1963, *54*, 57–62.

6 JULIAN HOCHBERG

Components of Literacy: Speculations and Exploratory Research

We must learn about the wide world that confronts us in install-ments, by very narrow glances in different directions, for our eyes register fine detail only within a very small region of the visual field. The inte-gration of these serial glimpses into a single, apparently stable perceived world, with fine detail apparently equally distributed throughout, is usu-ally very good, and the perceived world normally contains little hint of the continual changes of retinal image that occur as the eye sweeps the optic array confronting it. In consequence, the psychologist can often ignore the sequential nature of the sensory input by choosing the outer environment as his starting point when he analyzes the perceptual proc-ess (the optic array, the "picture plane," the distal world itself). Where one is concerned with looking behaviors per se, however, this simplifica-tion is impossible. Especially in the case of the reading process, the limits of the single glance, the nature and determinants of the succession of glances, and the rules by which the contents of successive glances are integrated into a single perceptual structure are questions that cannot be disregarded.

To put together the information obtained by the eye in successive glances, the effects of all of the following must be taken into account by the integrating mechanisms of the visual system: the direction in which the eye is pointed during each glance; the order in which the glances occur; and the station point of the head and body as a platform for the eye throughout all these glances. Thus, if the reader fixates in turn each of three letters, *a, b, c,* he must be able to register and to store both the visual data about shape gained in each fixation, and about the shapes' relative locations in outer space—that is, their "distal addresses"—if he is to perceive the spatial array as *abc* rather than as *cba* and so on. He must also be able to treat as completely equivalent the various different sequences of successive glances by which he arrives at a given distal address, so that regardless of how his eye arrives at a given fixation point (for example, whether he fixates in the ordered sequence *abc, cba, acb,* and so on), and regardless of that fixation point's position relative to the shape to which some distal address must be assigned, the same spatial array is perceived.

The spatial framework within which a distal address is assigned to any given shape by the visual system need not be at rest with respect to the reader—for example, at least in some circumstances, the various points on a sheet of paper, which is itself in random short-excursion movement, are nevertheless assigned to fixed and rigid distal addresses on that paper, as when one reads a mildly fluttering newspaper. This point is sufficient to distinguish that property of a shape that I am here calling its "distal address" from the similar term of "visual direction."

The sequential fixations must be guided by the distributions of information within each visual display if any economy of search is to be achieved. Such guidance of the search pattern by the visual display itself can only be of two kinds:

1. The low-acuity information picked up in the periphery of the eye can suggest to the optic search system where it must move its point of clearest vision in order to get detailed view of some potentially interesting region; call this "peripheral search guidance," or "PSG."

2. Knowledge about what he has seen so far should provide the observer with some hypotheses about where he should look in order to obtain further information; call this "cognitive search guidance," or "CSG." I'm not talking about real or consciously reported hypotheses, but about *constructs*—the observer acts *as though* he had hypotheses.

Visual perception requires such complex directional guidance and record-keeping in a very general way that we should expect to find the implied visuomotor abilities to be highly developed even in early childhood. Because CSG will in general depend heavily on both the immediate and the long-term personal history, looking sequence patterns should vary from one observer to the next, and perhaps from one time of perusal to the next (Buswell, 1935). However, because the number of points of informational value in the view is determined by the display, as well as by the observer's own patterns of CSG, we should expect that the general selection of regions that will be fixated, if not the order of their fixations, should be similar from one observer to the next, and this also seems to be the case (Brooks, 1961; Hochberg, 1962).

I know of no studies in which eye movements were recorded in normal environments without the subjects' knowledge. In fact, I do not know of any practical method by which this can be done without either fettering the head and trunk in an exquisitely unnatural manner or generating records that are extremely laborious and expensive to read. However, it seems reasonable to believe that something like the following occurs.

First, the major potentially informative points of the scene are scanned, probably with as much information gathered from one position of head and trunk as possible, that is, with as small a ratio of head movements to eye movements as possible. Then, where small detail is needed to determine some aspect of the scene's meaning, saccades will bring the appropriate regions to the fovea, followed by whatever small excursions may be needed to answer questions raised by the major glimpses and to confirm conclusions thus formed about the contents of the array.

This should produce a high ratio of large saccades to small ones, with successively more detailed expectations being tested by smaller saccades, up to the limits dictated by the task and by the stimulus display. The mechanism for keeping track of distal addresses over large excursions should be well practiced; the mechanism for keeping track of small, sequential excursions need not be, because these are merely filling in forms that have already been surveyed roughly by large movements.

There is nothing at all in this posited ability, however, as we have discussed it so far, that should make it possible for a subject to keep precise track of the order in which any search course has been traversed, mapping spatial order into temporal sequence. The mechanisms have been developed to keep track of spatial structures regardless of the sequence of glimpses by which that structure has been sampled. Keeping track of the temporal order of letter-by-letter fixations should not be an easy task with this set of skills. Yet this is just what beginning readers have to do, and, I shall argue, it is only much later, when the reader becomes expert at traversing a large spatial array of text by a relatively small number of fixations, that he can apply to the perusal of the printed page the habits of eye movements practiced so long and continually in looking at the world.

The first new task introduced by reading is the necessity of translating spatial into temporal order. Assume that the reader starts by learning to put together groups of one or two letters into the sequences comprised by words. Whether or not the reader actually learns this way, or by some more "molar" method of instruction, seems to me to be largely immaterial; even if he started with a visual vocabulary in which each word had been learned as a unique pattern, he would still have to put together the successive glances necessitated by words and phrases that are longer than can be encompassed in a single glance. Assume next that such small sequential fixation movements are very difficult and tiring to execute and to keep track of because they run counter to the normal demands that the visual environment has trained the oculomotor system's search functions to fulfill. Common usage has it that children need to learn with large letters and words because these are easier to discriminate. Why are they easier to discriminate? Certainly not in terms of visual acuity, of which the child has plenty to spare. My explanation is that if larger letters are in fact easier for beginning readers, it is at least in part owing to the difficulties in hobbling the eyes to make shorter and more systematically sequential saccades than those to which they are accustomed and suited.

The advanced reader, on the other hand, should need much less in the way of short saccades, making relatively long sweeps directed by PSG and CSG. That is, the practiced reader should learn to sample a page or text (rather than to "read it" in the strict sense of the term), moving his eyes in ways much closer to those used in viewing the normal world, therefore closer to the long and irregular excursions of normal vision. Skilled, directed reading should be a process closer to an open-ended expectancy-testing than to decoding a string of symbols.

What has the skilled reader learned that makes fewer fixations and longer eye movements possible? Originally, with one letter or letter group as a stimulus, and with an overt vocalization or subvocalization as his response, the beginning reader must make many fixations. After skill in directed reading has been achieved, far fewer fixations per block of letters are made, and it looks as though the reader is "picking up" many more letters per fixation. What makes it possible for the skilled reader to do with fewer fixations?

For one thing, the skilled reader has acquired strong response biases, or guessing tendencies. Given a few cues, he will respond as though the entire word, or perhaps an entire phrase, had been presented. Does this mean that he now can see more letters at a single glance? Hardly, else "proofreader's error" would not be so prevalent and so easy to demonstrate. Instead of seeing more letters, what this implies is that the reader is more ready to make the response that would be appropriate were a whole word seen clearly, when in fact only a portion of it falls on the fovea. Why should he have been reinforced for doing this? Because under meaning-retrieval conditions, the reader is always concerned, not with what particular stimulus pattern momentarily confronts his eye, but with the provisional information that this fixation brings to him about the substance of what he's reading and about where it tells him to look next. This careless and premature response must be the very heart of what is learned in directed reading.

What I'm arguing here, in short, is that there are a number of very different response systems that change as a result of acquiring skill at directed reading, but that there's no reason to believe that there's any change in what the reader actually sees at any glance. What responses change with the acquisition of reading skill? The answer, one would think, would be found in the three response systems that are most important to speed of sampling for meaning:

1. The experienced reader must respond with a readiness to emit one or another spoken word or phrase, as a preplanned motor unit, that is, with an articulatory program appropriate both to some features of the printed word that falls within clear vision where he happens to be fixated and to the various meaningful expectations that his previous fixations have built up with respect to that text. Because vocalization is rarely called for, and because reading speed greatly exceeds articulation speed anyway, I envision such verbal responses as being more in the nature of programs to speak a given word—perhaps merely the preparatory set to vocalize the initial sounds—rather than actual verbal responses. I shall return to this point shortly. This response bias will not only produce informed guesses about partially glimpsed stimuli; it will also help encode, store, and retrieve the contents of even fully grasped fixations.

2. The experienced reader must treat each important printed cue, each distinctive visual feature of word or phrase, as a confirmation or disconfirmation of some class of expectations and must respond with a set

of expectations concerning what should follow the particular material he's reading. (This is a psycholinguistic problem, and I have no idea how one would go about studying this aspect of the reading process.)

3. The experienced reader must respond to the contents of one fixation by making plans as to where he will look next. At the very lowest level, he must pick up with his peripheral vision cues that tell him where regions of high informational value lie in the field. (I shall present some research to this point, too.)

But in addition to all of these responses, which obviously must change as reading skill develops, the subject should also be able to see the forms of the letters and words he looks at. Is there good reason to believe that this ability has changed?

Much of the relevant evidence has been obtained by tachistoscopic research. Let us briefly consider whether such research findings really imply perceptual change.

A major argument in favor of the thesis that familiarity has increased the ability to receive a greater number of letters during a single exposure is the long-attested fact that it takes fewer (and/or shorter) exposures to report familiar textual material (for example, letters, words) than to report unfamiliar material (for example, reversed letters, nonsense syllables). In tachistoscopic presentation, the subject looks very briefly at a particular stimulus pattern. Presumably, the reason tachistoscopic exposures are treated as being relevant to the reading process is that they simulate the momentary fixations that occur between saccades in normal reading. However, because they appear out of context, are usually not programmed by the subject's eye movements, and demand a response (namely, *What word do you see?*) that is very uncharacteristic of the reading process, the relevance of any tachistoscopic experiment to the normal reading process must always be questioned. What I'm saying may be a commonplace, but it means that the good reader—certainly the student who survives to become a college freshman, and provides our major subject population in tachistoscopic experiments—is trained to do all sorts of things with briefly glimpsed letter groups, but saying with precision the letters that he actually sees is not one of them. However, there is good evidence that under tachistoscopic exposure familiar graphic material is reported better than unfamiliar material (Henle, 1942; Solomon and Howes, 1951). It is not clear, however, whether this advantage of familiar over unfamiliar words is owing to improved reception, that is, to an increased sensitivity to the forms of letters or letter groups, or to response bias, either as expressed in a simple guessing tendency or in a greater capacity to encode and to remember meaningful rather than unmeaningful material.

Consider Henle's demonstration that familiar letters can be identified under briefer presentations than their unfamiliar mirror images. This advantage of familiar over unfamiliar letters disappears when subjects are asked to make a same-different judgment (SD) between pairs of letters or of mirror images presented simultaneously (Hayes, Robinson, and Brown, 1961). What about words? We know that familiar words can be recognized at briefer exposures than unfamiliar words. But tachistoscopic recognition experiments require the subject to compare his memory of the letter group he has just seen with some word memory. R. Keen, V. Brooks, and I adapted the procedure of Hayes et al. to demonstrate that the effects of familiarity appear when subjects have to make same-different judgments between words that they cannot view simultaneously, but that the effects may disappear when the displays permit simultaneous shape comparison (Hochberg, 1968).

In the set of experiments I shall describe here, pairs of words or pairs of paralogs were arranged in double columns of letters, with each member of any pair of corresponding letters falling within foveal distance of each other. Columns were used, instead of horizontal displays, to minimize distance between corresponding letters and to minimize responses to familiar word shapes. One member of each double column (that is, one word or paralog) was either the same as or different from the other member, in that a difference in two letters appeared in half the presentations. Each such member might be either meaningful and pronounceable by both adults and children (for example, *cowboy*); it might be pronounceable only by adults (for example, *bierre*); or it might be meaningless and unpronounceable. There were six different pairs; each appeared twice, with the two members of each pair the same, and twice different, for a total of twenty-four pairs. Pair members consisted of sets of letters varying in length from four letters (for example, *idol*) to six letters (for example, *serial*). Pairs were spaced with a one millimeter within-pair horizontal spacing. There were six such pages with a total of twenty-four different pairs per page. Order of presentation of pages was counterbalanced between subjects (sixteen adults; sixteen children of from five years eleven months to seven years of age). Subjects were instructed to say as quickly as possible whether the two members of each column pair were same or different.

Some pairs of columns were pronounceable, some were unpronounceable; one whole set of column pairs were printed in mirror-image letters, so that reading would normally be delayed.

No differences could be found, either for adults or for children, among any of these conditions. Adults averaged approximately one second per column pair (including response time and transfer of their attention to the next column), with an SD of one-third second; the children averaged about three and one-half seconds. On one page, one member of each pair was in capitals, whereas the other member was in lower case. These pairs took longer for fourteen of the sixteen subjects (averaging about two seconds per column pair, and SD of 0.64 seconds), whereas the remaining two subjects, for whom the order of the tasks was such that the effects of practice worked to counteract the difference otherwise manifested, showed no difference for this condition.

In summary, when each pair of words was simultaneously fixated, the findings were these: whether the words were meaningful or not, pronounceable or not, mirror image or normal—none of these factors resulted in longer times to perform the task. Only one condition hindered discrimination: a difference in form (letter case) between the two column pair members. These findings suggest two things.

First, within the obvious limitation that the subject had to be able to know at what level of detail he could consider two letters to be identical (that is, and not continue to search for changes below some detail size, which he might do in the case of some completely unknown alphabet or other arbitrary form-matching task), perceptual learning and experience did not enter into this performance. The judgment seemed to be one of symmetry, not "reading."

Second, when corresponding letters differed in shape (capitals and lower case), performance time increased because the letters had to pass through a decoding stage, one in which different shapes were equivalent in alphabetic or auditory meaning, in order to decide the sameness or difference of any given letter pair. This point is underscored by the results of the next set of experiments.

In the second set of experiments, the procedure was unchanged, except that the words were now not arranged in columns, but in horizontal tiers, so that subjects could not now read both members of any pair at one fixation (separation between words was now about 20 degrees). Because both words could not now be read at one fixation, comparison had to involve a memory of at least one of them. Otherwise, procedures were as in the previous experiment.

In this procedure, the effects of learning and familiarity became very evident. For all sixteen adult subjects (and for four of the children), comparison of the word pairs when they were in mirror-image form took longer (mn = 1.7 seconds, SD = 0.5 second) than when they were in normal orientation (mn = 0.8 second, SD = 0.3 second). The twelve children who showed no differences took as long with the normal orientation as the others took with the mirror images—that is, they were not yet able to store the words in larger units. No differences were obtained between word pairs in which one member was in upper and one in lower case, on the one hand, and those in which both were in the same case (mns = 0.8, 0.8 second), on the other. But now age level and reading skill made a difference, because those words that were unpronounceable to the particular subject took significantly longer in the case of each of those four children who could otherwise handle the words as units (p's ranging from <.08 to <.005).

To summarize the successive-comparison condition, no increase in average comparison time attended the difference in letter shape (upper case vs. lower case) between the two words to be compared, but comparison time did increase significantly for all subjects when the two words to be compared were printed in reversed letters (mirror image) and also tended to increase for words the subject couldn't pronounce.

In the first experiment then, a direct form-dependent judgment is being made (something like a response to symmetry), whereas in the second experiment, in which words had to be viewed successively, at least one of the two words must be compared as an encoded and stored memory. The effects of word legibility appear in the second and not in the first experiment, whereas the effects of the differences in configuration between letters appear in the first and not in the second experiment. Moreover, in the second experiment the reader was required to compare successively viewed words, whereas the first experiment permitted comparisons to be made within a single fixation. These facts suggest that learning to read long words is a function of encoding and storage, not of changes in immediate input processing. I assume that, in the first experiment, subjects could detect form differences in one or two fixations, as long as each letter pair was made up of same-case letters. However, with different-case letters, each pair had to be compared letter by letter, decoding them to a common form of storage. In the second experiment, all comparisons had to be made in terms of stored material anyway, and here the longer times obtained in certain conditions reflect the greater number of fixations required to compare material for which no larger storage units were available.

Several factors were uncontrolled in these experiments and offered possible sources of artifact. First, when a difference was introduced into a meaningful word pair, that difference usually made one of the two words meaningless. Second, the use of columns in the first condition, and of rows in the second, permitted subjects to rely on familiar word forms and on reading habits more in the second experiment than in the first, and we cannot therefore separate the effects of delay from those of word-form familiarity. Third, because subjects regulated their own looking behavior, we cannot be sure that the differences in comparison times are an expression of fixation, rather than, say, of decision times. Accordingly, these experiments have been replicated by R. Keen and myself, using tachistoscopic presentation conditions and more controlled stimuli, with essentially the same results.

All subjects were adults. Viewing times were approximately one and one-half seconds, and subjects called for as many presentations as were needed to decide whether the two columns were the same or different. Stimuli were pairs of nine-letter or ten-letter columns, with the two members of each pair being either identical or different in only one letter at the same place in each letter string. Both members of each pair were either meaningful or meaningless, either pronounceable words or unpronounceable anagrams of those words. As in the previous experiments, no differences were obtained in the number of exposures that subjects needed in order to make the same-different judgment for the pairs of nonsense words as compared to the pairs of real words, when the members of each pair were immediately adjacent. On the other hand, when successive comparison was enforced by lateral separation of the two columns, a significantly greater number of exposures was required to obtain correct same-different judgments for nonsense strings than for real words.

What do such findings imply about the question of why experienced readers require fewer fixations? They do *not* prove that familiarity does not increase the number of letters actually sensed during each fixation, because our technique might mask such an effect. But they do show that the characteristic effects of familiarity that are obtained in tachistoscopic recognition experiments may be explained, economically, as being the result of having available a library or repertory of well-practiced responses, each of which encodes the entire set of letters into a single response, thereby enabling the subject to store the whole set of letters without loss before his overt verbal response can be completed. This, of course, raises the question of what the attributes of such storage mechanisms are like. There is seductive evidence to the effect that tachistoscopic visual presentations leave a primary visual image that can be read off for about one-third second, after which the information is encoded in the form of auditory or subvocal rehearsal (Glanzer and Clark, 1963; Sperling, 1963; Conrad, 1964; Biemiller and Levin, 1965). I believe that good arguments can be made (Hochberg, 1966; Sperling, 1967) that such encoding is neither auditory nor subvocal, but consists, instead, of articulatory programs, that is, of the plans that, if executed, would result in the translation of printed graphemes into spoken words. However, I do not think this question is an important one to the understanding of normal reading, because in reading the continual, if saltatory, nature of the visual stimulation and its speed of intake change the conditions very substantially from that of the single tachistoscopic presentation. The primary visual image (or afterimage) then becomes an annoyance rather than a source of information, because it can only interfere with the contents of the next fixation. Auditory rehearsal or subvocalizations would similarly either slow down reading speed or interfere with the encoding of subsequent fixations and, in turn, be interfered with by any auditory storage they might produce. Surely the reader's storage of a 150-page novel is not a constantly expanding subvocal recitation of what he has read, and it is not necessary for him to listen to what such auditory rehearsal tells him in order to know what to expect next. Even if sheer subvocal rehearsal plays a role in tachistoscopic recognition, actual reading must demand something like the articulatory programs, contingent expectations, and whatever other mechanisms mediate the laying down of cognitive structure.

But this is a side issue. What is relevant here is the argument that the skilled reader makes fewer fixations not because he can process letters faster, but because he has better response availabilities. And this in turn means that his greater reading speed has to be explained in terms of sampling the text, not in terms of greater "graphemic sensitivities." Let us now consider some requirements of, and some evidence for, such guided sampling.

In order for sampling to be effective, that is, in order for anything less than step-by-step reading of each letter, word, or phrase to suffice, some degree of redundancy must be present. In fact, redundancy is impressively great in printed English. Resistance to spelling reform has been attributed to the fact that redundancy is pretty close to 100 per cent (in the middle of long sentences) with our present spelling and syntax. But redundancy has virtues only in conditions of transmission that are "noisy" in some sense—conditions in which parts of the message are likely to be lost.

Why do we need redundancy in printed English? What is the noise? Why should part of the message be lost, with good type on white paper in decent light? Because it is hard to make small and systematic saccades, and because it is easy and rewarding to make information-retrieving guesses that are confirmed—to sample as lightly as possible here and there in the text, putting the pieces together with as little actual reading as possible. Orthographic redundancy is the price of a weak grammar and the adult's substitute for large type. But it is also more than that. The length of a word, or of a phrase, or even of a paragraph is informative, and unlike a mere enlarging of letters (which permits the eye to make large excursions instead of small ones), the use of a spelling system that can be sampled at relatively widely separated strategic places also provides information that the periphery of the eye can use for guidance in the rapid perusal of type.

Normal practiced reading, then, is an active process, involving the continual generation and testing of hypotheses, not an automatic sequential decoding process. On the other hand, it should also be an extremely variable process. It would depend on the task of the reader, that is, what he is reading for; on his knowledge of the language and of its contingencies; on his knowledge of the world about which that language is talking; and on his memory and understanding at one moment of what he has read in previous moments. Thus, receiving instructions to read aloud would change the pattern of search in the mature reader, forcing him to do much closer sampling. Instructions to find spelling errors would change the nature of the task almost completely. Because such differences in recorded eye movements with differences in task have indeed been reported by Judd and Buswell (1922), the question of the implicit instructions in any reading experiment becomes particularly important. One must interpret very cautiously the results of any procedure in which the subject knows that eye movements are being recorded or that the experiment involves the quality of his reading.

In general, one would expect that the longer span search tasks, which involve expectancies that may not be confirmed for paragraphs or even for pages of reading, would provide the main impetus to continuing a book. Tell someone the contents of its last pages and you terminate his interest in the who-done-it. This kind of expectancy, which demands knowledge about the world, is clearly dominated by cognitive search guidance (CSG) and requires more knowledge about subject matter than about orthographic and syntactic redundancies. However, short-term CSG, exercised within sentences and even within words, demands some knowledge about the structure of the language. The reader cannot sample economically unless he is able to fill in the spaces between the points he samples and proceed to further sampling.

Yet, this kind of reading sampling cannot proceed under CSG alone. The reader also needs some degree of peripheral guidance from the stimulus display. What kinds of redundancy might be sampled on the basis of such PSG, and how would these differ at different stages of reader sophistication?

The first letter in any word probably carries the most information, for at least two reasons. Being next to a blank space, which can be picked up readily even by the low-acuity vision of the periphery, the fixation point can be programmed to center on or near the initial letter more readily than on any other letter except the last one, and the last letter is probably too subject to constraints to be as informative. Second, the first letter's shape offers a more characteristic and invariant pattern than does the same letter with its sides masked in the middle of a word. In fact, there is evidence (Marchbanks and Levin, 1965) that readers do pay more attention to the initial letters in words, as determined by the errors of confusion in reading when words are presented singly. If what I have just argued is true, we should also expect readers to tend to look at or near letters that immediately follow any blank space. Peripheral search guidance should be well able to accomplish this task.

There is another, more sophisticated function that PSG would seem likely to assist. Words differ greatly in length and the smaller ones are usually functors: *on, in, to, up,* and so on. In many cases, these words are probably redundant, because their meaning is completely recoverable from context once you know where they are in the sentence. In other cases, what the particular functor is may be critical. In either case, it should be possible for the reader to detect that a functor lies at some distance out along the line of text in the periphery, and then decide either to look at the word, or, if it's likely to be redundant, to look at the word after it. I have tried casually to determine the average information value of each common functor over a variety of common sentences, by determining reading time (1) with the functors present and clearly legible; (2) with the functors present but partially obscured; and (3) with *xx*'s substituting for functors, which had been deleted. In the last two cases, a list of functors was printed at the head of the page to help the reader. On the basis of data from a few readers of widely disparate reading ability, this technique does seem to be workable and might make it possible to test the assumption that word length operates as a fixation cue in accordance with the average uncertainty of that word length.

Although it seems plausible to me that PSG should be able to mediate CSG in reading sampling, as suggested above, the wherewithal must first exist. A child who is unable to guess what a word may be on the basis of its first letter or two, will have to spell out more of the word, in order to read it correctly. If the functors do offer peripheral information via their characteristic word lengths, fixation deployment can only capitalize on that information to the extent that the reader has acquired expectancies conforming to those contingencies. And so, if all the preceding is close to the truth, we should be able to test the stage of development of the component skills of a given reader by noting the effects of interference with each kind of redundancy sampling.

I shall sketch briefly a recent attempt at this indirect form of measurement of the search patterns. Short stories, graded roughly as to reading difficulty, were prepared in two typographical versions (Hochberg, Levin, and Frail, 1966). In the unfilled, or U version, normal spaces were left between words. In the filled, or F version, the spaces between all words were filled with a meaningless symbol made by superimposing an x on a. c, each typed at half pressure, so that the resulting contrast of the two characters together was roughly that of the surrounding letters. Seen in peripheral vision, the F version of the text looked like an unbroken line of type. Which story appeared in which version was balanced between two groups of subjects, who were matched in reading ability. The material was presented for silent reading. Two age levels of subjects were used, twenty-four subjects from first and second grades, and twenty-four subjects from fifth and sixth grades. The dependent variable was reading time per character. The F version took significantly longer to read. Of primary interest, however, were the results of the following analysis. The eight slowest and the eight fastest first- and second-graders, as determined by their base rates, t_U (reading speeds on the U stories), were compared with respect to the difference in reading time, t_F minus t_U, divided by the base rate, t_U. The beginning readers, who are still looking from letter to letter, with sparse knowledge of orthographic and syntactic redundancies, should be little affected by filled-in spaces. The more advanced readers, deprived of the blank spaces as cues about where to look, should show a marked deficit. In fact, the poorer readers did show little drop in reading rate induced by the F condition. On the other hand, we expected that the better readers, who normally direct their gaze more selectively, would show much more loss, and they did. We have since replicated this experiment (with slightly different conditions) and obtained essentially the same results. The slow, beginning reader shows significantly less deficit when the blank spaces are filled than the fast. The better reader makes the poorer showing in response to interference with PSG.

These findings are consistent with the present argument that one of the components of skilled, rapid reading is the use of peripheral stimulus patterns to guide the eye in sampling the text. This set of experiments is very primitive and nonselective and does not permit us to distinguish the possible points of interference with the sampling process (for example, orthographic, syntactic, or semantic redundancies). Our future plans are to interfere more selectively with the spaces between words while they are still in the reader's periphery, keeping ahead of where the subject is fixated at any moment and, hopefully, making the kind and locus of interference contingent on the subject's performance.

In summary, reading is a mix of many different kinds of activities sustained by different goals and mediated by different skills. It is not clear that learning to read is related in any simple way to changes in form perception as such. I have argued that the main task in skilled, literate reading is to extract information about some subject from an array of redundant and often irrelevant graphic symbols and that this ability is very different in goal, in methods, and in mechanism from the task of translating graphemes into speech.

With respect to goals and incentives, some of these must depend on readers' needs external to the reading material itself, and some must be generated by the interest-arousing and expectation-confirming characteristics of the stimulus display itself.

With respect to the perceptuomotor tasks and abilities implied by such rapid processing of graphemic material, it was argued that no present evidence strongly supports any hypothesized improved letter-form sensitivity. The fact that familiar words can be recognized at shorter exposures than nonsense words may be explained in terms of more available encoding responses for the former. Experimental findings consistent with this explanation were described. Rapid reading was therefore ascribed to effective sampling abilities, resting on hypothetical processes of cognitive search guidance (CSG) and peripheral search guidance

(PSG). The theory implies that poor beginning readers should be less affected than faster ones by interference with peripheral guidance cues, an implication supported by experimental findings.

REFERENCES

Brooks, V. Attention. Master's thesis, Cornell University, 1961.

Buswell, G. T. *How People Look at Pictures*. Chicago: University of Chicago Press, 1935.

Conrad, R. Acoustic confusions in immediate memory. *British Journal of Psychology*, 1964, *55*, 75–83.

Glanzer, M., & Clark, W. Accuracy of perceptual recall: an analysis of organization. *Journal of Verbal Learning and Verbal Behavior*, 1963, *1*, 289–299.

Hayes, W., Robinson, J., and Brown, L. An effect of past experience on perception: an artifact (abstr.). *American Psychologist*, 1961, *16*, 420.

Henle, M. An experimental investigation of past experiences as a determinant of visual form perception. *Journal of Experimental Psychology*, 1942, *30*, 1–22.

Hochberg, J. The psychophysics of pictorial perception. *A-V Communication Review*, 1962, *10*, 22–54.

Hochberg, J. Reading pictures and text: what is learned in perceptual development? *Proceedings of the Eighteenth International Congress of Psychology*, 1966, *30*, 18–26.

Hochberg, J. In the mind's eye. In R. N. Haber (ed.), *Contemporary Theory and Research in Visual Perception*. New York: Holt, Rinehart & Winston, 1968, pp. 309–331.

Hochberg, J., Levin, H., and Frail, C. Studies of oral reading:VII. how interword spaces affect reading. Mimeographed, Cornell University. 1966

Judd, C. H., & Buswell, G. T. Silent reading: a study of various types. *Supplementary Educational Monographs*, no. 23, 1922.

Levin, H. & Biemiller, A. J. Studies of oral reading: I. words vs. pseudo-words. In H. Levin, E. J. Gibson, and J. J. Gibson, *The Analysis of Reading Skill*, Cooperative Research Project No. 5-1213, Final Report to the U.S. Office of Education, 1968.

Marchbanks, G., & Levin, H. Cues by which children recognize words. *Journal of Educational Psychology*, 1965, *56*, 57–61.

Solomon, R. L., & Howes, D. H. Word frequency, personal values, and visual duration thresholds. *Psychology Review*, 1951, *58*, 256–270.

Sperling, G. A model for visual memory tasks. *Human Factors*, 1963, *5*, 19–31.

Sperling, G. Successive approximations to a model for short-term memory. *Acta Psychologica*, 1967, *27*, 285–292.

7 PAUL A. KOLERS

Three Stages of Reading

If anything is true of reading, it is that it is one of our most complex forms of information processing. This assertion is so obvious that it should not need proving. Merely consider the difference between a reader's picking up a page written in a language foreign to him and a page in a language he knows. The page in a foreign language is a visual design, a set of abstract shapes laid out on a surface. It has texture, organization, contour; a person may even, as with an ink-blot plate, see figures in the array. Yet, almost none of these visual properties is perceived when the page is written in a known language and held at reading distance. Then, one sees words, meanings, messages, and it is only when the page is held in a way that makes it illegible (too distant or parallel to the plane of the visual axis) that its pictorial aspects are seen.

Despite the obvious complexity of the reading process, the greater number of investigators have sought relatively simple, strictly causal explanations of it. By strictly causal, I mean such simplistic theses as reading is principally the activating of conditioned meanings, reading is principally a matter of discriminating the geometry of letters, and reading is a matter of translating graphemes into sounds. There have been few efforts since Huey's masterpiece in 1908 to deal with the whole phenomenon, to account for the variety of events that go into reading.

This work was supported principally by the National Institutes of Health (Grant 1 PO1–GM–14940–01) and in part by the Joint Services Electronics Program (Contract DA 28–043–AMC–02536 [E]), at the Research Laboratory of Electronics, Massachusetts Institute of Technology. I thank Mrs. Kathryn Rosenthal, who collected and scored many of the data.

The late J. Robert Oppenheimer (1956) once remarked that a characteristic of a developing area in science is the discovery that the units of analysis employed are too small. Surely this observation is appropriate to the study of reading, indeed, to the study of psychology generally. Without claiming that the "real units" for the study of reading have been captured, this chapter describes three different levels, or stages, of competence in the skilled reader that are revealed by the material he is working on and the task set him.

The experiments described were performed with temporal and geometrical transformations of text. In some cases, the subjects named letters, and in others, they read text. The description of the data is designed to illuminate three levels of performance and some of the differences between them: (1) perception of characters, or visual operations, (2) perception of syntax, or sensitivity to grammar, and (3) direct perception of the meanings of words. The description is relevant to a general model of the reader.

VISUAL OPERATIONS

Naming Sequences of Letters

In one experiment (Kolers and Katzman, 1966), words were presented one letter at a time so that every letter appeared on the same part of the viewing screen as every other. The experiment was restricted to sequences six letters long, and three kinds of six-letter words were used. One type of sequence, an "ambiguous" group, can be seen as one six-letter word or as two three-letter words, for example, *cotton, carrot;* another group was formed from six-letter words whose first three letters or last three make a word, for example, *single, before,* or which cannot be divided into three-letter words, for example, *dollar, knight;* and a third group came from pairs of unrelated three-letter words, for example, *six, row.* We made the stimuli this way because we were interested in the effect on their perception of interposing a blank interval of time between the third and fourth letters. The results of many psychophysical experiments suggest that whether a presentation is perceived as one word or two should vary markedly with the length of that interval.

When we varied the amount of time for which the letters were presented and also the interval between the third and fourth letters, we found that blank intervals that lasted as long as 22 per cent of the time taken to present six letters did not greatly affect whether one word or two was seen. When six letters were presented serially for 250 milliseconds each, for example, virtually identical results on perception were obtained from a pause between the third and fourth letters of 83 milliseconds as from a pause of 250 milliseconds. Clearly, sequences of letters are grouped by the nervous system in a way different from that in which sequences of simple geometric forms are grouped. The psychophysics of item perception cannot be generalized uncritically to the psychophysics of word perception.

We found also in this experiment that the likelihood that all six letters would be identified correctly increased as the duration of the individual letters was increased; but even at 250 milliseconds each, all the letters were not identified perfectly. Thus, serially presented letters must appear for something more than one-quarter of a second each (actually, between one-quarter and one-third of a second) in order for correct identification to occur. If normal reading proceeded by a serial scan on a letter-by-letter basis, its maximum rate would be between three and four letters per second, or, because English words average about five to six letters in length, between thirty and forty-two words per minute. Because college students read on the average at a rate of 300 words per minute, it must be clear that they do not proceed in such a serial way. One other comparison bears on this assertion.

When the letters were presented for 125 milliseconds each and the subjects were required to name the letters or to name the word they spell, subjects did better naming words than letters. But when the letters were presented for 250 milliseconds each, the reverse was true. That is to say, when the letters came very quickly, subjects could make out words better than they could letters; but when the sequences were slower, subjects could identify all the letters in a sequence better than they could the word it spelled. Sometimes one can make out a word when its letters are individually unidentifiable, and sometimes one can identify letters better than words, even though the sequences presented are identical in the two cases. It follows, then, that the recognition of words has only a limited dependence on the recognition or "discriminability" of the individual letters.

Seriation

When letters were presented at shorter durations—say 125 milliseconds each or less—the subjects would sometimes report all the letters correctly, but in the wrong order. For example, if we represent the sequence as *a-b-c-d-e-f*, the subjects would sometimes report *b-a-c-d-f-e* and other such distortions. What is particularly interesting about these disorders of seriation is that they never occurred at longer letter durations, even though subjects sometimes failed to identify letters correctly under those conditions. These results identify two distinguishable processes in the perception of sequence: item identification and item order. Initially puzzling is the fact that order errors ceased to be made as duration of the letters was increased, but identification errors continued to be made. How can the subject identify a sequence of items correctly until he has first identified the items themselves? Kolers and Katzman (1966) suggested that the two kinds of identification occurred in parallel and that each required a different amount of time to be completed. But this suggestion has certain difficulties about it, and I should like to propose an alternative explanation.

This alternative supposes that there are two aspects to the correct identification of items: an initial schematization and a subsequent impletion, or filling-in. The schematization provides only a general framework, a rough sketch, as it were, of what the visual system must construct in order to represent what has been presented. The actual work of filling in details is done later. The mechanism concerned with ordering the array works on the results of the schematization. Thus the perception of serial displays has three stages: *scanning,* to form a schema; *ordering* of the schematic elements; and *impleting* or filling in of the schematized but ordered items. This analysis implies that the identification errors that continue to occur when there are no further ordering errors are errors of the impletion stage rather than of the scanning or schematization stage. Note that both the initial suggestion and this alternative explanation assume a mechanism in the visual system that is concerned specifically with ordering items. The data of Kolers and Katzman, furthermore, limit the conditions in which this mechanism will produce distortions to rates of presentation of five items or more per second, but under certain conditions (for example, when the items are of unequal duration), slower rates may also produce the effect.

Disorders of seriation are characteristic of certain kinds of reading disability wherein some words, usually short ones, are anagramatized. For example, *was* may be read as *saw, much* may be read as *chum,* and so on (Money, 1962). It may be the case that errors of this kind are owing to the combination of a momentarily improper fixation on the end of a word and a slow regressive eye motion, or alternatively, a leftward scan of an internalized image. However, it may also be the case, and this is worth testing, that readers who frequently make errors of this kind perform equally poorly in other tasks involving seriation.

It is a reasonable conjecture that there is a specific mechanism of the nervous system concerned with the ordering of inputs and that this mechanism is defective in such people.

Naming Transformed Letters

In other experiments, I studied the ability of skilled readers to name letters that had been transformed geometrically. Eight examples of geometrically transformed material are illustrated in Figure 7–1, in which connected discourse rather than arrays of letters is presented. The top four pairs of rows in the figure illustrate text subjected to simple rotations in three-dimensional space: normal text (N), rotation in the plane of the page (R), mirror reflection (M), and inversion (I). The bottom four pairs repeat the top four with the additional transformation that every letter has been rotated on a vertical axis through itself, making rN, rR, rM, and rI. In one experiment, a single page of connected discourse was transformed by a computer into two kinds of arrangements, called "Letters" and Pseudowords." In Letters, the relative frequency of the letters on the original page was preserved, but their order was scrambled. In addition, every letter was followed by a space, for example, *e r t s v a j l* and so forth. Pseudowords, too, preserved the relative frequency of the letters and also kept the lengths of the words of the original page, for example, *buoss ra mgerf csltpekr* and so on. With both kinds of materials, subjects named the letters of the geometrically transformed sequences aloud as rapidly as they could. There were 832 letters on each page of Letters and about 1,170 letters on each page of Pseudowords. In both cases the amount of time taken was measured after the last letter on the first line had been named. Intuition would suggest that the different transformations require different amounts of time for their recognition; and intuition is correct, as the data of Table 7–1 show. The transformations are arranged as four pairs of geometrically identical characters. The upper member of each pair was named from left to right and the lower member from right to left. Data are shown for the 800 letters measured on each page of Letters, for an equivalent 800 letters of Pseudowords, and for full pages of Pseudowords minus the first line. Note that, although individual letters within a pair of transformations are identical, the time taken to name them varies with the direction of scan. Thus, it is not the geometry or discriminability of the letters alone that affects their recognition. The times, however, are not the main concern here; the patterning of errors is.

Examples of geometrically transformed text, arranged in eight pairs of lines. The letters in the left margin mark the pairs, and the asterisk shows where to begin reading each pair.

N
*Expectations can also mislead us; the unexpected is always hard to perceive clearly. Sometimes we fail to recognize an object because we

R
*Emerson once said that every man is as lazy as he dares to be. It was the kind of mistake a New England Puritan might be expected to make. It is

I
*There are but a few of the lessons ... be conscious of all his mental processes. Many other lessons can be

M
*Several years ago a professor who teaches psychology at a large university had to ask his assistant, a young man of great intelligence

N
*On his first day in topsy-turvy land he was thoroughly disoriented. His feet were above his head; he had to brace himself for when he

R
*A very young child on an ordeal as it comes were merely a visual test analysis and serves the belief of view prejudicially,

I
*Psychology became an experimental science during the decades of the nineteenth century, at a time when European thought was determined by

M
*Imagine two different pictures. One shows a bright red circle on a pale yellow background, the other a bright green circle on a gray background.

Figure 7–1. *Examples of geometrically transformed text. The upper four pairs of lines are rotations in three-dimensional space; the lower four add the transformation of letter reversal to the upper four. The asterisk shows where to begin reading each pair.*

Table 7–1. *Geometric Mean Times to Name Letters (Minutes).*

TRANSFORMATION	LETTERS	PSEUDOWORDS (800 letters)	PSEUDOWORDS (full page)
N	4.61	4.49	6.42
rM	5.64	6.13	9.11
rN	6.94	7.76	11.49
M	7.15	7.84	11.07
rI	7.14	8.23	12.03
R	6.69	7.48	10.56
I	7.90	8.57	12.54
rR	8.50	9.32	14.27

Table 7–2. *Distribution of Letters in Text and of Errors (Per Cent).*

SOURCE	a	b	c	d	f	g	i	n	p	q	s	t	u	FREQUENCY
Letters														
distribution	7	2.5	2	3	2	2	7	6	2	0.1	6	8	3	2944/5600 = 52%
errors	6	31	0	29	3	18	3	18	35	67	4	10	8	2337/2506 = 93%
Pseudowords														
distribution	7	2	2	3	2	2	7	6	2	0.1	6	8	3	4154/8190 = 51%
errors	9	46	1	42	3	12	2	9	38	56	4	3	8	3641/3894 = 94%

The subjects made many errors when they named geometrically transformed letters. Table 7–2 shows the percentage of occurrence of those letters on which the greatest number of errors was made and the percentage of errors. The thirteen letters illustrated comprised 52 per cent of the total number presented in Letters and 51 per cent in Pseudowords, yet more than 90 per cent of the errors were made on these letters in the two conditions. The errors themselves, of course, are not distributed haphazardly, nor are they distributed proportionately to their frequency of occurrence in the text. For example, *b* appeared 2.5 per cent of the time in Letters, but on 31 per cent of the occasions it appeared it was misidentified. Conversely, *f* appeared 2 per cent of the time, but was misidentified on only 3 per cent of its appearances. Clearly, then, frequency

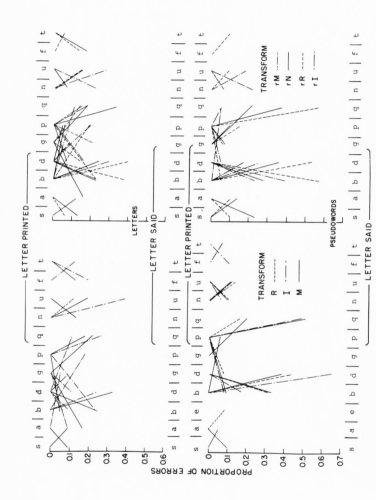

Figure 7-2. *Maps of letter substitutions. The lines of the figure show the proportion of times another letter was said for what was printed, in the two experiments, Letters and Pseudowords. The letters illustrated are examples of the type face used in the experiments.*

of occurrence and the associated opportunities for error thus provided are not the basis of making errors with the letters. It is the ambiguity of their appearance that establishes the likelihood of error. This is brought out in Figure 7–2. The figure shows the proportion of times something else was said in place of the letters that were printed. The upper half of the figure is for Letters, the lower half for Pseudowords; the left half for transformations R, M, and I, and the right half for the transformations involving letter reversal (r). Very few errors were made on normally oriented letters. Some were made with transformation rM, which is geometrically identical to N in Pseudowords but not in Letters.

Examining Figure 7–2 will reveal systematic patterns of substitution in the errors. When a subject makes an error, he does so by sampling from a small set of alternatives rather than by choosing an alternative haphazardly. Thus, *p-d-b-q* form one subset, *n-u* another, *t-f* a third, and so on. Although *bee-dee-pee* sound alike, *you-en, ay-ess,* and *tee-ef* do not; furthermore, *tee* sounds more like *bee-dee-pee* than it does like *ef,* but was never called *bee, dee,* or *pee.* The errors made, therefore, are based on visual appearance, not on sound similarity. For example, an inverted *p* looks like a *b* and is often called *bee,* an inverted *t* looks like an *f* with a short leg is called *ef,* and so on.

The hypothesis to explain these results is rather complicated; it involves the subject's supposition about orientation and the existence in his mind of orientation-related reference letters. I will not go into its details now except to say that in general the data indicate that a judgment of the orientation of the letters is a precondition for their correct identification and that this judgment, an integral part of the recognition process, lapses from time to time. This assertion follows from the consideration that though all the letters of a single page appear in the same orientation, the subject sometimes calls a given letter *you,* and sometimes he calls an identical letter on the same page *en.* This kind of error clearly involves a momentary change in the subject's sense of the orientation of the material he is looking at. A close analysis of the data of Figure 7–2 suggests that there is an order of power in the maintenance of orientation: our subjects found it easier to maintain the sense of up-down orientation than left-right orientation. Another way to say this is that the disorders of orientation, such as those sometimes attributed to dyslexics, are not all of a piece. Left-right orientations are perceptually more labile than up-down orientations. This difference in their lability—for example, the ease with which *b* and *d* can be confused compared with the lesser confusability of *b-p* or *t-f*—suggests that the visual system may have several different mechanisms for maintaining the sense of orientation of objects.[1]

In summary, we may say that, when subjects err while naming geometrically transformed letters, they tend to name a letter in terms of another untransformed one (for example, an inverted *b* is called *p* or *q*) and that the patterning of these errors reveals the prior judgment of orientation of the material. Further, this judgment of orientation is not made just once for the whole transformed page, but is a continuing aspect of letter identification, which lapses from time to time.

Position Errors

It is well known that familiar words are perceived as wholes rather than piecemeal by the skilled reader. Indeed, as was shown above, if he perceived them piecemeal, he would be unable to read as fast as he does. It is well known also that in this perception, the various parts of words—beginning, middle, end—do not contribute equally to the identification. Generally, the beginning of a word conveys more information than later parts, largely, it is thought, because of the constraints built into the language. We were curious to learn whether this lesser sensitivity to the internal structure of a word than to its beginning represents some inherent difficulty in the visual system's ability to process a dense array or whether it is truly a linguistic effect. One way to examine the question is to find whether certain parts of Pseudowords are misidentified more often than other parts. If the selective sensitivity to parts of words is owing to the action of cognitive or linguistic variables, there should be no clustering of identification errors in different parts of Pseudowords; conversely, if the effect is owing to a limited ability to operate visually on a dense array, the errors should predominate in the interior of a Pseudoword.

Table 7–3 shows the number and location of errors subjects made in naming the letters of Pseudowords. The length of the Pseudoword is shown across the top of the table, and the location of the letter on which the error was made is indicated along the side. Scanning down any column reveals that about the same number of errors was made on every letter of a Pseudoword N letters long. Thus, the visual system does not have some special difficulty in identifying the letters in various

---

[1] The subjects were tested on two days. The results reported here are for the first day only. More detailed analysis and exposition of the hypothesis suggested can be found in Kolers and Perkins (1969).

parts of a word. The advantage to recognition of the beginning is owing to linguistic, not visual, factors. Some of these linguistic factors will be described in a later section.

In this discussion of visual operations, I have shown that the identification of letters is dependent on a prior recognition of their orientation and that the identification of orientation is a variable and continuing

Table 7–3. *Number and Location of Errors in Naming Letters of Pseudowords.*

LETTER LOCATION	\multicolumn{17}{c}{NUMBER OF LETTERS IN PSEUDOWORD}

LETTER LOCATION	1	2	3	4	5	6	7	8	9	10	11	12	13	14	15	16	17
1	27	111	163	154	95	43	21	34	15	23	6	0		1			1
2		119	169	134	93	49	36	40	22	20	7	4		0			0
3			160	149	65	38	36	39	26	22	9	1		1			3
4				131	118	47	44	40	31	7	12	0		0			1
5					84	53	33	43	23	17	15	4		3			2
6						54	30	22	24	14	8	1		1			1
7							39	47	29	20	10	3		0			2
8								36	30	25	8	3		0			1
9									35	18	10	0		1			1
10										28	6	2		0			1
11											12	1		4			4
12												0		0			7
13														1			0
14														0			1
15																	1
16																	0
17																	0

process. In discussing some of the temporal characteristics of letter and word recognition, I pointed out that the recognition of words cannot typically proceed by the serial integration of letters, for word recognition is often independent of letter recognition. I have also discussed the problem of seriation and suggested that seriation, like orientation, may involve the action of distinctive mechanisms in the visual system. I turn now to the reading of connected discourse and will show that just as recognizing words does not occur by the piecemeal recognition of their letters, reading connected discourse does not proceed by the piecemeal recognition of words.

SENSITIVITY TO GRAMMAR

In other experiments, college students read pages of text in each of the kinds of geometric transformations illustrated in Figure 7–1. On each of eight successive test days each of thirty-two subjects read one page in each of the eight transformations, reading different pages and in different orders on the various days. All sixty-four pages of text came from a single source (Miller, 1962).

As one may imagine, the subjects made many errors when reading the transformed text. Analyzing them reveals a good deal about the sensitivity to grammar that characterizes normal reading. The chief kind of error was the substitution of some recognizable English word for what was printed. Substitutions accounted for more than 82 per cent of the errors made on both the first and the eighth day of testing. Other kinds of errors were omissions, intrusions, neologisms, and words begun wrong but then corrected. The total number of errors made over the eight days declined by about one-third, but their relative distribution, both among kinds and among the transformations, remained the same. Approximately equal percentages of error occurred on each of the transformations, but fewer words in N were misread. Three analyses of substitution errors will be described.

Parts of Speech

The part of speech that the subject substituted for what was printed was tallied for all errors. The parts of speech used for the analysis were the eight classical ones: noun, verb, adjective, adverb, pronoun, preposition, conjunction, and article. Contemporary linguists prefer to analyze words by the functional role they play in a sentence rather than by their taxonomic categories, and, in fact, it is very often difficult to categorize a word uniquely as a single part of speech. Nevertheless, some useful information was obtained with this old-fashioned kind of analysis, even though certain ambiguities restrict its complete interpretation.

The first analysis revealed the number of times that a substitution was the same part of speech as the printed word. About three-quarters of the time, errors in reading nouns, verbs, and prepositions substituted other nouns, verbs, and prepositions. About half of the time, errors in the remaining five categories substituted identical parts of speech for what was printed. If the substitutions had been made completely haphazardly among the eight parts of speech, identity of printed and spoken form would occur only about 12 per cent of the time by chance. Thus, the actual percentages of identities are well above chance level. By itself, this coincidence in part of speech between printed form and spoken substitution shows that the reader is not reading "just words," but is sensitive as well to their grammatical category.

A second aspect of this sensitivity to grammar is revealed by considering what substitutions are not made. Table 7–4 shows the percentages of substitutions for all eight parts of speech. The columns of the table represent the word that was printed; the rows, the part of speech that was substituted by the subjects. Reading down the column called "noun" indicates that a noun was substituted for a noun 76 per cent of the time, an adjective was substituted 16 per cent of the time, and so forth. The bottom row indicates the number of times that a mistake was made. The table is based on a total of 721 errors—those made on the first day of testing, excluding repetitions of an error by the same subject on the same page, and excluding changes in tense and number.

Table 7–4. *Substitution of Parts of Speech* (*Per Cent*).

SAID	NOUN	VERB	ADJ.	ADV.	PRINTED PRON.	PREP.	CONJ.	ARTICLE
Noun	76	4	18	4	0	5	0	0
Verb	3	82	0.5	6	2	7	10	0
Adjective	16	2	57	12	14	4	2	5
Adverb	2	3	10	45	6	4	2	6
Pronoun	0.5	4	2	10	56	2	12	16
Preposition	1	2	6	12	0	73	10	5
Conjunction	1	2	1	4	18	6	66	22
Article	0.5	0	7	8	4	0	0	45
Frequency of errors (721)	180	163	160	61	31	61	40	25

Table 7–4 shows that adjectives are the second most likely substitution for nouns; similarly, the column marked "adjective" shows that nouns and adverbs are most likely, after adjectives, to replace adjectives. Nouns are almost never replaced by pronouns, nor are pronouns, conjunc-

tions, or articles ever replaced by nouns. Verbs never replace articles, nor do articles replace verbs, and so on. Thus, when he makes an error the reader not only tends to replace a given part of speech with another word of the same kind (shown by the diagonal of Table 7–4), but even when he does not do that, there is a selective patterning to his substitution. His replacement tends to have a syntactic similarity to what is printed. The precise degree of patterning cannot be accurately assessed, however, for the reason alluded to earlier: classifying words as parts of speech is often a delicate and is sometimes an ambiguous process. The reason for this is that just as letters do not have single sounds in English, words do not have single category memberships as parts of speech. A word ending in *ing* may be classifiable equally as noun or adjective, *your* and *our* can be pronouns or adjectives, and so on. In the greatest number of cases, of course, the categorization of a word into its part of speech is not ambiguous, given its context; but even when following an authority such as Curme (1931, 1935), enough ambiguities remain (about 10 to 15 per cent of the total) to make precise statements impossible. Therefore, though the overall patterning of the table is clear, some accidents must necessarily have crept into the scoring. I mention them here, but do not worry about them, and recommend anxiety-free contemplation of the tables to the reader as well.

Examining the frequencies of the last row of Table 7–4 might lead one to think that certain parts of speech are more likely to be erred on than others. For example, almost three times as many errors are made on nouns as on adverbs or prepositions. Is there something about a noun that induces a subject to make errors on it when reading aloud, or is this finding an artifact of the statistical distribution of parts of speech in the written language? To answer the question the same criteria were applied to pages of the printed material that had been applied to the errors in order to find the frequency of occurrence of parts of speech in the original. The findings were clear-cut: the frequency of errors in Table 7–4 is in good accord with the frequency of occurrence of parts of speech in the original. The errors are made according to their opportunities for being made rather than according to a selective bias by the reader. Thus, readers make part-of-speech-preserving errors, but are indifferent to the part of speech they choose to err on.

Grammatical Relations

Functionally, grammar is a matter of sequences rather than isolated words, that is, the relations that parts of speech have to each other rather than the parts themselves. The thesis of this chapter is that the reader, even when reading aloud, is doing much more than identifying or discriminating letters, or translating them into sounds, or even recognizing the internal structure of words. The preceding analysis showed that the reader is sensitive to the grammatical category of words taken individually. I will now show that he is sensitive also to the relations words have to those that come before and to those that follow what he is saying at any time. To do so I will again deal with the substitution errors the subjects made when they were reading transformed text aloud.

Imagine that the sentence to be read is *Emerson once said that every man is as lazy as he dares to be* and that it was misread in the following ways by different subjects:

1. Emerson once paid that. . . .
2. Emerson once bias that. . . .
3. Emerson has said that. . . .
4. Emerson once suggested that. . . .
5. Emerson once say that. . . .

Errors 1, 3, and 4 are grammatically acceptable at the place they occur: 1 could be the first part of a sentence describing Emerson's payment of a bill; 3 merely changes the tense of the verb; and 4 offers a synonym for the verb. However, though 3 and 4 remain grammatically correct when the remainder of the sentence is considered, 1 violates both syntax (it is the wrong kind of verb) and sense. Error 2 violates syntax and semantics of the preceding words; and error 5 violates syntax but preserves meaning. These examples illustrate the way errors were evaluated for their grammaticality: with respect to the words preceding the substitution and with respect to the whole sentence.

The words *paid* and *bias*, furthermore, look somewhat like *said* when it has been transformed geometrically, but *has* looks different from *once*, and *suggested* looks different from *said*. Therefore, the substitutions can also be evaluated for their visual similarity to the printed word. And finally, the readers sometimes corrected their errors and sometimes did not. These three variables make a $2 \times 2 \times 2$ table for classifying substitutions: whether they were corrected or not; whether or not the substitution looked like the original; and whether or not they were grammatically adequate with respect to preceding words and with respect to the sentence as a whole. Grammatical adequacy, in turn, has two components: syntax and semantics, which themselves form a 2 × 2 table. These five variables were used to classify the data in a manner I shall now illustrate.

Table 7–5 shows the data from the first test day for corrected errors that looked like the original, called "corrected visually similar errors." On that day, the subjects made 714 substitutions, of which 374 fell within this category. Eighty-eight per cent of them were syntactically and semantically acceptable with respect to the preceding words of the sentence. Nine per cent were acceptable syntactically but distorted the meaning of the passage (*Emerson once paid that*. . . .). One per cent

Table 7–5. *Analysis of Corrected Visually Similar Errors (Per Cent).*

	ANTECEDENT WORDS		WHOLE CLAUSE	
	Syn +	Syn −	Syn +	Syn −
Sem +	88	1	19	1
Sem −	9	2	20	60

preserved the meaning but were wrong syntactically (*Emerson once say that*. . . .), and the remaining 2 per cent were neither syntactically nor semantically acceptable (*Emerson once bias that*. . . .). When the whole sentence was taken into account, 19 per cent of the substitutions were considered acceptable grammatically, whereas 60 per cent violated both meaning and syntax. It is an obvious conclusion from such data that the error in grammar was a signal to the subject that he had made a mistake.

There is another side to grammatical adequacy, and this is illustrated in the complete table of data (Table 7–6). Comparing the data just described with their neighboring uncorrected visually similar errors shows that virtually the same percentage was grammatically acceptable with respect to preceding words (89 per cent compared with 88 per cent). However, 61 per cent of the uncorrected errors were acceptable in the whole sentence and only 23 per cent violated syntax and meaning. Thus, the other side to grammatical adequacy is that when the substitution was grammatically acceptable, the reader usually left it uncorrected. In other words, the reader was more sensitive to the grammatical relations of what he was reading than to the printed words themselves.

This hypothesis is borne out by considering the lower half of Table 7–6. There we see that an even larger percentage of substitutions was acceptable at the place they were made (98 per cent and 100 per cent of corrected and uncorrected errors). Forty-eight per cent of the corrected errors remained grammatically acceptable, but 89 per cent of the uncorrected ones were acceptable in the whole sentence. Thus, the discrepancy

Table 7–6. *Grammatical Analysis of Errors (Per Cent).*

	VISUALLY SIMILAR							
	CORRECTED				UNCORRECTED			
	ANTECEDENT WORDS		WHOLE CLAUSE		ANTECEDENT WORDS		WHOLE CLAUSE	
	Syn+	Syn−	Syn+	Syn−	Syn+	Syn−	Syn+	Syn−
Sem+	88	1	19	1	89	4	61	2
Sem−	9	2	20	60	8	2	14	23
	VISUALLY DISSIMILAR							
Sem+	98	2	48	5	100	0	89	0
Sem−	0	0	8	40	0	0	3	9

of what he said from the printed word acted as a signal to the reader to correct his error, but the higher percentage of visually dissimilar errors left uncorrected (89 per cent) shows that the grammatical adequacy of the substitution permitted errors to go uncorrected even though the substitution did not look like the original. The skilled reader who has not yet attained complete mastery of the visual code he is reading is nevertheless more sensitive to its grammatical regularities than to its appearance. He obviously is not reading words as such but, even at this stage of competence, words in terms of their grammatical relations to other words.

Grammatical Complexity

A third demonstration of the reader's sensitivity to grammar would describe the likelihood of an error as a function of the grammatical complexity of the text. I shall first discuss what we would like to do and then what we were able to do with this topic. There are several ways to decompose sentences into their tree structures, but, regrettably, these analyses work well only on sentences composed in the laboratory and not so well on sentences taken from the natural use of language. This is especially the case for decomposition of sentences into their surface structure, for many of the same problems that preclude the unequivocal classification of words into their parts of speech also preclude the unambiguous decomposition of sentences into their surface structure. Optimally, we would like to make such decompositions and then find whether the errors occur as a function of the nodal depth in the tree of the words erred on. Trees can be written far more easily for deep structure than for surface structure, but deep structure analysis leaves unclassified many words on which errors are made.

Grammatical complexity is somewhat correlated with the length of an independent clause, as the following examples show.

1. The autonomic nervous system controls the vegetative functions. (8)
2. On the other hand, so long as he does not talk, he will not contradict us. (13)
3. The dream of a single philosophical principle that explains everything it touches seems to be fading before the realization that man is vastly curious and complicated, and that we need a lot more information about him before we can formulate and test even the simplest psychological laws. (21)
4. When they talk about their sensations, they speak cautiously and try to say how their experiences would appear to someone who had no conception of its true source or meaning. (23)

Example 1 is a simple declarative sentence; 2 has one dependent clause. Example 3 contains several dependent clauses within one independent clause; and 4 is a complex construction, with a compound verb and dependent clauses. The number after each of the sentences indicates the total number of errors that were made in reading it on the first test day.

Obviously, however, the length of an independent clause is not perfectly correlated with grammatical complexity. For example, *The very, very, very, very, very . . .* can be extended infinitely without adding complexity; and a string of possessives can do the same, as *John's brother's uncle's father's sister's. . . .* However, sentences of these kinds almost never appear in normal connected discourse.

In the examples cited, the number of errors increased with the complexity of the sentence; but if one believes that 4 is grammatically more complex than 3, the total number of words in the sentence is not the crucial variable in this matter. In our experiments, we have found, in general, that errors do increase with complexity, but not simply as a matter of the number of words in a clause. At the present stage of linguistic analysis, there is unfortunately no unambiguous way to define grammatical complexity, and so the analysis we wish to perform cannot yet be carried out on natural discourse. (One could, of course, require subjects to read sentences constructed according to rule in the laboratory and examine errors as a function of preestablished grammatical complexity.)

Nevertheless, certain aspects of grammar function differently in the reader's mind from others. That is to say, a sentence is not merely a string of words, as the following results will show. Most of the sentences in the text we used were declarative. The first and the last parts of a declarative sentence typically name things, whereas the section surrounding the verb expresses an action or a relation. To study whether these different aspects of grammatical usage affected the subjects' ability to read, we tallied the number of errors subjects made as a function of fractions of independent clauses. The clauses were divided into fifths. Thus, a clause ten words in length has two words in each fifth, a clause thirty words in length has six, and so on. Figure 7–3 shows the likelihood of an error as a function of parts of a clause. The maximum number of errors occurs in the second fifth of a clause for all clauses except those fifteen words long. Given the kind of gross statistical analysis this figure represents, the similarities are all the more impressive. If, in fact, the second fifth of an independent clause contains the parts dealing with verbs, the data suggest that the perception of the relations a sentence expresses is more difficult to attain than the perception of the things being related. On the other hand, the decline in the curves after the second fifth shows that the more of a grammatical structure one has grasped, the less likely he is to make an error.

By now it should be obvious that any theory that attempts to account for reading in terms of translating graphemes into phonemes, in terms of the discrimination of individual letters, or in terms of a sensitivity to the morphemic structure of single words, is hopelessly insensitive to even the simplest kinds of linguistic processing the reader engages in. I have shown this by illustrating the potent role grammar plays in reading—and grammar by its very nature involves sequences of words rather than single words. I turn now to illustrate the case with other facts.

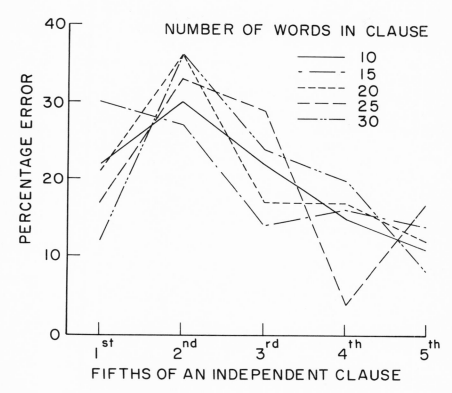

Figure 7–3. *The percentage of errors in various parts of an independent clause.*

DIRECT PERCEPTION OF MEANINGS AND RELATIONS

My argument is that the skilled reader does not operate in terms of words as such. His sensitivity to the grammatical relations of the text was described above. Now I will show that he operates on the semantic or logical relations of the text he is reading, even to the point of disregarding, in a certain sense, the actual printed text, and, further, that this kind of behavior must typify the skilled reader of normal connected discourse.

Coding of Isolated Words

Imagine that words are being presented one at a time on a screen, each word for about one second. What does one see? If the words are in a foreign script one sees visual designs. If they are in a foreign language written with the Roman alphabet, the reader of English sees sequences of letters or phonetic units. What if they are in a language and script that one knows? Some people believe that then one also sees sequences of letters, or morphemic units, or some such. My argument is that a person who knows the language in which the words are being flashed sees the concepts the words represent and not just the words themselves. I shall make this point by describing two experiments with bilingual subjects.

The first experiment was performed with lists of unrelated words. If a long list of words is presented at a rate of one word per second, bright undergraduates can remember about ten words from the list. If the list is arranged so that some words are repeated within it, the likelihood of recalling some word increases with an increase in its recurrence in the list. A word presented four times, for example, is twice as likely to be recalled as another word presented twice (Waugh, 1963, 1967). The experiment I shall describe used this finding and applied it to bilingual lists of words. Here is the paradigm of the experiment:

hat	*desk*	*neige*
shoe	*desk*	*snow*

The question is with what probability will a bilingual subject recall *snow,* which translates *neige?* Will he recall it proportionately to its frequency of occurrence—equal to the average, say, of recalling *hat* and *shoe;* or will its translation affect his recall in English, so that the recall of *snow* will equal the recall of *desk?* If each word in a list were seen only as a word—as a morphemic or phonetic unit—there is no way the occurrence of *neige* could affect the recall of *snow,* or *wheat* affect the recall of *blé,* because each word and its translation look different and sound different. On the other hand, if the words are perceived and stored in memory in terms of their meaning, then presenting *neige* would affect the recall of *snow,* and presenting *wheat* would affect the recall of *blé,* because the pairs of words have very similar meanings.

In the experiment (Kolers, 1966a), French-English bilingual subjects saw long lists of words; on each list, some words appeared in French only, some in English only, and some as translated pairs. In addition all of the kinds of words were distributed haphazardly throughout a list, so that the subject never knew whether a word would be repeated or whether its translation would also appear. Nevertheless, the results showed very clearly that the recall of a word in one language was aided by presenting its translation. Using the illustration above, the probability of recalling either *neige* or *snow* was exactly equal to the probability of recalling *desk* and not to the probability of recalling *hat* or *shoe*. The conclusion seems obvious that for a person who knows them, words are perceived and remembered preferentially in terms of their meanings and not in terms of their appearances or sounds. This will now be shown in another way.

Reading Bilingual Connected Discourse

In this experiment (Kolers, 1966b), French-English bilinguals read passages such as the following:

His horse, followed de deux bassets, faisait la terre résonner under its even tread. Des gouttes de verglas stuck to his manteau. Une violente brise was blowing. One side de l'horizon lighted up, and dans la blancheur of the early morning light, il aperçut rabbits hopping at the bord de leurs terriers.

or the following:

Son cheval, suivi by two hounds, en marchant d'un pas égal, made resound the earth. Drops of ice se collaient à son cloak. A wind strong soufflait. Un côté of the horizon s'éclaircit; et, in the whiteness de crépuscule, he saw des lapins sautillant au edge of their burrows.

In one part of the experiment, the subjects were tested for their understanding of such bilingual passages, compared to their understanding of similar passages in French only or in English only. Our tests showed that even when the time they were allowed to read the passages was always the same, the subjects were able to understand the mixed passages as well as they could unilingual ones. If the readers had had to make all of the words of a mixed passage conform to a single language before they could understand them, they would have had less time to work out the meaning of a mixed passage than of a unilingual one; and having less time, their comprehension would have been poorer. But it was not; and so we concluded that, as was shown in the preceding section, when a reader knows the words of a language, he perceives them directly in terms of their meanings.

This conclusion becomes all the more obvious when we consider another part of this experiment. There, the subjects were asked to read both unilingual and bilingual passages aloud as rapidly and as accurately as they could. In trying to do so, they made certain interesting kinds of errors, two of which are relevant to our discussion. One kind of error was a translation. For example, the reader might say, *Son cheval, suivi by deux hounds,* or *Drops of ice se collaient to his cloak.* He might say *door* when *porte* was printed, or the reverse; or *hand* for *main;* or *de sa* for *of his;* or *with* for *avec.* These translations of the word that was printed did not occur haphazardly. Most of them occurred as translations of the first word in language 2 that followed a sequence in language 1. However, others occurred as the translation of the last word in a sequence of language 1 that precede a sequence in language 2. Parenthetically, language 1 and language 2 refer equally to French and English. There was no difference in the results along these lines between Americans who knew French and native speakers of French who knew English. In both cases, the subjects were treating words in terms of their meanings rather than in terms of their appearance on the page.

In addition to translation errors, the subjects made order errors. The two passages illustrated contain distortions of normal French syntax as well as of normal English syntax (for example, *made resound the earth*). Many such syntactic anomalies occurred in the texts the subjects read, and many times the readers rectified the disordered syntax. For example, the phrase above was read as *made the earth resound;* the phrase *in a cell dark* was read aloud as *in a dark cell;* and so on. In the greater number of cases, these departures from the printed text were not noticed by the subjects; in a similar fashion, their translations of words were also not noticed. At least, this is what the subjects said when we questioned them, and the data show that they did not often go back to correct their errors. And so again I have shown that the skilled reader of a language is not operating in terms of a passive but faithful mouthing of the text before him. He is not trying to translate graphemes into phonemes, and he is not responding especially to the morphemic structure of the words. He is not even able to see all of the words on the page, as I have shown elsewhere. Instead, he is treating words as symbols and is operating on them in terms of their meanings and their relations to other symbols.

This is probably the usual mode for the skilled reader. The skilled reader, however, is a highly sophisticated system performing a highly sophisticated act. It is a characteristic of sophistication that when the need arises, performance may proceed on less sophisticated levels, as in identifying unfamiliar words or reading proof. Thus the sophisticated practitioner of a skill has a hierarchy of options available to him. An accurate representation of any complex skill must account for the various levels at which it can be executed and for the conditions that determine any level of performance. This task cannot be performed inductively, by studying the most primitive aspects of the reader's performance and working up, because there is no principle to guide the induction. The more primitive behavior can be understood only as a part of the more sophisticated behavior. We will never come to understand reading if we concentrate our experimentation on the ability to distinguish geometric forms, or the ability to translate graphemes into phonemes, or similar tasks. Most of the experiments conducted in the last sixty years have proceeded in that way, and we are no more able to understand from them what the skilled reader is doing than we would be after another sixty.

THE REPRESENTATION OF WORDS

Perhaps one reason there have been so few advances in the understanding of reading during the last sixty years is that investigators have not appreciated fully what the nature of written language is. One way in which science develops is by understanding the role of the stimulus it manipulates. That understanding does not seem to be widely dispersed among investigators of reading. Of central importance is the nature of linguistic symbol systems, and I shall present a brief review of this topic. This exposition is intended especially to show why certain kinds of theories of reading are necessarily wrong, and it does so by examining the nature of written languages. It is not intended as ordered argument but as observation.

There are two major writing systems in use in the world today, the semantic and the phonetic. They are also referred to as the logographic and the alphabetic systems. The semantic system is represented by contemporary Chinese, in which stylized abstract designs have particular meanings. The contemporary designs are derived in part from pictorial representations of objects and the relations between them; but the logograms have been so changed over the years that the contemporary reader of Chinese only rarely sees any of the original pictorial quality in the symbols he is reading. All pronunciations of all symbols in all languages are of course conventionally determined. There is no natural relation between symbol and sound. In some languages, such as the alphabetic, the convention is such that the reader who knows the correspondence rules of the language can usually sound out a written word that is new to him with a fair approximation to the way it is normally sounded. This is not the case with Chinese logograms, however, for they are semantic only and convey no explicit information about pronunciation. Two contemporary languages of China, for example, are Mandarin and Cantonese. In spoken form, these are mutually unintelligible, but they are written with identical characters whose meanings are the same in the two languages. Speakers of English have a similar semantic system, which they share with the Chinese and most other literate peoples, namely, the number system. The symbol *417*, for example, represents the same quantity to the Chinese, the American, and the Russian, but is obviously sounded out very differently in the three languages. The same is true for the Mandarin and Cantonese readers of Chinese and, indeed, for the Japanese who use some Chinese logograms in their own writing. The meaning of the symbol is retained in all cases, but its pronunciation is vastly different in each of them.

Learning to read a semantic system therefore requires one to memorize each logogram as a separate entity. This fact, incidentally, is alleged to be a severe inhibitor of literacy among the Chinese, for there is no simple rule that establishes the equivalence of written characters and spoken words. Thus, the reader and writer of Chinese has to learn a spoken language—a vocabulary of many thousands of words—and then another entirely arbitrary vocabulary of symbols for representing in writing the words he knows. Semantic systems have certain advantages with respect to informational density, however. A single logogram or a pair of them can represent the same information that it takes several words of English to convey. The principal disadvantage of a logographic system is that it imposes more severe strain on the reader's memory.

The second major system in use is the alphabetic or phonetic. In this system sounds rather than meanings are represented. The chief advantage of the alphabetic system is that a small number of symbols—the letters—can be permuted to represent the entire vocabulary of the language, for letters have conventional classes of sounds associated with them. This restriction in the size of the symbol set of alphabetic languages—the twenty-six letters of the English alphabet, for example—is associated with a great savings in memory and a relative ease in decoding unfamiliar words into approximations of their pronunciation, but with a greater length of the array on the printed page. The following rule seems to be quite straightforward: the fewer the elements that the user must carry in memory, the greater the spatial extent will be of the message symbolized and vice versa. Given the strain on learning and memory that acquiring large numbers of independent elements represents, it is clearly easier to become literate with alphabetic systems than with semantic systems. The number of words that must be learned can be the same in the two languages, but the ease of representing the words gives an advantage to the alphabetic system.

A saving of space was not of course the chief motive for the development of semantic systems. The argument has many times been made, in fact, that the letters of the Roman alphabet were themselves originally derived from a pictorial system of writing. The letter M, for example, is thought by some to be derived from an Egyptian word, *mulak* 'an owl', whose stylized representation eventually took the form of our M; and some historians of the alphabet believe that the *alpha* and *beta* of the Greek alphabet are derived from stylized versions of a Semitic *eliph* 'ox' and *bayith* 'house'. Gelb (1963) disputes this idea of a pictorial origin of the alphabet; he thinks that all of the characters were abstract representations of sound classes from the beginning. Whether the origin is pictorial or not, certainly no reader of any contemporary language that uses the Roman alphabet derives information from any pictorial quality of the letters. When he meets a new word, he sounds it out more or less according to the rules he has learned for assigning kinds of sounds to kinds of symbols and not according to the pictorial resemblance of its letters to objects.

The fact that there is a correspondence between the written symbol and the sound has suggested to some students of the subject that reading is a matter of simple translation: the reader scans the sequence of printed letters and translates them more or less automatically into their appropriate sounds and thus has the word. This theory has two assumptions built into it. One is that the regularity of relation of symbol to sound is virtually complete, and the second is that reading is accomplished by forming an auditory representation of the printed word. However, reading does not need to proceed by the reader's forming auditory representations of printed words; the fact that many readers do that may indicate only that they have not mastered the skill of reading to a very high degree. And of course it is impossible that reading at the rate of 2,000 words per minute or more be dependent on auditory representations because auditory representations cannot be formed so quickly. The first assumption, in turn, that there is a simple consistent regularity between symbol and sound, is simply not correct for many languages, notably English and French. In both languages, given symbols are sounded very differently in different contexts. The differences are so great, in fact, that it is quite clear that the reader must first recognize the part of speech a word is before he can sound it out correctly. In English, such words as *refuse* and *lead* are pronounced quite differently when they are verbs or nouns. In French the letters *nt* are sounded in a certain way when they occur as the adverbial suffix and are not sounded at all in the third person plural of a verb in the present tense. Further, the sounding of *nt* in the adverb has no sound quality of *t* to it, anymore than there is any quality of *b* at the end of the English words *plumb* and *bomb*.

Nevertheless, it should not be thought that English does not have sound-to-symbol regularities. It does indeed, and rules for describing them can be formulated. Furthermore, the discrepancies from the major rules can always be accounted for by special rules, just as any event that occurs in nature can be described by some mathematical equation. The equation may be ridiculously long, running to thousands of terms; but the fact remains that all events can be described by equations and all forms of writing-speaking equivalents can be described by rules. The questions of interest to the student of reading are not whether all correspondences can be characterized by rules, for they can, but whether the reader learns his skill by explicitly mastering those rules, and whether reading is merely their application. Here the answer is decisively negative.

The skilled reader has learned many rules indeed, and he uses them when he comes to words he is not familiar with. The rules are usually applied successfully, but this is not always the case. For example, words such as *eyrie, phthisic,* and *syzygy* may cause even the skilled reader who is unfamiliar with them some trouble in pronunciation; and of course the word PECTOPAH can be pronounced correctly in two quite different ways depending upon whether it is taken as a sequence in English or a sequence in Russian. How it is pronounced depends on what symbol set the reader recognizes it to belong to. PECTOPAH in the Cyrillic alphabet is the phonetic equivalent of *restoran* 'restaurant' in the Roman alphabet. Clearly, its correct pronunciation requires a prior recognition of its linguistic membership. Thus, prior recognition of linguistic membership and of grammatical category are both required for correct pronunciation. Correct pronunciation cannot result only from translating individual symbols or even groups of them (for example, *refuse* and *lead*). The skilled reader recognizes the grammatical relations and reads meanings directly from the words within a language; he does not read the words themselves. A simple analogy can help make the point.

Imagine a policeman who suddenly holds up his hand to traffic. Most drivers stop when the policeman does this. Yet few drivers would recall whether the policeman held up his right or left hand, whether he was wearing gloves or not, how many fingers were extended on the hand, or the like. They get the message of the signal, but they are relatively indifferent to the actual details by which the signal was generated. They see the gesture in terms of its meaning directly, without first telling themselves, "Ah, there is a policeman, and he is holding up three fingers of his white-gloved right hand. A policeman holding up his —— hand means 'stop'. Therefore as I see a policeman holding up his hand I will stop." Knowing what the signal means directly comes after long practice, of course. It is long practice that characterizes the skilled reader, and it is in direct apprehensions of meaning that the skilled reader's performance must be understood.

It has often been alleged that written language has been derived from and is a representation of spoken language. This assertion is probably wrong. Though alphabetic languages represent discourse by establishing some correspondence between printed character and sound represented, semantic languages have no correspondence rules at all between written character and spoken word in the sense of the above. Furthermore, the arrangement or linear sequence of the symbols on the page of pictorial languages bears no necessary relation to the syntax of the spoken language: Chinese characters used to be written principally in vertical arrays, which permits a fair transformation to spoken syntax, but Egyptian hieroglyphs were written in more complicated arrangements of rows and columns (Gelb, 1963). Meaning was sometimes signified by spatial position, so that the sequential arrangement of words may be significantly different in pictorial writing and speech. Even alphabetic languages may use a different syntax in written and spoken forms, as witness the style of scholarly composition, legal documents, the variant of American English called "Federalese," and formal German. Korean, an alphabetic language, writes its words partly in horizontal and partly in vertical arrays. In this case, the written language is represented in two spatial dimensions, whereas all spoken languages are represented only by the temporal ordering of words in one dimension. Further, developmentally, children scribble and mark at ages near to those at which they begin to speak. In no meaningful sense can the marking be called a representation or surrogate of babbling, for example. Rather than regard the written as derived from the spoken language, logic requires that we regard both as abstract structures, two different means in the skilled practitioner for representing relations between objects and between concepts, which may have more or less similarity in their arrangements.

Thus, what I have suggested is that the skilled reader regards words as symbols which function as clues. Some of them are principally substantive; others are relational. The idea that the skilled reading of even alphabetic languages involves the interpretation of symbol systems implies that the reading of Chinese and the reading of English have more in common than would at first appear. It implies also that the understanding of the mechanisms of reading can illuminate the means by which any symbolic information (instrument dials, road signs, musical scores, circuit diagrams, paintings) is interpreted and used. Proper attention to these facts should facilitate the further study of reading and locate that study in terms of the analysis of cognitive functions. This information is basic also to a theory of symbols.

REFERENCES

Curme, G. O. *A Grammar of the English Language.* Vol. 3. *Syntax.* Boston: Heath, 1931.

Curme, G. O. *A Grammar of the English Language.* Vol. 2. *Parts of Speech and Accidence.* Boston: Heath, 1935.

Gelb, I. J. *A Study of Writing.* Rev. ed.; Chicago: University of Chicago Press, 1963.

Huey, E. B. *The Psychology and Pedagogy of Reading* (1908). Cambridge, Mass.: M.I.T. Press, 1968.

Kolers, P. A. Interlingual facilitation of short-term memory. *Journal of Verbal Learning and Verbal Behavior,* 1966, *5,* 314–319. (a)

Kolers, P. A. Reading and talking bilingually. *American Journal of Psychology,* 1966, *79,* 357–376. (b)

Kolers, P. A. Reading temporally and spatially transformed text. In K. Goodman (ed.), *The Psycholinguistic Nature of the Reading Process.* Detroit: Wayne State University Press, 1968.

Kolers, P. A., & Katzman, M. T. Naming sequentially presented letters and words. *Language and Speech,* 1966, *9,* 84–95.

Kolers, P. A., & Perkins, D. N. Orientation of letters and errors in their recognition. *Perception and Psychophysics,* 1969, *5,* 265–269.

Miller, G. A. *Psychology: The Science of Mental Life.* New York: Harper & Row, 1962.

Money, J. (ed.). *Reading Disability.* Baltimore: Johns Hopkins Press, 1962.

Oppenheimer, J. R. Analogy in science. *American Psychologist,* 1956, *11,* 127–135.

Waugh, N. C. Immediate memory as a function of repetition. *Journal of Verbal Learning and Verbal Behavior,* 1963, *2,* 107–112.

Waugh, N. C. Presentation time and free recall. *Journal of Experimental Psychology,* 1967, *73,* 39–44.

8

HARRY LEVIN

ELEANOR L. KAPLAN

Grammatical Structure and Reading

"A good reader is a good cheater." This aphorism reflects the common observation that readers, at least beyond the initial mastery of the skill, do not attend equally to every element of the text. In fact, they sample the text, attending to some elements—letters, syllables, words, phrases, and so forth—sometimes in great detail, at other times less densely. The consideration of reading as a sampling process leads us to study reading within the context of information processing. What are the relevant units? Further, how do the units vary with the nature of the materials, the task, and the characteristics of the reader?

That the skilled reader does not sample the text letter by letter or word by word can be taken for granted. A recent study by Hochberg, Levin, and Frail (in preparation) supports this assumption. Children in the second and fifth grades read texts in which the spaces between words were filled by a consistent but meaningless symbol. Compared to untreated texts, second-graders were little influenced by the absence of interword spaces. On the other hand, the older children were strongly retarded by the doctored texts. We interpret these results to mean that the younger children are reading the text word by word, so that the lack of spaces does not hamper their relevant processing units. Older children, who are apparently forming units that are larger than a word, are unable to use these higher order units when important cues—interword spaces—are not available.

In this chapter, we shall review three studies dealing with the nature of units that depend on the material being read, namely, the grammatical

This research was supported in part by funds from the U.S. Office of Education.

structure of sentences. A model to account for the findings will also be advanced.

The difficulty of studying reading lies principally in the private nature of the process. It is difficult to externalize and observe the process without disturbing it. To study some outcomes of the process is not the same thing as studying the process itself, for example, the degree of comprehension of or memory for what has been read. From time to time, the study of eye movements has had a vogue; yet we are skeptical about the naturalness of reading under the conditions of eye-movement recording. Although the problem of the ecological validity of reading research may not be soluble to everyone's satisfaction, we have chosen one method, which we have used in a number of studies. The consistency of the findings among a number of investigators has been encouraging, although we make no claim that we entirely understand the behavior we have externalized.

The technique is the "eye-voice span" (EVS), which has a substantial history in reading research. In reading aloud, the EVS is the distance, usually measured in words, that the eye is ahead of the voice. There are two general procedures in studying the EVS. Eye movements are recorded while the person is reading aloud. Or more simply, the text is made unavailable at some point, and the subject is asked to give as much of the text as he is able, beyond the point at which he no longer saw the text. Interest in the EVS began at the end of the last century. One consistent finding has been that EVS tends to increase with age (Buswell, 1920; Tinker, 1958). Moreover, the EVS is readily affected by the difficulty of the reading material (Buswell, 1920; Anderson, 1937; Fairbanks, 1937; Huey, 1922; and Tinker, 1958). The more difficult the reading material, the shorter the EVS. Similarly, reading rate and EVS increase with more structured or constrained materials (Lawson, 1961; Morton, 1964a, 1964b). Thus, the EVS would be shorter for a word list than for sentential material or, in other words, the greater the redundancy of the material the longer the EVS.

There is contradictory evidence as to whether the position within a line of text has any effect on the EVS. Buswell (1920) found no effect of position within a line. Quantz (1897) and Fairbanks (1937), however, both reported that the EVS was longest at the beginning of a line, of medium length in the middle of a line, and shortest at the end. Fairbanks (1937) found, nevertheless, that the length of the EVS was more dependent on the difficulty of the reading material than on the position within a line. Both Buswell (1920) and Fairbanks (1937) found that position within the sentence affected the EVS: the EVS was longest at the beginning of the sentence and shortest at the end. Buswell reported this effect for good readers only, whereas Fairbanks found it with both good and poor readers. Because in most instances subjects were reading paragraphs and because little statistical analysis was presented, it is unclear as to how position in sentence and position in line were separated. Moreover, if we assume that sentences are more constrained, in general, at the ends than at the beginnings, several of the above findings are contradictory.

Having selected good and poor readers on the basis of a standardized reading test, Buswell (1920) found that the good readers had longer EVS's and read more rapidly. Morton (1964a), using reading rate as the criterion for good and poor readers, found that the EVS for good (fast) readers was longer than for poor (slow) readers. Quantz (1897) also reported that the higher the reading rate, the longer the EVS. Thus, fast rate and long EVS seem to go hand in hand. This would seem to be owing to the fact that most of the time spent in reading is in fixation or pausing. The fewer the pauses, the more rapidly the subject reads and the more he sees in one fixation pause. Schlesinger (1969) looked at the number of times EVS's ended at a phrase boundary and did not find a difference between good or poor readers.

Most investigators have noticed that readers make fewer stops or pauses (fixations) per line than there are letters in the line. From this they concluded that reading is accomplished in terms of units of some sort and not just in terms of letters. Buswell (1920, p. 41) suggested that the function of the EVS was to allow the mind to grasp and interpret a large meaning unit before it was necessary for the voice to express it. Thus, he hypothesized that the EVS takes in units of meaning similar to phrases or sentences. Although he had evidence to support the fact that chunks larger than individual letters are involved, he did not have any evidence to substantiate the hypothesis that these larger chunks were in fact meaningful units such as phrases. Cattell (1889) thought that the reading units could be words, phrases, or even sentences, because he found that subjects could recognize tachistoscopically presented individual words, phrases, or even short sentences just as easily as they could recognize one letter. Anderson (1937) suggested that the reader's eye movements are regulated by the content of the reading material so that the reader progresses by phrase units and not word by word. Along this same line, Tinker (1958) wrote more recently that reading is in terms of "units," in terms of groups of words and not in terms of spelling or syllabizing. Words and word groups form perceptual "wholes." Schlesinger (1969) stated that "the span of the eyes . . . ahead of the voice represents a unit of decoding." He predicted that the units of reading could be defined in terms of syntactic structure, that is, that subjects would read ahead to the end of a group of words that could exist alone as a unit or phrase. The results of Schlesinger's studies supported the hypothesis that people read to the end of units, chains, or phrases, which are both syntactic and semantic wholes. However, the exact nature of his stimulus materials is unclear.

In spite of the volume of research on the EVS, it is fair to say that we do not understand the details of the behaviors that result in longer or shorter spans. Input, processing, and performance are implicated, and the final behavior is likely a complex amalgam of all three. Short-term memory plays a part. We are certain that the reader is not picking up the span peripherally as he focuses on the word he is reading aloud. Rather, as he reads aloud, he actively scans the succeeding text, and this active process determines the length and nature of the span. Likewise, we are convinced that the span represents something more than simple guesses about what is likely to be the text, given the materials already read. For one thing, it is highly improbable that a string of words could be guessed correctly.

STUDY I. EYE-VOICE SPAN FOR SIMPLE ACTIVE SENTENCES[1]

The intent of this study was to repeat Schlesinger's (1969) work, using English sentences and several age groups. We were particularly interested in determining whether readers did indeed report phrase units and whether we could see at which levels of reading sophistication this tendency occurred. This interest derived partly from our inference on the basis of the Hochberg, Levin, and Frail study that older children read in larger than word units.

Ten subjects at each of six grade levels were studied: second, fourth, sixth, eighth, tenth grades and adults. Four types of sentences were used, three of which will be considered here: (1) active sentences made up entirely of two-word phrases; (2) active sentences of three-word phrases; and (3) of four-word phrases. There were enough sentences

---

[1] Dr. Ann Turner, now of the University of Edinburgh, is the coauthor of this study.

of each type so that the light could be turned off at all possible between-word points in the first two phrases. A different sentence content was used for each of the light-out positions. Thus, there was a total of eight two-word phrase sentences, twelve three-word active sentences, and sixteen four-word phrase active sentences. The fourth sentence type was a structureless word list; there were eight of these.

Sentences were constructed with enough phrase units in them so that there would always be at least ten words in the sentences beyond the light-out position. With sixth-grade children and older, each of the critical sentences was embedded in a paragraph of four sentences. The critical sentence occurred an equal number of times in the first, second, third, and fourth sentence positions. For the second- and fourth-graders, the paragraphs contained two sentences and the critical sentence occurred in either the first or second position. The light tended to be turned out toward the beginning of the line so that there would be at least ten words remaining in the critical sentence on that line for any one given sentence.

Two similar sets of sentences were used. One set was made up with the vocabulary of a second-grade reader and was used with second and fourth grades; another set was made up with the vocabulary of a sixth-grader and was used with the sixth grade and all older subjects.

The paragraphs were exposed in a box with a one-way mirror in the lid so that the subjects could see the text when the light was on. At predetermined points, the experimenter turned out the light, and the subject was asked to report all the words he had seen beyond the word he was saying when the light went out.

A comparison was made between the mean length of the EVS on the unstructured word lists (mean span = 2.19 words) and the mean length on all of the sentences (3.91 words). This difference is highly significant. The results can be generally summarized as follows:

1. Older subjects had longer EVS's than younger subjects did.
2. There was a tendency for the EVS to be longest on the three-word phrase sentences.
3. Faster readers had longer EVS's than slower readers did.

We were able in this study to replicate Schlesinger's findings (1969) that the EVS tended to extend to a phrase boundary. This tendency was not related to the age of the reader (except in the second-grade sample) nor to the phrase sizes. Also, when readers inserted words in their spans that were not really in the text, these insertions usually completed phrases.

The results of this study supported the hypothesis that subjects read in phrase units. This suggests that readers have an elastic span, which stretches or shrinks to phrase boundaries. There was no difference in the number of times subjects read to phrase boundaries on the different types of sentences; thus, the finding that subjects read to phrase boundaries cannot be a function of the facilitative effect of a particular phrase length. The finding that older subjects read to phrase boundaries more often than did the second-grade subjects suggests that beginning readers tend to read more word by word than do older subjects.

The phrase-unit reading hypothesis was further supported by the observation that not infrequently subjects made up unit or phrase endings so that they stopped reading at the end of a completed unit even if they had not actually seen the end of the phrase boundary on the printed page.

Fast or good readers read to the end of phrase boundaries more often than did slow or poor readers. Thus, good readers seem to be processing more in terms of units or phrases, and their EVS seems to be more adaptable to the structure or content of the reading material. The slow readers, like the beginning readers, may be reading more in terms of what Anderson and Swanson (1937) call "perceptual" factors, that is, they tend to be reading every word individually, not taking advantage of the contextual constraints.

Our findings also tended to support earlier findings. The EVS did tend to increase with age. Also, the EVS for unstructured or word-list material is significantly shorter than for structured sentences. The fact that this difference exists suggests that all readers, both slow and fast, must take advantage to some degree of the contextual constraints of the material they are reading.

STUDY 2. THE EYE-VOICE SPAN FOR ACTIVE AND PASSIVE SENTENCES

There is ample evidence to indicate that the phrase has unitary qualities in various psychological tasks. The findings that oral reading makes use of the phrase unit can be explained, in part, by the strong constraints that exist within a phrase compared to the constraints across phrase boundaries. Some evidence for this assertion comes from the consistently short EVS for word lists and from Morton's (1964a) finding that EVS size was directly related to the order of statistical approximation to English of his materials. Because the manipulation of statistical approximations is equivalent to the manipulation of sentence redundancies, it seemed likely to us that the EVS should also be sensitive to the variation of other structural variables that have been shown to affect within-sentence constraints.

Two classes of sentences within which the constraints were known to be differently distributed were selected for study. Clark (1965) had found that the pattern of contingencies between major sentence parts was quite different for active and passive sentences. His subjects generated sentences from active or passive sentence frames from which two or three of the major sentence parts—the actor, verb, or object—had been deleted. An uncertainty analysis of the results yielded a measure of both the diversity of each of the sentence parts and the extent to which the sentence parts covaried. The uncertainties associated with the actors, verbs, and objects, and the patterns of constraint between them, were found to be different within the two forms. The important finding here is that the latter part of passive sentences, the verb and the actor, is highly constrained by the first part, the object; this was not true for the corresponding parts of active sentences. The latter part of active sentences, the verb and actor, were relatively independent of the first part, the actor. In addition, Clark (1966) and Roberts (1966) later demonstrated that recall for different sentence parts could be predicted from these uncertainties and contingencies.

It was hypothesized, therefore, that if the EVS is sensitive to within-sentence constraints, it should become larger toward the middle of the passive form. A corresponding increase in EVS was not expected in the active form. More specifically, the EVS should increase in size when the reader reaches information that specifies that the sentence is passive. Although this information is signaled by the form of the verb phrase, direct confirmation comes only when the eye reaches the *by* phrase. There is no reason to believe that there is unequivocal information for this decision prior to either of these phrases.

In this study (Levin and Kaplan, 1968), eighteen college students attending Cornell University served as subjects. Two different phrase lengths and two different sentence types were selected for study, which in combination comprised the four sentence types used: active sentences composed of four-word phrases; passive sentences composed of four-word phrases; active sentences composed of five-word phrases; and passive sentences composed of five-word phrases. The four-word sentences contained nineteen words, broken up into five phrases or constituents: four words, four words, three words, four words, four words. The five-word sentences contained eighteen words divided into four phrases or constituents: five words, five words, three words, five words. The short three-word phrase represented the *by* phrase in the four- and five-word active sentences. The sentences were constructed so that the first half of both active and passive sentences is structurally identical. For example:

Passive: The cute chubby boy was slowly being wheeled by the maid along the pebbled lane to the quaint store.

Active: The brash tall man was certainly being loud at the rally of the new group on the main campus.

Differences in the size of the EVS could thus be attributed to the presence or absence of the passive form.

Each sentence was embedded in a separate paragraph of either four or five sentences. The sentences within each paragraph were unconnected in order to prevent inflation of the EVS by the subject's ability to guess succeeding words on the basis of context. Because exploratory data indicated that subjects seemed to scan the first line before beginning to read aloud, the experimental or target sentence was never first. The target sentences were positioned so that there were at least three words preceding the critical word on the same line and at least eleven succeeding it for the four-word sentences and eight for the five-word sentences. Few subjects extended their EVS to the last word in the sentence.

In addition, ten paragraphs made up entirely of lists of unrelated words were included in order to ascertain the relative contribution of syntactic structure to the variation in the EVS. Finally, an additional twenty paragraphs were included as fillers. The first sentence in these paragraphs was treated as the target sentence in order to encourage subjects to attend equally to all sentences. These sentences were not included in the data analysis. Thus, there was a total of 142 paragraphs. Subjects were assigned to one of six different random presentation orders.

In order to examine differences in processing strategies that occur as a consequence of differential linguistic constraints, the EVS was systematically measured at numerous places (referred to as critical positions) within the set of experimental sentences. EVS scores were obtained at various points starting after the third word and after every succeeding word up to the *by* phrase in the passives and to the corresponding point in the active sentences (a prepositional phrase).

The paragraphs were exposed on a small ground-glass rear projection screen directly in front of the subject, who was positioned so that he could scan the lines with minimal head movement. The size of the letters when projected on the screen was approximately equivalent to that found in texts. A fixation point indicating where the beginning of each paragraph would appear eliminated the problem of having the subject search the screen each time a new paragraph was exposed. The contrast between the letters and the background was sufficiently low as to eliminate any afterimages.

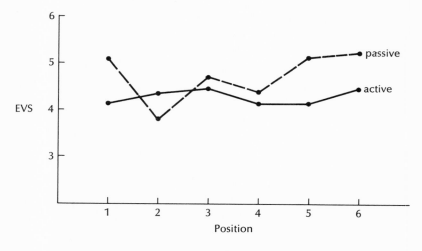

Figure 8–1

As soon as the paragraph appeared on the screen, the subject began to read aloud at his normal reading rate. When the subject reached the predetermined place in the target sentence, the projector shutter was closed, removing the material from view. The subject then proceeded to report all material seen but not yet read aloud. The number of correct words reported was taken to be his recall EVS for that sentence.

The results of this study can be seen most clearly in Figures 8–1 and 8–2. Each point on the curves represents the mean EVS after the light was turned off at that position in the sentence. In the four-word phrase sentences, active and passive sentences do not differ for positions 1 through 4, but they do differ for critical positions 5 and 6. Within the active sentences there are no differences among the critical positions.

Among the passives, however, positions 1 through 4 differ significantly from positions 5 and 6. The results for five-word phrase sentences are comparable.

The findings, then, are (1) in sentences composed of four- and five-word phrases, the EVS span is longer in the passive sentence at the two terminal critical positions than in the active sentence; (2) within the active sentences, the position at which the shutter was closed had no effect on the EVS; and (3) in the passive sentences, the EVS at the two final positions was larger than at critical positions earlier in the sentence. These findings support the major hypothesis that the EVS varies in accordance with intrasentence contingencies. The results showed

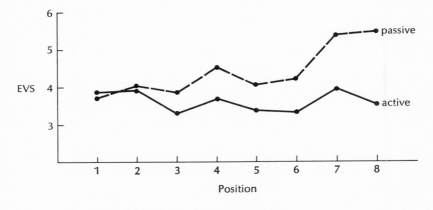

Figure 8–2

that the EVS is longer for passive sentences at that point where the active and passive forms begin to be differentially constrained (Clark, 1965). Because (1) the first portions of both active and passive sentences were identical and (2) the short three-word phrase in the active sentence was a prepositional phrase where the intraphrase contingencies would not be expected to differ from those within the passive *by* phrase (Aborn, Rubenstein, and Sterling, 1959; Treisman, 1965; Fillenbaum, Jones, and Rappoport, 1964), these differences must be attributed to the structure of the sentence as a whole.

That these data represent differences in decoding that are dependent on differential linguistic constraints is further supported by three additional findings. First, and this is indeed an important point, is the low false alarm rate for the recognition test. The ratio of correct to incorrect word choices on the recognition test was well over 1,000:1. Considering the way in which these lists were constructed, it seems most improbable that the EVS represents the subject's ability to guess. Rather, it is more likely that the reader was utilizing the structure present in the written material. This is supported by a second finding that the EVS was constant at all positions in the strings of unrelated nouns and verbs.

STUDY 3. EYE-VOICE SPAN FOR RIGHT-
AND LEFT-EMBEDDED SENTENCES[2]

This study represents a cycle of research from the development of sentences whose internal constraints are empirically known to the processing of these sentences by the EVS technique.

The constraints in thirty-seven right embedded and twenty-seven left-embedded sentences were ascertained using a modified Cloze procedure. Sixty-seven subjects were given the sentences with various positions deleted, and they were asked to fill in the blanks so as to form grammatical sentences. In general, the blanks to the left were completed by a variety of forms, whereas the blanks after the verb were rather consistently filled in by an embedded phrase. For example, in those cases in which the entire embedded phrase was omitted, embeddings were supplied on the right 70 per cent of the time for six blanks and 78 per cent for four blanks. On the left, only 33 per cent of the completions were embeddings. To take another example, the frame in which all of the sentence except the initial noun phrase and the final prepositional phrase was deleted can be completed as either a right- or left-embedded sentence. In fact, embeddings occurred 34 per cent of the time, of which 77 per cent were right embeddings and 23 per cent were left. From these findings, we conclude that embedding in a sentence is more often expected after the main verb than before it, and the forms this type of structure takes is more restricted on the right.

The sentences used in the EVS part of this study were similar to those on which the constraints were earlier studied. We, of course, expected that the EVS would be longest in the region of the embedding after the main verb. Notice, however, that this form of embedding occurs further into the sentence than the left-embedding type, so that the longer EVS may be owing simply to position in the sentence. To control the position of embedding, left-embedded sentences were formed with a three-word adverbial phrase, making the beginning of the critical phrase

---

[2] Jean Grossman and Raymond Yang are coauthors of this study.

the sixth word in both types of sentences. But what if the initial filler phrase affects the EVS? A second set of right-embedded sentences with an initial adverbial phrase was added.

Twenty sentences of each of the above three types were placed in paragraphs as in the earlier studies. The subjects were nine undergraduate students. Even with so few subjects, the results are clear. First, neither the initial adverbial phrase nor the number of words into the sentence affects the length of the EVS. The important effects are due to the position of the embedding in relation to the main verb. An embedded phrase before the main verb produces a markedly lower EVS than does an embedding after the main verb. This difference is substantial—on the average, two words.

The subsequent study included a denser sampling of light-out positions, particularly at the end of the initial NP. Together with the earlier studies, these findings indicate that the size of chunk in reading is related to the grammatical constraints within the sentence.

DISCUSSION

An explanatory model must account for the following facts: (1) reading, as indexed by the EVS, proceeds by phrase units; (2) the size of chunk processed in word lists is much smaller, and is amazingly regular, than for meaningful, connected discourse; and (3) the EVS is sensitive to constraints within sentences. In general, these findings may be summarized by the statement that the size of unit processed in reading is determined by various constraints in the sentence. That is, there are no constraints in word lists, constraints are greater within phrases than across phrase boundaries, and where there are constraints across phrases they influence the EVS.

How do such constraints affect language processing? Constraints allow the decoder (listener or reader) to anticipate, predict, or formulate hypotheses about what comes next. These hypotheses not only permit the reader to limit the range of possible alternatives, but also provide him with a set of tentative interpretations for what he has read and what is likely to appear next. In a sense, the decision-making mechanism tells the eyes where to look next.

The important point is that constraints facilitate processing only insofar as they lead to the formation of successful anticipations. The reader then can test for the confirmation or disconformation of his hypothesis. If it is confirmed, the previously assigned interpretation is accepted and the material can be easily and efficiently processed. Disconfirmation involves backtracking and the reassignment of interpretations; this seems easier to do in reading than in listening. The "garden path" sentences first used by Quantz in 1897 and recently popularized by Hockett are good examples of the commitment-disconfirmation relationship. Early commitment to a particular interpretation leads to surprise and misunderstanding when the reader or listener comes to the end of the sentence. The sentence must be reread or repeated to be understood.

A recent study (Wanat and Levin, 1967) using normal passive and agent-deleted passives is easily interpreted in terms of successive predictions of grammatical structure and their confirmation or disconfirmation. The sentences were of the types *John was hit by the stick.* and *John was hit by the park.* We assume that to English speakers the first form is the more usual; that is, given a passive verb form, the reader expects *by* + agent. He is surprised when he reads, or hears, *by* + locative adverb. In fact, the EVS is longer on the first compared to the second form. Also, on the basis of preliminary eye-movement data, the fixations on and regressions to *park* are longer than on *stick*.

To this point, we are saying that language processors form and confirm or disconfirm successive guesses about what is coming next. Confirmation permits efficient processing; disconfirmation involves backtracking and the reassignment of interpretations. This implies a two-step process: confirmation/disconfirmation and then the processing of the input. We might expect that, with confirmation, the implicated text may be sampled more loosely and hence show a longer EVS. Disconfirmation results in rereading or denser sampling of the text.

There is a third possibility: delayed confirmation. For example, an active, affirmative self-embedded sentence of the form *The man that I like brought the package.* illustrates an instance in which the status of the initial NP is delayed by the intervening modifying phrase. If the interpretation assigned to a portion of the message cannot be confirmed more or less immediately, then it must be held in some readily accessible form until confirmation is possible. Therefore, the greater amount of material intervening between the proposed hypothesis and its fate, the greater the burden on memory and the more difficult processing will be. The EVS for left-branching and right-branching sentences supports this interpretation.

We have used "constraints" rather loosely, and we should be more specific about what we mean by the bases of hypothesis formation. Some of the more obvious constraints result from the direct realization of formal linguistic rules. For example, NP follows *the;* adjective signals a noun or NP; and words such as *that* and. *by,* depending on the context, signal the occurrence of specific constructions. That these syntactic markers are important for understanding sentences is well illustrated in a recent study by Fodor and Garrett (1967). Subjects were presented with simple, self-embedded sentences in which the relative clause was introduced by a relative, for example, *that,* or without the relative. Sentences in which the embedded phrase was introduced by the relative were more easily paraphrased and the reaction time to give the paraphrase was shorter.

Another order of constraints is more difficult to describe, but these follow no less obviously from the expectations of readers and speakers. These relate the subject and predicate of a sentence. That is, given the subject, the predicate must follow, and vice versa. In turn, the language user makes use of the syntactic markers to formulate hypotheses about which is the main NP and VP.

In summary, we have suggested that the reader, or listener, continually assigns tentative interpretations to a text or message and checks these interpretations. As the material is grammatically or semantically constrained he is able to formulate correct hypotheses about what will come next. When the prediction is confirmed, the material covered by that prediction can be more easily processed and understood. This model of reading, that is, understanding written material, is in its important aspects applicable also to understanding spoken language.

REFERENCES

Aborn, M., Rubenstein, H., & Sterling, T. Sources of contextual constraint upon words in sentences. *Journal of Experimental Psychology,* 1959, *57,* 171–180.

Anderson, I. H. Eye-movements of good and poor readers. *Psychological Monographs,* 1937, *48,* 1–35.

Anderson, I. H., & Swanson, D. E. Common factors in eye-movements in silent and oral reading. *Psychological Monographs,* 1937, *48,* 61–69.

Buswell, G. T. An experimental study of eye-voice span in reading. *Supplementary Educational Monographs,* no. 17, 1920.

Cattell, J. McK. *Mind.* 1889.

Clark, H. Some structural properties of simple active and passive sentences. *Journal of Verbal Learning and Verbal Behavior,* 1965, *4,* 365–370.

Clark, H. The prediction of recall patterns in simple active sentences. *Journal of Verbal Learning and Verbal Behavior,* 1966, *5,* 99–106.

Fairbanks, G. The relation between eye-movements and voice in oral reading of good and poor readers. *Psychological Monographs*, 1937, *48*, 78–107.

Fillenbaum, S., Jones, L. V., & Rappoport, A. The predictability of words and their grammatical class as a function of rate of deletion from a speech transcript. *Journal of Verbal Learning and Verbal Behavior*, 1964, *2*, 186–194.

Fodor, J. A., & Garrett, M. Some syntactic determinants of sentential complexity. *Perception and Psychophysics*, 1967, *7*, 289–296.

Huey, E. B. *The Psychology and Pedagogy of Reading*. New York: Macmillan, 1922.

Lawson, E. A note on the influence of different orders of approximation to the English language upon eye-voice span. *Quarterly Journal of Experimental Psychology*, 1961, *13*, 53–55.

Levin, H., & Kaplan, E. L. Eye-voice span (EVS) within active and passive sentences. *Language and Speech*, 1968, *11*, 251–258.

Morton, J. The effects of context upon speed of reading, eye-movements and eye-voice span. *Quarterly Journal of Experimental Psychology*, 1964, *16*, 340–351. (a)

Morton, J. A model for continuous language behavior. *Language and Speech*, 1964, *7*, 40–70. (b)

Quantz, J. O. Problems in the psychology of reading. *Psychological Monographs*, 1897.

Roberts, K. The interaction of normative associations and grammatical factors in sentence retention. Paper read at Midwestern Psychological Association, Chicago, 1966.

Schlesinger, I. M. *Sentence Structure and the Reading Process*. (Janua Linguarium Ser., No. 69), New York: Humanities Press, 1969.

Tinker, M. A. Recent studies of eye-movements in reading. *Psychological Bulletin*, 1958, *55*, 215–231.

Treisman, A. Verbal responses and contextual constraints in language. *Journal of Verbal Learning and Verbal Behavior*, 1965, *4*, 118–128.

Wanat, S., & Levin, H. Reading efficiency and syntactic predictability. Mimeographed, Cornell University, 1967.

9 THOMAS G. R. BOWER

Reading by Eye

Reading is one of the most fascinating skills a psychologist can study, and it is an important skill of great cultural relevance. For generations, it was taught by people who were uninterested in the machinery they were programming. Today, there is a great interest in the machinery of the skill, though much of the interest, it seems to me, is somewhat misplaced. The psychological study of reading skill was begun fairly recently. It is thus not an established area with an existent set of problems and techniques. This is an advantage, because one can pause to ponder the extrinsic aims of one's research before becoming absorbed in its intrinsic attraction. This is hardly possible in more traditional fields, where the extrinsic aims that motivated the first generation of research workers are probably unknown to the present generation.

The extrinsic aims that motivated me were both practical and theoretical. The theoretical aim was to understand how it is that the visual system can carry out this entirely unnatural task with the fluency it does. Reading, above all, makes one realize the truth of the late Lord Brain's dictum that if anything distinguishes the human visual system from any other, it is what is done with it. Note that this assumes that reading is a visual skill. This is a not inconsiderable assumption, but I shall attempt to defend it. As a practical aim, I hoped that an improved understanding of the reading process would facilitate the teaching of reading to children and adults, both normal and handicapped. I also hoped that an understanding of what a reader does when deciphering a text would enable one to plan the production of texts for easy reading. It seemed likely, from a theoretical point of view, that one could improve and manipulate the reading skill in all of its aspects, by contrast with other verbal skills that seem to have such a strong constitutional component as to be beyond experimental control (Lenneberg, 1967).

Given this set of aims, it is natural that attention was focused on the skilled reader. Skilled readers are what we want to produce. It is more sensible to work from them back to the raw material rather than to take the reverse course and begin with children or handicapped adults and work up as many investigators have done. This seems like trying to find out how to build computers by playing with cans of logic modules. From the practical point of view, then, it is important to define our product before experimenting with the production process. From the theoretical point of view, the skilled group is also the most interesting. Consider the fact that a skilled reader can read with comprehension at rates of more than 1,000 words per minute. Such a reader is processing, say, 6,000 characters per minute, each of which is defined by a bundle of ten distinctive features. The data rate of such performers is truly awesome; it presents an irresistible challenge to theoretical explanation.

The study of reading begins in the armchair. From this secure base, one produces an informal theory to guide subsequent research. A number of these theories already exist. For example, one theory or group of theories takes as its starting point the seeming fact that a written text is speech made visible (Levin, 1965). This theory about the production of text is then inverted to provide a theory about the reception of text. The seen word is allegedly transformed into a heard word or some early central representation of a heard word. The reading process is then carried on by whatever mechanisms are used to process heard speech. A related hypothesis asserts, on the contrary, that visual text is not transposed into an auditory surrogate, but rather that it is transformed into subvocal speech, so that the reader understands what he is reading either by hearing himself or feeling himself reading it aloud (Hochberg, 1965). There are other possible frameworks for reading (see Table 9–1), but the two listed are currently the most popular. It is interesting that proponents of these two frameworks argue with one another and with proponents of the visual framework (Bever and Bower, 1966), each managing to produce data in support of his own hypothesis.

My own predisposition, which will be supported later, is to believe that all of these frameworks could be valid for some subjects and that any of them could be made to seem valid for any subject by the use of an appropriate experimental task. Task effects will certainly warrant more study than they have so far received (Bower, 1965a). It can be no accident that proponents of auditory transformation theories rely heavily on short-term memory paradigms, whereas visual theorists rely most on same-different designs. Be that as it may, consider the first point, that all of these frameworks are possible. After all, text is a human invention. It was not arrived at through evolutionary pressures and so should not display any of the rigidity associated with more primitive processes. It is with textual material that we should see the full docility of the human perceptual system. This suggests that we should not waste time trying to find out which process framework is true but, rather, we should try to find out which one works most efficiently.

As a first step toward this goal, we can dismiss the auditory and motor strategies previously described. The data rate of these two systems is simply too low for them to handle the kind of processing that fast readers go through. Indeed, the figure of 6,000 characters per minute seems high even for the visual system. It would, in fact, be an impossible rate if certain current assumptions about the visual system's mode of operation in reading had any validity. Among these are the general set of ideas stemming from the neo-Wundtian theorizing of Hebb (1949) and his associates. Two ideas in particular would militate against fast reading: (1) that reading initially and ever after is a letter-by-letter process, (2) mediated by external eye movements or their covert equivalents, which means that the eye of a reader, or his mind's eye, must roll from left to right along every letter and every letter space in a page of text. We noted earlier that this would mean that a fast reader must be handling 6,000 characters per minute, one after the other, each one defined by a bundle of ten distinctive features, processed one after the other, making an incredible total of 54,000 operations per minute. Because, according to Sternberg (1966), it takes forty milliseconds to process one character, the mere existence of fast readers is enough to discredit this theory. For an experimental disproof of the idea that the theory is necessarily true of all readers, see Bower (1965b). This does not, of course, imply that it is not true of some readers.

The most significant impetus in the psychological study of language comes from current work in linguistics, particularly the theorizing of Chomsky (1964). No real acquaintance with his work is pretended; indeed, most of the research reported here was done in willful, deliberately maintained ignorance of Chomsky's formal theory. That there seems to be some correspondence between my research and the theory is all the more gratifying, if the correspondence is at all real. I was initially predisposed to believe that there could be no correspondence, because the formal theory is represented as being about the production process. There is good reason to believe that perceptual processes are basically quite different from production processes (Bower, 1965(b)). The formal theory has dealt with ways of analyzing strings of words that are felt intuitively to be acceptable sentences. For our purposes, we can isolate three levels of structural analysis: the analysis of the apparent phrase structure of a sentence; the analysis of its underlying or logical structure; and the final stage, semantic analysis. The most interesting thing about this progression is the economy of the final input to semantic analysis. A great deal of input has been shed between the levels. This is interesting because it would seem that some kind of shedding process is necessary for fast reading.

The question is whether the visual system can accomplish this kind of shedding process and, if so, how. Alternatively, can the visual system use orthographic information to decide on the form of a sentence before processing any of the words of the sentence, and can this decision control subsequent processing so that only task-relevant information is processed? Take these two sentences: (1) *The dog bit David.* (2) *David was bitten by the dog.* They are, from one point of view, equivalent descriptions of the same event. However, the second sentence has far more characters than the first and would take much longer to process if every character were processed. However, the second sentence's additional characters serve to indicate with a high probability that this is a passive sentence. If they were deleted, the sentence would read: (2) *David . . . bit . . . the dog.* Now, if this sentence were read in left to right order the meaning would be changed. However, if the primary decision—that this is a passive sentence—controlled subsequent processing, the input order would be *The dog bit David,* which preserves the meaning perfectly.

For this kind of processing, information about syntactic form can be discarded completely. In processing interrogatives, however, it would seem that the syntactic information would have to be preserved, if meaning were not to be lost. However, it would not have to be carried iconically, but could accompany the stripped-down sentence as an elemental marker.

There are other ways in which the visual system could shed information. For example, the time reference of sentences within paragraphs does not usually change, nor does their thematic subject, save within quite narrow limits. Actually, the advantages accruing to making a decision about syntax before beginning to process characters and words are so many that it is pointless to enumerate them. The full advantage of context can only be enjoyed by a reading device that uses this strategy. The major advantage of context is that it allows one to define the subsets from which the subjects and predicates of consecutive sentences are going to be drawn. The only way in which this can help is if the perceptual system knows that the word it is trying to process at the moment is the subject of the sentence, or its verb, or whatever. The advantages of context are lost entirely if word identification is made to precede syntactic decisions. Knowing that a passage is about soldiers, say, is not going to help one decide, for example, whether a word is *fight, tight, light, flight,* and so on, unless one knows the part of speech of the word being processed. This seems to me to be an obvious point that is, however, often missed in discussions of context.

None of this would facilitate fast reading if the visual system had to go through the whole sequence of stages given earlier, that is, if grouping into words were followed by grouping by surface structure, which was only then followed by detransformation to deep structure. This kind of process would mean that the visual system still had to absorb every character before it and hold them until everything else was complete. Nor can we assume that the reader has any mystical communion with the writer so that he can "apprehend deep structure directly." Only if there is stimulus information for sentence form could the visual system economically do the kind of shedding or partialing out described previously. Though we cannot specify this information at the moment, we should be able to imply its existence in a number of ways, for example, by constructing illusions where reliance on this hypothetical form information leads to errors.

The foregoing argument is intended to delimit the framework of ideas that guided the sequence of attempts at experiments presented here. The main points may be stated as follows:

1. Reading can be a visual process, which does not involve mediation by other input systems with a lower data rate.

2. Visual texts contain complex stimulus information that specifies the grammatical form of sentences, with high probability. This information, along with contextual information, minimizes the amount of character-by-character processing that must be done.

3. Reading is a sequential process in which ongoing processing is affected by prior processing and will determine future processing.

In planning this research, it would have been possible to try first to disprove the various theories described. Because I believe that all of them are probably true, at least partially, this would have been a pointless exercise. A more appropriate program was to try to furnish evidence that my broad assumptions have some foundation in fact. The first hypothesis that required testing was that fast readers can in fact make use of high-order textual information to facilitate the processing of text.

The subjects in this experiment were eight fast readers (speeds of 1,000 words per minute or more) and four slow readers (speeds of 300 words per minute or less). All were college students in good standing. Subjects were run in a matching task with reaction time (RT) as the measured variable.

The stimuli used were sentences. The following list of ten simple active sentences was prepared:

1. Kennedy will beat Keating.
2. The police surrounded the bridge.
3. They threw him in the gorge.
4. The farmers support Goldwater.
5. I will support the Fayette project.
6. The students boycotted the Straight.
7. Poachers are killing the cranes.
8. A deer wrecked the car.
9. Hunters shot our pet raccoon.
10. The snow stopped the traffic.

Each of these was reproduced as a negated (N) version of itself, as a passive (P) version of itself, and as a negated passive (NP) version of itself. Each of the resulting actives and passives was then subjected to lexical transformation. Briefly, each sentence was reproduced once with the subject of each of the other sentences inserted in place of its own subject; with the verb from each of the others inserted in place of its own verb; and with the object from each of the others in place of its own object. Only a single lexical item was changed at a time. These sentences were then presented in pairs consisting of a sentence and an alternation of itself. The subjects were told that they were going to be shown pairs of sentences. Their task was to indicate whether the two sentences have the same or a different meaning. A trial was initiated when the subject pressed down on two keys, one of which was a same key and the other a different key.

The target sentence was presented for 1,000 milliseconds. After a 1,000 millisecond gap, a test sentence was flashed on the screen. The reaction time began with the appearance of the test sentence and was stopped when the subject raised a finger from a key to indicate his choice. The sentences were presented in a tachistoscope. Each sentence subtended a visual angle of about 3°. RT's were recorded by a digital counter, with increments of five milliseconds. Pairs were presented in blocks of twenty. Each pair was separated by a five-second gap. Three-minute rest periods were given between blocks. The total number of trials was completed in four hour-long sessions, each separated by a twenty-four-hour gap. Before the experiment began, each subject was given twenty training trials with correction.

The results were rather complex. First, the accuracy of both groups of subjects was extremely high. The total number of false negatives was twenty-four, all contributed by the slow group. The total number of false positives was six, three from each group.

Second, it was possible to produce a very simple description of the behavior of the slow readers. Their response latency was a simple function of the length of the test sentence.

The behavior of the fast group was considerably more complicated. The first thing that stands out is that same judgments took about the same time regardless of whether the subject was matching pairs of the same or different syntactic form. Next, let us examine different judgments where the change was lexical. Here, the relative form of target and test sentence made no difference if results were plotted disregarding surface structure relations and concentrating on deep structure relations. If the logical subject of a sentence was changed, this change was detected very rapidly whether the logical subject appeared at the beginning of test and target (as in A-A pairs), at the end (as in P-P pairs), or at the beginning of one and at the end of the other (as in A-P and P-A pairs). Note that the processing seemed to be truly sequential. Latency of response did increase in an orderly way. Does the order of increase tell us something about the nature of processing here? The data are as follows. The latency of detection of a difference is least in going from a negated to a nonnegated version of a sentence; next are those cases where the deep structure subject of a sentence is changed; next come lexical changes involving a verb; then, changes involving the object; and, slowest of all, changes with nonnegated to negated versions of sentences.

This pattern of results suggests that the steps in processing the test sentence are as follows: (1) Decide on syntactic form of sentence. (2) Use the information to locate deep structure subject. If same in test as target, (3) go to verb stem. If same in test as target, (4) go to deep structure object. If same in test as target, (5) check whether steps 1, 2, 3, and 4 have accounted for all the words in the sentence. At this point, negatives would be (6) discovered. If none left, (7) respond *same.*

This hypothetical processing model can account for the results obtained in the present restricted situation, with one glaring exception, that being the amazing speed of discovery of absence of negation in the second, test, sentence when the first, target, sentence was negated. According to the model I have presented this detection should take as long as its inverse, whereas in fact it took about half as long. A probable reason for this discrepancy is that negated target sentences were rather rare in this task and that the most probable difference between a negated target and the subsequent test was the negation. Because this was so, any subject who was optimizing probabilities in this situation would naturally check for presence of the negative before going on with the rest of his routine. If this explanation is valid, it suggests that the subjects in this experiment devised and adopted a strategy specifically for this experiment. This, in turn, means that the strategies manifested here may all have been specific to this one experiment, which would imply that the experiment has shown nothing of any absolute significance. In my eyes, this is not a defect. I firmly believe that reading is a docile skill. This experiment has shown one way in which the reading system can be made to operate. The fact that the reading system can operate in other ways is irrelevant. What matters is that it can be made to operate this way and that this is an efficient way to operate.

The results seem to constitute a promising, if shaky, first step on the way to an understanding of the process of skilled reading. However, the situation was extremely restricted and differed from the normal reading situation in many ways. One obvious difference was in the amount of context provided. In normal reading, one does have a context that specifies future information to some extent, but not to the extent it was specified in this last experiment. The matching experiment thus has too much context by comparison with normal reading.

An identification design, by contrast, has far too little context. In that design, one simply presents subjects serially with an item from an unspecified set, with no context. When the items are sentences, we have a design that grossly underplays the role of context by contrast with normal reading. With the vague hope that there might be some invariants across the two tasks that might then be said to be characteristic of sentence processing in general, a series of identification experiments were performed. Before the reader goes any further, I must confess that I could not master the intricacies of the identification experiment. In a series of experiments, interesting hints followed suggestive trends that trooped after almost significant differences, all to no avail. I was unable to bring any of the rich store of effects in this design under proper experimental control. Indeed, the more interesting the effect, the more difficult it was to bring under control! A sample experiment may illustrate the kinds of results which were almost obtained.

A stock of 100 sentences was taken from *Time* magazine. The sentences were typed on cards and exposed in a rotating shutter tachistoscope. The sentences were not selected, but were taken at random in an attempt to get a representative sample. Subjects were encouraged to give any response they could. They were encouraged to indicate abstract features of the presented sentences. The subjects were five fast and five slow readers. Interesting effects certainly occurred. The fast readers, after a little practice, were very good at indicating sentence structure, whereas the slow readers were not. Some other interesting effects also occurred, occasionally, such as reports of a sentence in simple present active form when what was presented was a passive past, for example.

The hoped-for invariances between matching and identification did not amount to much. Both experiments indicated that fast readers can and do use the high-order information in text that specifies the form of sentences. If the information does control further processing, it does so differently in the two tasks. The subject-verb-object order of the matching experiment was not repeated in this experiment. If there was any precedence of one part over another, it was a precedence of the verb, but the effect was not significant.

The one striking invariant between the two experiments was the obvious ability of the fast readers in both experiments to pick up the structure of sentences before picking up the individual constituents of the sentences. That they were doing this in the matching experiment was shown by the direction of the subsequent processing, the uniformity of which clearly implied that some primitive decision about sentence form had been made. In the identification experiment, the evidence was more direct, because there were many correct form responses that were not accompanied by correct element responses. These two results together seem to indicate that some skilled, comparatively fast readers take their first step toward processing a sentence by deciding what kind of sentence it is. This decision seems to be based on information spread out over a sentence, the kind of information that could be picked up by the visual system with its capacity for extended simultaneous scans. This kind of decision could not be primary if these readers were encoding sentences one word at a time into some time-ordered, auditory surrogate.

The studies reported thus far have shed some light on processing, but they have not really touched on the modality issue. The sequences of steps revealed in these experiments could occur in any modality, although they do seem more appropriate for the extended visual sense. The following two studies were aimed more specifically at the modality issue. One involved an extension of behavioral techniques into a different language, modern Greek. This study took advantage of two of the many peculiarities of articulographic correspondence in modern Greek, the facts that (1) five written symbols, η, ι, v, $\epsilon\iota$, $o\iota$ map into a single sound, the English /ee/ and (2) two written symbols o and ω map into the sound /o/. Greeks themselves complain that this mapping leads to the majority of the difficulties involved in learning to read and write. From my point of view, these difficulties were a godsend because they provided me with a way of altering the appearance of a word without altering the way in which it mapped into articulatory or auditory space.

For the experiment, ten passages from a newspaper were altered by substituting randomly within a group of /ee/'s and by replacing one /o/ with the other. Forty subjects read one normal passage and one altered passage. Initially, speed of reading aloud was the only measure taken. A later group of four bilingual subjects were asked to translate one normal and one mutilated passage into spoken English. Only two passages were used. Speed of translation was the variable measured. The results, though crude, showed quite clearly that the look of a word is more important in reading than its sound. On the average, it took one and one-half times as long to read a mutilated passage as it did to read a normal passage. More noticeable, though unquantifiable, was the way in which fluency tended to crack in reading the mutilated passages. Translation seemed to take twice as long when the text was mutilated. Indeed, it was obvious that in the mutilated case, subjects were interposing an extra loop in the process, a vocalization of the Greek prior to translation. In other words, in the mutilated but not in the normal case, subjects had to produce auditory-articulatory surrogates before they could begin semantic analysis. None of these readers was a fast reader by the standards used in my American studies. Yet, all of them seemed to exemplify the visual approach to reading, except when mutilations forced a detour. Note that mutilation did introduce detours, hence the increase in processing time. The mutilations would not have done this had the normal processing procedure involved a loop into auditory or articulatory space, because the mutilations produced no change in the auditory or articulatory correlates of the passages. Only the appearances were changed.

The second study attempted to get more directly at processing, if EEG records can be considered in any way direct. The reasoning that led to the study was as follows. It is possible to record activity in primary sensory receiving areas. Reading must involve the visual cortex. If visual input is transformed into an auditory surrogate, then presentation of text should cause activity in both primary visual and auditory cortex. If reading is a purely visual affair, then there should be no activity in the auditory cortex while it is going on. In any task that involves internal auditory rehearsal there should be auditory activity to be picked up. If this kind of breakdown does occur—auditory activity during internal auditory rehearsal but not during reading—it would be convincing evidence that auditory mediation plays no role in the reading process.

In the following experiment, diminution of activity rather than activity was studied, for a number of reasons. Subjects were seated facing a screen on which periodic (1.6 cps) pulses (9 sec duration, 15,000 candela luminance) were superimposed on a steady 30 ft L luminance. Subjects wore earphones through which a click, simultaneous with each flash, was fed in. The intensity of the click was adjusted for each subject so that the amplitude of the two evoked potentials, one auditory and the other visual, was approximately the same. Then the subject was presented with a projected sheet of text for ten seconds. The luminance of the text background was 30 ft L, so that gross conditions of stimulation were not changed. The flashing light was superimposed on this display. The subject was instructed to read the text as fast as possible (this took longer than ten seconds, the texts being 300 to 350 words long) and then to rehearse it until given a signal to repeat the text. The signal was given thirty seconds after the text disappeared. During reading, the periodic EEG signal from the visual cortex was almost washed out. During rehearsal, on the other hand, it was the auditory signal that lost definition. The initial results for two subjects were extremely impressive, and these results seemed to indicate that reading is a visual process and rehearsal an auditory one. However, since that time I have discovered that there were defects in the equipment that could have produced the results obtained.[1] I mention the experiment only because I feel it could yield interesting results if properly carried out. Unfortunately, I am no longer in a position to do such experiments.

These forays into the reading process seem to indicate that reading can be, and for skilled readers often is, a visual process. That is to say, it follows a sequence like that shown in Table 9–1. It would also

Table 9–1. *Hypothetical Sequence of Events in Reading in Visual and Auditory Readers.*

VISUAL READERS		
Central representation		
Processing rules		
Visual store	Auditory store	Articulatory programs
Visual receptors	Auditory receptors	
AUDITORY READERS		
Central representation	Processing rules	
Visual store	Auditory store	
Visual receptors	Auditory receptors	

suggest that the processing that goes on is hierarchical, with large-scale decisions about the form of sentences coming first and controlling subsequent operations. There can be no doubt that these large-scale decisions are under stimulus control. The definition of the stimuli requires an ecological sample. Egon Brunswik to the contrary, this is a job for a computer. My only stab at it was a demonstration that any string of words with a capital letter at the beginning and a period at the end with —— *ed by* in the middle will be taken for a passive sentence if exposed briefly enough. This is hardly an ecological sample, hardly even a functional validation. However, I am sure this kind of research could be done. We are used to teaching children to spell by familiarizing them with probable letter sequences exemplifying standard spelling to sound correlations. Might we not be able to teach reading by exposure to probable word patterns, exemplifying correlations between stimulus patterns and grammatical forms?

---

[1] I am grateful to David Bender and Dr. Charles Gross for drawing my attention to these defects.

REFERENCES

Bever, T., & Bower, T. G. R. How to read without listening. Project Literacy Report No. 6, ERIC No. ED 010 312, January 1966.

Bower, T. G. R. Visual selection. *Psychonomic Science,* 1965, *3,* 361–362. (a)

Bower, T. G. R. The parameters of performance of two perceptual tasks. Doctoral dissertation. Cornell University, 1965. (b)

Chomsky, N. *Aspects of the Theory of Syntax.* New York: Wiley, 1964.

Hebb, D. O. *The Organization of Behavior.* New York: Wiley, 1949.

Hochberg, J. E. Toward a general theory of graphic communications: I. The component perceptumotor skills at different literacy levels. Project Literacy Report No. 5, ERIC No. ED 010 311, November 1965.

Lenneberg, E. H. *Biological Foundations of Language.* New York: Wiley, 1967.

Levin, H. Studies of various aspects of reading. Project Literacy Report No. 5, ERIC No. ED 010 311, November 1965.

Sternberg, S. High speed scanning in human memory. *Science,* 1966, *153,* 652–654.

10 ROSE-MARIE WEBER

First-Graders' Use of Grammatical Context in Reading

To demonstrate that early readers use context to facilitate their identification of words in a passage would only confirm the experience of anyone who has observed a child learning to read. But little can be said specifically, for example, about the interplay between the use of graphic cues on one hand and the use of contextual cues on the other, about the developmental stages in the exploitation of cues by the novice or about the relative import of various linguistic and extra-linguistic features that comprise context. In particular, grammatical structure as an aspect of context has hardly been considered in regard to reading, despite its central position in the language as the vehicle for semantic as well as extralinguistic content and despite the well-known restrictions on the occurrence of words in sentences that grammar entails. It is obvious from their abilities to speak and understand that first-graders control the grammar of their language with only minor substantive differences from the way their parents do. The extent to which they bring their grammatical competence to bear on the reading task is another matter, however. In the studies of errors during oral reading reported below, the sensitivity of first-graders to grammatical structure is described in an attempt to assess the grammatical dimension of their reading performance.

These studies were supported by funds from the U.S. Office of Education of the Department of Health, Education, and Welfare. Assistance from the staff of the Ithaca City School District, Project Literacy, and the Laboratory for Research on Language Skills at Cornell is gratefully acknowledged.

147

The contribution of verbal context to adults' reading has been investigated from several points of view, but all in all has received little attention. The facilitating effects of preceding context have been reported by Tulving and Gold (1963) and Morton (1964), who found lower recognition thresholds for tachistoscopically presented words exposed in the context of a meaningful sentence compared to anomalous contexts or in isolation. Salzinger, Portnoy, and Feldman (1962) and Coleman (1963) are among those who have analyzed the improvements in subjects' cloze test scores with increasing statistical approximations to English— that is, decreasing contextual distortions—and have thus complemented the evidence from perception and learning studies for the integrative power of linguistic structure. In the literature on children's reading abilities, the cloze technique has been used as a measure of comprehension, but consideration of the use of context in and of itself is almost entirely absent. One exception is Goodman's report (1965) that young readers were less accurate in reading words presented in a list than when the same words were incorporated into stories.

Context in these studies usually refers not only to the grammatical structure of sentences, but also to their communicative content, including such features as truth value. Although semantic and syntactic features have been separated in perception and memory studies, their differential effects on reading have come to attention only recently. Ford and Levin (1967) compared the recognition of homographs in a syntactic frame and in the context of a word with high associative value and found that the syntactic frame had greater effect on eliminating the ambiguity of the stimulus. Ruddell (1965) constructed passages in accordance with the grammatical structures found in the speech of fourth-graders and reported higher comprehension of the passages composed of high-frequency patterns than of those made up of infrequent patterns.

Our approach to young readers' use of the constraints imposed by their grammar is through the analysis of oral reading errors. The degree to which an error approximates a correct response can be gauged at several linguistic levels. Consider the sentence *He shook the pig and out came some money.* The erroneous response *dimes* for *money* would suggest that the reader ignored the graphic display and responded in terms of the context established by reference to a situation involving a piggy bank and by the expectation that a word following *some* at the end of a sentence would complete a noun phrase. On the other hand, the response *many* for *money* would indicate that the reader attempted to respond in terms of the relations between letter and sound patterns, but at the expense of attention to the preceding context, including the specific grammatical restrictions within a noun phrase beginning with *some*. Such an analysis emphasizing the correct features of an erroneous response can reveal a reader's appropriate strategy in the use of graphic and grammatical cues in spite of his imperfect handling of some feature or other. Therefore, as a first step in assessing how early readers bring their grammatical competence to bear on the reading task, we consider the acceptability of oral reading errors to their preceding grammatical context within the sentence. The assumption here is that an acceptable response demonstrates the readers' sensitivity to grammatical constraints. The distinction between such a response and one that upsets the grammatical structure of a sentence, for instance, *many* for *money* in our example, is significant simply because the grammatical structure of a sentence is central to its communicative function. Although not all ungrammatical sentences are incomprehensible, their lack of coherency often precludes interpretation. Next, in order to demonstrate young readers' handling of graphic and grammatical cues relative to one another, we report the degree to which responses approximate written words in terms of graphic similarity and with this index we show the interaction of graphic similarity and grammatical acceptability. Finally, from another perspective on children's sensitivity to grammatical constraints, we note how the grammaticality of a set of errors affects the readers' own correction of these errors.

The first corpus of oral reading errors was collected in a first-grade class of twenty-one children in the Ithaca City School District, Ithaca, New York (Class 1). From December through May, two observers noted the errors as the children read from their texts during daily small-group instruction. Scores on the Lorge-Thorndike IQ test (n = 20) averaged 109.2, s.d. = 14.5. The 1950 series of the New Basic Readers (Scott-Foresman) served as the principal reading materials; high achievers went on to supplemental readers (*The Reading Caravan*. Boston: Heath, 1964). Instruction largely followed the recommendations of the teacher's guides, supplemented by the presentation of all consonant sound-letter correspondences to the class as a whole. During most of the observation period, the class was divided into four instructional groups according to the teacher's judgment of the children's abilities. For purposes of this discussion, the two groups that showed the most progress are combined into the high group (n = 12) and the other two into the low group (n = 9). By May almost all the children in the high group could handle unfamiliar materials, but the low group did not have the skills to transfer to words that they had never seen before. This difference shows up on the results of the Metropolitan Achievement Test: the high group (n = 11) scored at mean grade levels 2.6, 2.9, and 2.8 on the word knowledge, word discrimination, and reading subtests, respectively, whereas the low group (n = 8) scored 1.8, 1.8, and 1.6 on these subtests.

Another corpus of oral reading errors was collected in a second Ithaca class of twenty-four children (Robinson et al., 1966). The mean Lorge-Thorndike score of 110.5 (n = 23, s.d. = 9.2) was not different from that of class 1, but the significantly smaller variance (F = 2.48, 19, 22 d.f.; p < .025) reflects the greater homogeneity of these children. Here the data were collected under conditions that allowed rechecking. The children's reading was tape-recorded monthly in the presence of a familiar adult. The selections, drawn from the various texts that comprised the instructional materials, showed a greater range of vocabulary and style than the basal readers used in class 1. The reading program in this class was deliberately eclectic, including a rather thorough phonics program involving auditory and visual discrimination, attention to consonants in various positions, and early introduction of vowels. For most of the data-collection period, November through June, the class was divided into three main instructional groups. In June, they numbered eleven, seven, and six children, in order of decreasing achievement. The Metropolitan Achievement Test scores indicate that the over-all progress in this class was greater than in class 1. On the word knowledge, word discrimination, and reading subtests, the high group (n = 9) scored 3.0, 3.1, and 3.4; the mid group (n = 7) scored 2.5, 2.8, and 2.6, and the low group (n = 6) scored 1.8, 1.9, and 1.8.

The first-grade reading materials were not especially designed for the investigation of errors, but were selected as representative of the materials that the children faced every day. This means that few children read identical passages and the selections were not necessarily well matched to the children's abilities. This lack of control may obscure many of the variables that deserve attention. It is defensible, however, on the grounds that these data reflect the behavior of children learning to read under typical circumstances.

Several categories of erroneous responses were identified and errors were classified according to these categories. Only responses that differed overtly from the text were considered. That is, no hesitations or refusals to respond were taken into account. The substitution of an erroneous single word response for the expected response was taken as the basic error type. Several other types were also identified: a word omitted impulsively from the response, a word spoken although no corresponding written word appeared on the page, and a reversal in word order, possibly in combination with other types of errors. Note that though these categories could be applied to letter-sound discrepancies, they were applied only to whole words here. Table 10–1 shows an example of each type of error.

Table 10–1.

TYPE	PRINTED WORD/RESPONSE
1. Substitution	funny/family
2. Omission	the *black* umbrella/the umbrella
3. Insertion	down the creek/down *to* the creek
4. Scramble	In went the animals/In they all went

A total of 1,072 errors were recorded in class 1 and a total of 871 in class 2. As will be seen, the achievement groups within each class are more or less evenly represented in these totals. However, it should be noted that the higher groups covered much more reading material than did the low groups in making comparable numbers of errors. From the distribution of the types of errors presented in Table 10–2, it can be seen that substitutions are by far the most frequent.

Table 10–2. *Frequency of Error Types.*

CLASS	SUB.	OMIT.	INSERT.	SCRAMBLE	TOTAL
1	79.9	8.5	9.2	2.4	100.0
	(856)	(91)	(99)	(26)	(1,072)
2	93.9	3.2	2.6	.2	99.9
	(818)	(28)	(23)	(2)	(871)

Judgments on the grammatical acceptability of an error were to be made in terms of the words in a sentence that preceded the error. Therefore, because not all errors are amenable to this analysis, certain errors had to be eliminated from consideration. First, errors of omission, although they can be judged in terms of their effect on the entire sentence, are not subject to judgment within preceding context only. Second, words that stand at the beginning of the sentence are hardly subject to any grammatical restrictions, so that including them in the sample of errors to be judged would inflate the total of grammatically acceptable responses. In class 1, 23 per cent (241) of the total number of errors occurred at the beginnings of sentences. When these were eliminated along with the omission errors (some omissions were initial), a total of 753 usable errors remained. In class 2, 15 per cent (125) of the errors were made on the first word. With the elimination of these and the omissions, 718 errors remained.

In order to assess the use of grammatical context by the children in these classes, the errors were judged with respect to grammatical acceptability within the preceding context of the printed sentence. All the printed sentences were accepted a priori as grammatical, although some sequences in the atrophied language of primers may be questioned. The analysis was undertaken on the assumption that any error that maintained the sentence as a grammatical sequence would share a significant grammatical property of the printed word that was misread: privilege of occurrence in a syntactic construction. An error was judged acceptable if the printed sentence could be completed after the point of the error in any way, not necessarily by the remainder of the printed sentence. Consider the examples of errors shown in Table 10–3.

Table 10–3.

PRINTED SENTENCE	ERRONEOUS RESPONSE
1. Spot *can* help Dick.	Spot *and*. . . .
2. Puff did not say what she wanted.	Puff did not say *that*. . . .
3. I will see what *it is*.	*I will see what *is it*.
4. She looked and looked, but she *could* find no food at all.	*She looked and looked, but she *cold* . . .

Of these four examples, the first two errors were judged as grammatically acceptable with respect to the preceding context of the sentence; the sequence with the error could be completed into a grammatical sentence. The second two, on the other hand, were judged as grammatically unacceptable. By their very occurrence, they upset the grammatical structure of the sentence.[1]

The analysis for grammaticality in the performance of the children in class 1, who read from basal readers, shows that an overwhelmingly large proportion of the errors (91 per cent, n = 753) were grammatically acceptable to the preceding context. The differences in achievement between the high and the low groups in reading, as reflected not only by progress through textbooks, scores on tests, but also over-all classroom performance, led us to expect that the groups would differ in the use of preceding verbal context. However, the difference in grammatical acceptability between them is negligible: 92.3 per cent (n = 465) for the high group as compared to 88.9 per cent (n = 256) for the low group.

In class 2, we might expect that the more varied style of writing and the greater range of vocabulary that the children faced would affect their use of grammatical context. Again, however, the proportion of grammatical responses approaches 90 per cent. For the class as a whole, 87.7 per cent (n = 718) did not violate preceding grammatical constraints. Among the three ability groups within the class, the proportions show that the strong readers are no more successful in this respect than their weaker classmates: high 87.5 per cent (n = 192); mid 87.0 per cent (n = 299); low 89.4 per cent (n = 227).

Given the slots in the sentences where the errors occurred, we do not know the proportion of random words that would be grammatical in these contexts. It is clear from the 90 per cent figure, however, that words are not identified by these children without reference to preceding syntactic constraints and that this aspect of context is exploited, perhaps sometimes overused, by them. Moreover, the high proportion of grammatically appropriate errors reflects the strong expectations by first-graders that written sentences will conform to the restrictions that the grammar of their language imposes. These findings, then, do not support the characterization of the relatively low achiever as a word-by-word reader. Rather, they suggest that children—no matter what their potential for acquiring literacy skills—bring to the task a fundamental linguis-

---

[1] Scorers were familiar with the notion of grammaticality as it has been elaborated in grammatical theory. As acceptable strings, they included only those that they judged grammatical. It should be noted, however, that violations of selectional rules, as Chomsky has formulated their characteristics (1965, pp. 149, passim), were allowed as grammatical. Ten per cent of the classroom data from class 1 and the tape data from class 2 were double-scored for reliability; the entire corpus from the tape-recordings in class 1 was double-scored. In all cases, agreement among scorers on the judgment of grammatical acceptability was over 90 per cent.

tic ability, which in its rigidity shapes their reading responses into familiar language structure.

Many of the substitution errors are grammatically acceptable to preceding context as well as graphically and phonologically similar to the printed words, for examples, the substitution of *that* for *what* in the sentence *Puff did not say what she wanted.* However, there are instances of errors that are grammatically acceptable—even semantically appropriate—but graphically dissimilar, such as the substitution of *tell* for *say* in the same sentence. Such errors would indicate a heavy dependence on contextual cues and disregard of the graphic display and its relationship to the sound system of English. On the other hand, there are errors—such as *cold* for *could* in the sentence *She looked and looked, but she could not find any food at all*—that suggest close attention to the spelling and its correspondence in sound, but at the expense of the information provided by the preceding context. The interplay in the use of information from the stimulus display itself as opposed to the information from context has been investigated by Tulving and Gold (1963) and Morton (1964). In both studies, evidence was found to confirm the hypothesis that the amount of information needed about the stimulus for its identification varies inversely with the amount of available contextual information. From our analysis of the grammatical acceptability of reading errors, we have seen that first-graders exploit contextual information to a high degree. How might this aspect of their performance relate to their use of graphic information? With the hypothesis about the inverse relation between context and stimulus in mind, we might suppose that in the relatively rare cases when the readers disregarded the grammatical constraints of preceding context, their attention was directed to analyzing the details of the graphic display, or even to working out the relationships between the letters of the stimulus and its pronunciation. Evidence for this attention to graphic information could be demonstrated if the errors that did not conform to preceding context approximated the stimulus words more closely in terms of graphic features than did the contextually appropriate errors.

In order to describe the degree to which an erroneous response approximates the stimulus in terms of graphic patterns and therefore phonological patterns, an "index of graphic similarity" was devised. By this measure, various graphic characteristics of the stimulus are compared with characteristics of the erroneous response word, transcribed in traditional orthography. The features taken into account are the number of letters shared by the stimulus-response pair, the position of shared letters within the words, the position of shared letters relative to each other, the average length of the words, and the difference in length between the stimulus and response words. Two features have not been taken into account: the similarity in the shapes of letters, such as *o, c,* and *e,* and the distinction between upper and lower case letters. It should be noted that these features have no obvious phonological correlates.

The graphic similarity scores were computed according to the following formula:

$$GS = 10\left[\left(\frac{50F + 30V + 10C}{A}\right) + 5T + 27B + 18E\right]$$

F = the number of pairs of adjacent letters in the same order shared by S and R:

$$\text{S HOUSE / R HORSE} \qquad F = 2$$
$$\text{S EVERY / R VERY} \qquad F = 3$$

V = the number of pairs of adjacent letters in reverse order shared by S and R:

$$\text{S WAS / R SAW} \qquad R = 2$$

C = the number of single letters shared by S and R:

$$\text{S SPOT \quad / R PUFF} \qquad C = 1$$
$$\text{S FAMILY / R FUNNY} \qquad C = 2$$

A = average number of letters in S and R:

$$\text{S EVERY / R VERY} \qquad A = 4.5$$

T = ratio of numbers of letters in the shorter word to the number in the longer:

$$\text{S EVERY / R VERY} \qquad T = 4/5$$

B = 1 if the first letter in the response is the same as the first letter in the stimulus; otherwise B = O:

$$\text{S FAMILY / R FUNNY}$$

E = 1 if the last letter in the response is the same as the last letter in the stimulus; otherwise E = O:

S FAMIL*Y* / R FUNN*Y*

Examples include:

SPOT/PUFF	75	FAMILY/FUNNY	528
ARE/EAT	117	BUMPED/BANGED	633
WILL/LIKE	175	DUCK/DUCKS	732
THE/TO	343	BEGAN/BEGUN	780
WANTS/BOATS	390	THREE/THERE	860

The weights assigned to the selected features reflect our intuitions about the significance of various cues for the identification of words. For example, the greater weight given to shared beginning letters over end letters, and in turn the weight given to shared end letters over common letters elsewhere in the word, reflect the importance of the positions of letters for word recognition. The literature has shown (for example, Marchbanks and Levin, 1965) that readers, as they master left-to-right orientation, exploit the letters in the end positions as salient cues yielding high information. Because common adjacent letter patterns reflect the formation of units of a higher order than common single letters, special value is assigned to adjacent pairs, especially if they are in the same order. Because the number of adjacent pairs is a function of word length, the average number of letters is included in the formula.

Some validation for the usefulness of the index was provided by adult rankings of word pairs. Two lists of ten words and their misreadings were selected from the errors in our study. The pairs on one list were chosen arbitrarily, whereas those on the second differed by roughly 100 points according to the graphic similarity index. Fifteen college students were asked to rank the word pairs on a list in terms of the similarity of their appearance. The rankings within the arbitrary list correlated .93 with rankings based on the graphic similarity index; within the selected list, the rankings correlated .89.

In and of themselves, the graphic similarity scores for the classes under study are of interest, for they reveal the expected differences between the high and low achieving subgroups. The mean score for all the substitution errors in class 1 (n = 856, including 146 with no shared letters and therefore scores of 0) was 350.79. The low group mean of 265.47 (n = 353) is well over a hundred points below the high group mean of 407.87 (n = 503). The mean graphic similarity score for class 2 was similar to the mean for class 1: 356.44 (n = 818, including seventy-nine with no shared letters). The means for the various ability groups were: high 396.11 (n = 215); mid 363.36 (n = 340); low 315.05 (n = 263).

However, we are not concerned only with the evidence for the more or less successful use of graphic cues, but rather with the evidence for the interplay between the use of such cues and the carryover of information from the preceding context. The hypothesis on the inverse relation in the use of contextual and stimulus information suggested that grammatically unacceptable responses would on the whole share more graphic features with the stimulus words than would the responses that conformed to preceding grammatical context. Table 10–4 shows the mean

Table 10–4. *Mean Graphic Similarity Scores According to Grammatical Acceptability.*

GROUP	GRAMMATICAL	UNGRAMMATICAL
1. high	379.81 (365)	550.47 (32)
low	255.26 (218)	467.33 (30)
TOTAL	333.24 (583)	507.02 (62)
2. high	392.17 (159)	414.39 (23)
mid	347.13 (254)	452.85 (39)
low	294.09 (198)	433.76 (25)
TOTAL	341.66 (611)	437.20 (87)

graphic similarity of the substitution errors of classes 1 and 2 according to their grammatical acceptability. Support for the hypothesis is indicated by the fact that the mean for ungrammatical errors exceeds the corresponding grammatical mean in every comparison.

From these results we can infer that when the readers neglected the constraints of the preceding grammatical context they were attending to the task of identifying and perhaps decoding the features of the graphic display. Thus, the inverse relationship found in adults' handling of the two types of information is demonstrated by our findings with children also. It should be noted, however, that Morton's (1964) and Tulving and Gold's (1963) adult subjects compensated for an experimentally distorted context by exploiting the stimulus information; the experimental materials were manipulated so that an imbalance between the contextual and stimulus information was created. The performance of the children in this study, however, indicates an emphasis on one of the two sorts of information in a situation in which both are available. The errors, of course, demonstrate the misuse of available graphic cues. But the increase in graphic similarity scores when preceding grammatical context is disregarded suggests that a relatively intensive analysis of the graphic display sometimes results in the neglect of contextual information. For these beginning readers, the ability to use information from both sources efficiently is not entirely in hand. But it should be recalled that disregard of preceding grammatical constraints shows up in only about 10 per cent of the errors; the children seldom neglected grammar for letters.

Up to this point, we have considered only the verbal context that precedes an error. But, although an error may be appropriate to what precedes, it may not fit into the subsequent context of a sentence as it is written. The effect that an error may have on the entire sentence is also interesting, for the coherency of the sentence as it continues after an error is certainly significant to a reader's comprehension of the sentence. Thus, in order to assess the children's sensitivity to the grammatical effects of the errors they have made, we noted their own corrections of their errors in light of grammatical acceptability of the error with respect to the entire sentence.

Errors made in the presence of a prompting teacher are not amenable to the analysis of children's own spontaneous corrections of their errors. For this aspect of our study, five weekly readings by twenty members of class 1 during the last two months of instruction were tape-recorded. Each child read a selection into a microphone. No one was present to interrupt, look critical, or supply corrections, and so the children could ignore or correct whatever errors they made. Each passage was a familiar page from the regular instructional materials (New Basic Readers, Scott-Foresman, 1950's; *The Reading Caravan*, Boston: Heath, 1964) that had been covered in small-group instruction during the previous week. As before, the class is divided into the high (here n = 11) and low (n = 9).

Of the total 200 errors under consideration, 54 per cent (107) were made by the members of the high group. Their rate of errors per 100 words was 3.9 in contrast to the low group's 6.7, indicating that the better readers read much longer texts to accumulate a comparable number of errors. The proportion of substitution errors for the class was 84 per cent; omissions, insertions, and scrambles comprised the rest.

In order to describe the grammatical acceptability of an error in the context of the entire sentence, the error was first scored for its acceptability within the preceding context and then for its effect on the remainder of the sentence. Consider Table 10–5. Judgments of grammati-

Table 10–5.

PRINTED SENTENCE	RESPONSE
1. Spot can *help* me.	Spot can *hear*/ me./
2. He said, *"Can* I help you?"	He said, *"Come*/ I help you?"/
3. Down comes the *car*.	*Down comes the *cars*.//

cality were made in the response sentence immediately after the occurrence of the error and at the end of the sentence, that is, at the points indicated by the slashes, although the children did not necessarily read to the end of the sentence after making the error. All in all, the effect on the grammatical structure of each sentence in which the errors occurred was scored as (1) grammatical up to and including the error and grammatical to its end. (2) grammatical up to and including the error, but ungrammatical to its end. (3) ungrammatical up to and including the error, and therefore ungrammatical to its end. The 200 errors occurred in 167 sentences. In cases of more than one error in the sentence, the written sentence was, as usual, taken as the right-hand context. However, for second or third errors in cases of more than one, the partial sentence as it was read, that is, including earlier errors, was taken as preceding context. For instance, if the printed sentence was *Where did Bunny go?* and the child responded *Where is Bunny going?* the response *going* was scored within the context *Where is Bunny* . . . It should be noted that because this analysis was concerned with both the preceding and following contexts of the errors as well as children's sensitivity to the errors, misreadings at the beginning of the sentences and omission errors were not discarded. Rather, for these errors the preceding context was scored as grammatical.

The distribution of the errors according to their effect on the grammaticality of the entire sentence is given in Table 10–6 for the high and low groups as well as for the class 1 as a whole. The proportion of errors that were judged grammatically acceptable with regard to the preceding context, as shown in columns 1 and 2, is similar to the corresponding proportion presented earlier: 94.5 per cent (91.0 per cent of 134 if 46 beginning errors and 20 omission errors are discarded). The high and low groups show no significant differences. Although only about 6 per cent of the errors in this corpus immediately upset the grammatical

Table 10–6. *Frequency of Various Grammaticality Judgments.*

GROUP	(1) GRAM. TO ERROR; GRAM. TO END.	(2) GRAM. TO ERROR; UNGRAM. TO END.	(3) UNGRAM. TO ERROR AND TO END.	TOTAL
high	68.2	28.0	3.7	99.9
	(73)	(30)	(4)	(107)
low	55.9	36.6	7.6	100.1
	(52)	(34)	(7)	(93)
total	62.5	32.0	5.5	100.0
	(125)	(64)	(11)	(200)

structure by their occurrence, another 32 per cent render their sentences ungrammatical when the context following the error is taken into consideration.

The evidence for the children's sensitivity to preceding grammatical constraints suggests that they would bring their knowledge of structure to bear on the correction of these errors. Here the problem is not simply to identify a word, but to notice that a response is incorrect, to locate the error, and usually to reidentify a word. We would expect that the errors that violated the grammatical structures of the sentence would be more frequently noted than those that did not. Those errors that conformed to the grammatical structure, on the other hand, would be passed over because, on the grammatical level at least, they would not be noticeable.

Table 10–7 shows the frequency with which the children disregarded or corrected the errors that maintained the sentence as a grammatical string in contrast to those that rendered the sentence ungrammatical. A greater proportion of all errors was disregarded rather than corrected. But whereas the grammatical errors were disregarded more than twice

Table 10–7. *Corrections According to the Grammatical Effect of the Error.*

GRAMMATICALITY	DISREGARDED	CORRECTED	TOTAL
grammatical to end	70.4	29.6	100.0
	(88)	(37)	(125)
ungrammatical to end	38.8	61.3	100.1
	(29)	(46)	(75)
TOTAL	58.5	41.5	100.0
	(117)	(83)	(200)

as often as they were corrected, the ungrammatical errors were corrected nearly twice as often as they were ignored. The effect of the error on the grammatical structure of the sentence, then, is indeed recognized by young readers. Again they demonstrate their sensitivity to the structure of the language, but in this case they are evaluating their responses rather than anticipating them.

We noted that there was no significant difference in the use of preceding context between the high and the low groups. However, a breakdown of the data as shown in Table 10–8 indicates that the above effect

Table 10–8. *Corrections According to the Grammatical Effect of the Error—High and Low Groups.*

GROUP	GRAMMATICALITY	DISREGARDED	CORRECTED	TOTAL
high	grammatical to end	72.6	27.4	100.0
		(53)	(20)	(73)
	ungrammatical to end	14.7	85.3	100.0
		(5)	(29)	(34)
	TOTAL	54.2	45.8	100.0
		(58)	(49)	(107)
low	grammatical to end	67.3	32.7	100.0
		(35)	(17)	(52)
	ungrammatical to end	58.3	41.5	100.1
		(24)	(17)	(41)
	TOTAL	63.4	36.6	100.0
		(59)	(34)	(93)

of ungrammaticality on corrections is created almost entirely by the performance of the high group. The high group passed over 73 per cent of the grammatical errors, but ignored only 15 per cent of those that upset the grammaticality of the sentence. In contrast, the low group passed over 68 per cent of those that maintained the sentence as a grammatical string, a figure comparable to the high group's, but passed over an almost equally high proportion of errors that upset the syntactic structure, 58 per cent.

Having made a response that was incorrect, the better readers showed by their corrections that they were sensitive to the grammatical context of the entire sentence. The fact that the poor reader did not correct their ungrammatical errors to the same extent does not necessarily indicate that they were insensitive to deviant grammatical structures. Perhaps such readers do not have efficient strategies for finding errors that upset syntax, or perhaps they simply have a different standard of what is acceptable as oral reading.

The basically linguistic nature of the reading task has not received adequate formulation that would point up its fundamental similarity to the perception of spoken language. These analyses of oral reading errors have provided substantial evidence that beginning readers use their knowledge of grammar to narrow down the words that compete for a given sentence slot, just as they surely do in understanding speech. The materials that the children read here were not adjusted to the skills of the individuals; their handling of easy materials in contrast to difficult ones was overlooked. The shifts in strategy that might have taken place with maturity were also ignored. But from a broad perspective, the notable finding was that weaker readers do not differ from their more skilled classmates in respect to the use of grammatical constraints for the identification of words in a string. It is as though the children resisted uttering a sequence that did not conform to an acceptable sentence. Having made errors that did not fit into the grammatical context of the written sentences, however, only better readers consistently demonstrated their rejection of ungrammatical sentences by correcting themselves.

REFERENCES

Chomsky, N. *Aspects of the Theory of Syntax* (Cambridge, Mass.: M.I.T. Press, 1965).

Coleman, E. B. Approximations to English: some comments on the method. *American Journal of Psychology*, 1963, *76*, 239–247.

Ford, B., & Levin, H. Studies in oral reading: VII. homographs in a semantic context. Mimeographed, Cornell University, 1967.

Goodman, K. A linguistic study of cues and miscues in reading. *Elementary English*, 1965, *42*, 639–643.

Marchbanks, G., & Levin, H. Cues by which children recognize words. *Journal of Educational Psychology*, 1965, *56*, 57–61.

Morton, J. The effects of context on the visual duration thresholds for words. *British Journal of Psychology*, 1964, *55*, 165–180.

Robinson, J. The first grade study, 1965–66. Project Literacy. Mimeographed, Cornell University, 1966.

Ruddell, R. B. The effect of oral and written patterns of language structure on reading comprehension. *Reading Teacher*, 1965, *18*, 270–275.

Salzinger, K., Portnoy, S., & Feldman, R. S. The effect of order of approximation to the statistical structure of English on the emission of verbal responses. *Journal of Experimental Psychology*, 1962, *64*, 52–57.

Tulving, E., & Gold, C. Stimulus information and contextual information as determinants of tachistoscopic recognition of words. *Journal of Experimental Psychology*, 1963, *66*, 319–327.

Psychology and Reading:
Commentary on Chapters 5 to 10

For some decades, reading research concentrated on just two processes: the discrimination of letters or words as visual forms and the translation of such forms into speech sounds. The two processes together were what psychologists and educators meant by reading. The six chapters I have been invited to discuss have rather little to say about letter discrimination and letter sounding. They are concerned instead with such matters as the role of orthographic constraints in word recognition, the identification of perceptual strategies for sampling the text, and the size of the syntactic unit that is processed in reading. Much that is asserted in these essays would be as true of speech perception as of reading. Clearly, there has been a major change in the kind of process psychologists take reading to be. What is the nature of the change? We shall return to that question when we have reviewed the individual chapters.

GIBSON, SHURCLIFF, AND YONAS: UTILIZATION OF
SPELLING PATTERNS BY DEAF AND
HEARING SUBJECTS

Eleanor Gibson (with Shurcliff and Yonas) has produced conclusive evidence against her own earlier hypothesis that spelling-to-sound invariance accounts for the fact that pronounceable pseudowords, such as *dink*, are more likely to be correctly identified on brief visual exposure than are unpronounceable pseudowards, such as *nkid*. It seems to me that the authors are correct, incidentally, in believing that this outcome does not reduce the importance of the linguistic research (Hockett, 1963; Venezky, 1963; Venezky and Weir, 1966) showing that there are many ways in which English spellings are regular if graphic units larger than the single letter are considered. What the new results with deaf subjects show is that knowledge of rules that map spelling into sounds cannot be the essential factor that makes pronounceable words more easily recognized than unpronounceable words. The higher-order spelling-to-sound invariances are not essential here. They may, nevertheless, function in other ways for hearing subjects—in sounding out new words, for instance.

For an earlier study (Gibson, Pick, Osser, and Hammond, 1962), Gibson had subjects rate her pseudowords for pronounceability. She used the method of Underwood and Schultz (1960), by which subjects are directed to try saying the words to themselves and when they have a good feeling for the range of difficulty to rate each word from 1 (easy) to 8 (hard). Some sample ratings are: *dink* (1.06), *nkid* (5.85); *sprilk* (3.21), *lkispr* (7.40); *glurck* (2.94), *ckurgl* (6.59). These pronounceability ratings predict visual identification scores for hearing subjects and also for congenitally deaf subjects. The question is, really, what factor, underlying the pronounceability ratings, causes them to be powerful predictors of visual identification. It cannot be the extent to which a pseudoword suggests a single invariant pronunciation in terms of spelling-to-sound rules because the sounds were not known to the deaf subjects. Gibson and her coauthors believe that the pronounceability ratings are reflecting English orthographic regularities, which they conceive of as grammar-like rules. The competing possibility that one feels the authors would very much like to discard is "dat ol' debbil" frequency. More properly, the alternative possibility is that the pronounceability ratings reflect some statistical property of English and that it is the statistical property that really causes the visual identification effects.

The authors are able to show that there are four kinds of frequency that predict less well than do pronounceability ratings. The four are summed bigram frequency and summed trigram frequency taken without regard for word length or letter position within the word (Underwood and Schultz, 1960) and bigram and trigram frequencies that take account of word length and letter positions (Mayzner and Tresselt, 1965; Mayzner, Tresselt, and Wolin, 1965). Because pronounceability is a better predictor of perceptual identification than any of these four frequencies, it seems reasonable to conclude that none of the frequencies is the actually determinative variable. What cannot be concluded is that no sort of frequency is the determinant.

Among the four frequencies considered, bigram and trigram sums, taken without regard for word length or letter position, have only a very rough relevance to the perceptual task. Most obviously, they fail to distinguish between clusters that can occur initially but not finally and vice versa. Consider the pair *dink* and *nkid*. The bigram must have the same value in either case if the Underwood and Schultz tables (1960) are used, because these tables disregard position. In the Mayzner and Tresselt tables, on the other hand, *nk* that is word final in a four-letter word has a count of twelve, whereas *nk* that is initial in such words has a value of zero. Not surprisingly, the more relevant frequencies, those of Mayzner and Tresselt, are the better predictors.

The difficulty with concluding that no frequency would predict the perceptual results better than pronounceability ratings do is that the frequencies used are not the only ones that might conceivably be relevant. One might hypothesize that the perceptual device incorporated a model of the structure of English in which letter strings have the bigram frequencies of English but no other constraints and further hypothesize that the perceivability of a letter string would be proportional to the logarithm of the probability of the string in the model. To find the frequency of a string in the model (which is a single-stage Markov process), one would take the product of the bigram frequencies of all the bigrams and divide it by the product of the frequencies of all the letters in the string except the end letters.[1] There are other possibly relevant frequencies; the one you pick depends on what you think happens perceptually. Suppose we believe that subjects may register the initial two letters but that order is an independent feature that may not be registered. In that case, the relative frequencies of *di* and *id* as initial digrams in four-letter words would be relevant.

Eleanor Gibson and her coauthors favor the view that pronounceability ratings reflect orthographic rules. Such rules exist, in the case, for example, of initial and final consonant clusters, and one can see that the pronounceability ratings do reflect them. However, pronounceability appears to be a continuous variable rather than an either-or judgment and so, if rule determined, must be a complex resultant of multiple

---

rules. So far as I know we do not have a set of rules that would do this job. At this point, then, there is an open choice: one can believe either that an unspecified set of orthographic rules or an unspecified set of language statistics underlie the perceptual effect.

There is, in this fine essay, an incidental point of much interest. The authors note that, in writing answers to an open-ended question, their deaf subjects made numerous grammatical errors and that these seemed unlike the grammatical errors that are made by hearing children in the years when they are acquiring English. They seem so to me also, and it is a difference I have noticed before; in the sentences on black-boards in schools for deaf children, one sees grammatical errors that appear to be drawn from an entirely different population than the errors of hearing children. Perhaps these differences are, in part, a function of differences in the clarity with which some grammatical features (for example, inflections) are marked in print and in speech. There is a more interesting possibility, however. Normal errors are probably linked to a normal order of progression in grammatical knowledge. And for the normal order of progression to obtain, it may be essential that the acquisition of syntax begin in the second year of life when neurological growth is incomplete and the child operates under limitations that seem to impose simplifying transformations on the adult speech he hears. If the linguistic input that activates grammar-discovery routines is not delivered until a later age, as is the case with deaf children, then it may be that the routines must work somewhat differently than in the normal case.

HOCHBERG: COMPONENTS OF LITERACY: SPECULATIONS AND EXPLORATORY RESEARCH

"Components of Literacy" is a richly suggestive analysis of the skills acquired in learning to read. One observable difference between skilled and unskilled readers is in the number of fixations required to take in a line of text. The skilled reader uses fewer fixations and larger saccades. His visual system is deployed on text somewhat as it is deployed on the visible world generally; he appears to sample information rather than to read in a letter-by-letter or word-by-word sequence. The neophyte reader makes many fixations; saccades are small and he seems to proceed unit by unit. A large part of Hochberg's discussion consists of an effort to specify the skills that underlie the change in fixation style.

Hochberg sees no reason to suppose that the number of fixations goes down because the skilled reader can actually see more letters or words in a given fixation. He thinks that reading skill is not primarily a matter of improved processing of immediate input. The experiments discussed in this connection as described in his chapter seem to me to bear only rather obliquely on the main point. Essentially, the experiments compare the ability to make same-different judgments on textual material presented in a fashion that should activate a reading-like process with judgments of the same material presented in a fashion that should activate a perceptual process unlike reading. In this second case, two strings of letters are presented as two vertical columns close enough together so that the two members of any letter pair are within foveal distance. Comparison in these circumstances is rather like a judgment of symmetry. It seems to make no difference in these circumstances whether the paired strings of letters are pronounceable words or unpronounceable anagrams nor whether the letters are presented in the usual orientation or in reversed (mirror-image) orientation. As I understand the argument, it is that if reading skill were importantly dependent on an improved perceptual sensitivity to familiar forms (letters in normal orientation and real words), then that perceptual sensitivity should be manifest in perceptual tasks that are unlike reading as well as in reading.

Same-different judgments were also made in conditions that brought the subject nearer to reading. The strings of letters were presented in horizontal tiers. They could not be directly compared without changing fixation and so it was necessary to encode and store the first string while scanning the second—even as in reading. In these circumstances, unpronounceable anagrams required more trials than pronounceable words, and mirror-image letters were more difficult than normal letters. On the other hand, the task was not made more difficult when one word in a pair was in upper-case letters and the other in lower-case. This last variation did make the task harder in the perceptual-symmetry circumstances. The implication seems to be that when a subject reads he samples the letters of a word just to the point where he can retrieve the engram of the complete word and then samples the second word comparing the data he receives against the engram of the first. With familiar text, all this can be done without examining each letter of each string for the reason that familiar text is partially redundant text. And so in a reading situation differences are found between familiar and unfamiliar material that do not obtain when the circumstances produce a kind of perceptual symmetry judgment.

If not increased form sensitivity, what then makes possible the larger and less regular saccades of the skilled reader? It seems to me that Hochberg's answer may be summarized as follows:

1. The skilled reader develops the ability to use redundancy to project full text (or meaning) from minimal visual samples. In a very general sense, the skilled reader knows in advance a large proportion of what is in any new text; he knows what is there because he knows English, he knows writers, and he knows about the world.

2. The skilled reader develops the ability to sample text strategically, looking where the information is. This ability develops, with respect to the visible world generally, very early in the preschool years. Hochberg suggests that sampling is guided by two sets of factors. Peripheral search guidance (PSG) is possible because low-acuity information picked up in peripheral vision can suggest to the optic search system where it must move its point of clearest vision in order to get a detailed view of a potentially interesting region. Cognitive search guidance (CSG) is possible because the movement of the point of clearest vision could be governed by implicit hypotheses or guesses about the full text or meaning that derive from the past data sample and that require new samples to confirm or disconfirm them.

In connection with PSG, an experiment (Hochberg, Levin, and Frail, 1966) of high interest is described. Short stories for children were printed in two versions. In one version, called "filled" (F), the spaces between words were all filled with the same single symbol, a symbol created by superimposing the letter x on the letter c. The resultant text looked perfectly continuous in peripheral vision. The second version, called "unfilled" (U) was simply normal text with spaces between words. The stories were to be read silently, for comprehension. Some readers (first- and second-graders) were new at reading and slow; others (fifth- and sixth-graders) were skilled and fast. The dependent variable was reading time per character. Filled text slowed up reading for subjects generally, but, most interestingly, it produced far greater relative impairment in the fast readers than in the slow. Hochberg takes this result to mean that fast readers ordinarily pick up interword space in peripheral vision and use it to program the next fixation "to center on or near the initial letter," which would be a good thing to do for the reason that initial letters convey maximum information. Consequently, for fast readers, removing the cue interferes seriously with the efficient sampling of the text. Slow readers, he suspects, do not use spaces for PSG, but rather proceed one word at a time and so are very little disturbed by the filled version.

Hochberg speculates a bit about a second cue available for PSG—the length of words. Impressions of length are easily obtained from peripheral vision and might serve, for example, to distinguish functors from other words. Hochberg proposes that "it should be possible for the reader to detect that a probable functor lies at some distance out along the line of text in the periphery, and then decide either to look at the word or, if it's likely to be redundant, to look at the word after it."

It seems likely to me that interword spaces and word lengths play a more important role in reading than Hochberg assigns them. He appears to believe that spacing and length function only so as to aim the next fixation—at a functor or not and at the first and most informative letter of whatever word. I suspect that there is a "noticing order" that operates within a single fixation in such a way as to process, first, word lengths and (guided by spacing) initial and final letters. In other words, I am proposing that with no change of fixation a sizable stretch of text is processed but not letter-by-letter and left to right. On the contrary, I think the text is processed in terms, first, of the features of length and terminal letters. Initial and final letters are the most informative in the sense of being the least predictable and by processing from the ends toward the middle the reader could make optimal use of redundancy. Indeed, terminal letters and an impression of length will often uniquely characterize a word.

There is some evidence that a noticing order that begins with the two ends of a word does operate within a single fixation. Relevant experiments include Bruner and O'Dowd, 1958; Harcum and Jones, 1962; Crovitz and Schiffman, 1965. The last of these is, I think, the most powerful. Adult subjects received tachistoscopic exposures too brief (100 milliseconds) to permit a change of fixation. A preexposure fixation dot and then a string of eight letters, sometimes positioned so as to fall entirely to the left or entirely to the right of the fixation point and sometimes so that the fixation point fell in the center of the string, were exposed. In all these circumstances, the initial letter was correctly reported much more often than any other. When the string of letters was entirely to the left or the right of the fixation point, the last letter in the string had the second best score. In general, the data showed a bowed serial-position effect such that performance was poorest in the middle of the sequence.

In reading silently, for meaning, as in the Hochberg, Levin, and Frail experiment, the only function of the printed word is to serve as an unequivocal address for a semantic entry, the meaning of the word. Addresses generally become unequivocal well short of the complete letter-by-letter form. Suppose one read the sentence *The navigator dropped his sextant.* How much of a sample would a skilled reader have to make of the word *sextant?* Suppose he processed first the features: initial *s*, final *t*, and two syllables. This would leave him with a small set of "hypotheses," or projections, which might retrieve the meanings of *serpent, sextet,* and *silent* as well as *sextant.* However, semantic context (for example, *navigator*) and syntactic context (for example, a noun is required) would set aside most hypotheses other than *sextant.* If context did not quite set aside all other hypotheses, then the processing of another letter or two inward from either end would do the job and retrieve the meaning: 'a navigational instrument used to measure the altitude of sun, moon, and stars'. In reading for meaning, there would be no necessity at all to process the complete word including the middle letters. If one were reading aloud, rather than for meaning alone, it would be necessary to process the complete word. It would not, however, be necessary visually to process all the letters on the page. For the terminal letters and impression of length that serve to retrieve the semantic entry would serve equally well to retrieve (or alternately to synthesize) the complete word entry. However, the whole middle portion of the entry would have been "guessed," as it were, or retrieved from memory, and then vocalized. It would not have to have been processed visually.

It seems likely that the sampling skills that, for the skilled readers, were disrupted by filled text in the Hochberg, Levin, and Frail study, included more than the use of peripheral cues to steer fixations. Specifically, I think the skills may have included a within-fixation noticing order that gave priority to word ends and word lengths. The filled text would have camouflaged the ends and also the lengths.

The experimental evidence from reading studies that suggests a noticing order for word features other than the letter-by-letter linear order makes contact in an interesting way with certain experiments on memory for words. Brown and McNeill (1966) have studied the familiar "tip of the tongue" phenomenon by supplying subjects with definitions of uncommon words and asking them to try to recall the word. When a subject was sure he knew the word but just could not get it, though he felt it was on the verge of coming to him, on "the tip of his tongue," in fact, he was asked certain questions about the word he could not retrieve. Among other things he was asked the initial letter of the word and the number of syllables in it. The study showed conclusively that when subjects cannot retrieve a word in its entirety they often do know how many syllables it has (general impression of length) and also can often supply its terminal letters. In general, across words and subjects the likelihood of correctly guessing letters within a word shows a bowed, within-word, serial position effect strikingly like the effects found for reading by Crovitz and Schiffman. Are the effects related? They may be.

Suppose that in reading for meaning (and perhaps also listening for meaning) one ordinarily perceptually processes only length and terminal letters. These features serve to retrieve semantic entries and redundant portions of the word are not processed at all. Suppose, further, that an associative network is built up, from reading and listening for meaning, which relates each word to various other words, meanings, settings, and so forth. But suppose that each associative increment is limited to just those features of the word that are processed on a given occasion. It would then follow that the features of words that are most often processed would be wired more firmly and more widely into an associative network than the more redundant features, which are only occasionally processed. It would, furthermore, follow that the usually processed features—end letters and length—would be retrievable by definitions, settings, and associations that would not suffice to retrieve the less usually processed features. Ergo—the "tip of the tongue" phenomenon as we all know it.

KOLERS: THREE STAGES OF READING

Kolers has reviewed results, from his extensive research program, concerning reading processes at three levels: the visual operations involved in letter recognition; the sensitivity to grammar that is evident even when reading conditions are very unnatural; the fact that meanings, not word forms, are what the reader apprehends. Numerous experiments, some of them quite complex, are described, and so my discussion has to be selective.

One method that Kolers has used particularly captures the imagination. It is the presentation of text as a temporal succession of letters appearing at a fixed point in the visual field. In these circumstances Kolers has found that for full intelligibility each letter must be exposed for 250 milliseconds or a bit more. This comes to a maximum reading rate of about forty-two words a minute. Because the average college student in normal circumstances reads about 300 words a minute Kolers reasons that skilled reading cannot be a process of successive (left to right) identification of each and every letter. Though the reading rate in the temporal succession situation is probably somewhat depressed by visual masking, no doubt the calculations are about right and also the conclusions. Using letter-by-letter successive processing as a kind of baseline, which may be something like the first stages in reading but cannot be much like skilled reading, there is an exciting general possibility, I think, of modifying the procedure so as to test the reality of the various heuristics we suspect that skilled readers employ.

Most hypotheses about advanced reading concern either the size of the unit processed (for example, Levin and Kaplan on the role of phrases) or the order in which features of a unit are processed (for example, Bower on the rule of syntactically crucial words and Hochberg on the role of initial letters). The method that Kolers and others have used, if it is extended a bit, offers a general strategy for testing hypotheses concerning unit size and processing order. It does so by externally controlling the possibilities.

Suppose one thinks that a sentence such as *The boy hit the ball* is processed by a skilled reader as two subroutines corresponding to the high level constituents: NP (*the boy*) and VP (*hit the ball*). We might modify the successive presentation method so as to preserve left-to-right order in the visual field (rather than presenting all letters at one point) and then contrast a temporal order preserving phrase units with one violating phrase units. In the former case a reader would first see *the boy* and then see *hit the ball;* in the latter case he might see *the boy hit the* and then *ball.* Suppose one had the further hypothesis that there was a scanning order for letters in a word (see Crovitz and Schiffman, 1965, for tachistoscopic evidence) such that initial and final letters were scanned first with successive scannings moving toward the middle of the word. This might be combined with a notion that more time is given to the maximally informative terminal letters than to the more redundant central letters. These ideas could be tested for single words, controlling order and time allotment for letters. If a hypothesis about normal skilled reading is correct, then when the baseline condition of letter-by-letter succession is changed so as to make available to the reader a particular heuristic, his reading rate should increase above the baseline rate. If the method of presentation makes available multiple correct heuristics—perhaps presenting text as successive phrases and the letters of words-within-text according to an optimal sequence and allotment of time—reading rate should move closer to the normal rate of 300 words a minute. The general research strategy then would be to build up from the letter-by-letter method of exposure toward a realistic externalization of skilled reading by laying on additional heuristics.

Kolers has already obtained interesting results with the successive-letter method. He has found that temporal gaps do not function for segmentation into words quite as they do for unit formation with geometrical forms. He has found that when letters are presented at short durations, 125 milliseconds or less, subjects sometimes report all the letters correctly but get the order wrong. This latter fact suggests that item identification and item ordering may be distinguishable processes in reading. I am reminded of comparable results obtained, not often but occasionally, in the "tip of the tongue" experiment (Brown and McNeill, 1966). A subject trying to retrieve the word *ambergris,* for instance, thought of *Seagrams* which contains all and only the letters of *ambergris,* except *b* and *i*; however, the order is wrong.

Kolers has extensively experimented with another method—the reading of text subjected to various kinds of geometrical transformation. The main results are quite well known. Some sort of judgment about the orientation of letters is a prerequisite to recognition but, when the orientation is abnormal, the judgment cannot be made once and then perfectly maintained for long stretches; it repeatedly lapses and results in errors of recognition. These errors are predictable from visual appearance (*u* as *n* or *t* as *f*) rather than from similarity of sound. Here is evidence, and by no means the only evidence, that subvocalization is not an essential aspect of reading. Using transformed text Kolers also finds evidence that within-word position effects for letters do not simply result from the perceptual difference between letters that have a space adjacent to them and letters that are in the middle of a dense array. Position effects fail to occur when transformed text is read letter by letter though spaces are normally placed.

The interaction, in reading, of hypothesis formation and visual sampling is dramatically illustrated by results with transformed text. Even when such text is read aloud, rather than simply for meaning, it appears that what a word is taken to be is rather more a matter of what it ought to be than of what it visually is. Kolers found that, when one word was mistaken for another, the incorrect reading was consistent both semantically and syntactically with the antecedent text in about

90 to 100 per cent of the cases. Incorrect readings that as visual forms resembled the actual text were inconsistent, either semantically or syntactically, with prior text only 12 per cent of the time. Whether or not a mistake, once made, was corrected, proved to be primarily a function of consistency with subsequent text rather than of visual similarity to the actual printed form. These dramatic results make one wish for corresponding data on normal text when such text is read for meaning rather than aloud. With what order of syntactic unit would a misreading have to be consistent? Would it be everything antecedent to the word or would it be just the phrase, partly antecedent and partly subsequent, of which the word was a member?

Finally, there are Kolers' fascinating experiments on reading in bilinguals and, particularly, the one that shows that the presence, in a list, of semantic equivalents in two languages (*snow, neige*) heightens the probability that either will be recalled, exactly as if one word had appeared twice (*desk, desk*). I think that the conclusion Kolers draws from this experiment is too strong. Certainly the result shows that words in familiar languages are not perceived simply as strings of graphemes or phonemes, because there is no reason why *neige* as a string of letters should strengthen *snow* as another string. However, Kolers draws the conclusion that "for a person who knows them, words are perceived and remembered in terms of their meaning and not in terms of their appearances or sounds." I am not clear what can be meant by "perceived" in this conclusion. In one sense, *neige* and *snow* certainly are "perceived" as appearances, because it can only be the appearances that retrieve the common meaning. Kolers cannot mean that the appearances go unprocessed perceptually. Presumably he means that appearances are not in consciousness, but then they never are except in special experimental tasks. We are not ordinarily explicitly aware of the cue structure of the world we experience.

The possibility that words are stored in memory only as meanings and not as forms or sounds is more interesting. It reminds us of recent experiments (Sachs, 1967) showing that in sentence recall meaning is retained whereas surface structure is lost. Whether a sentence was *He put on his coat,* or *He put his coat on,* is likely to be forgotten. It is certainly probable that both words and sentences are usually stored as meanings rather than as forms, but I am not convinced that forms are always lost. In Kolers' experiment, for instance, he did not try including *beige* on the same list as *neige*. I should think they might have strengthened each other though perhaps only because any characteristic uncommon enough to be noticed would, if it were repeated, increase the probability of recalling the items sharing it. It is just possible, however, that word forms are sometimes recalled for more interesting reasons. When a word is not very familiar (for example, *numismatics* or *cloaca* or *egregious*), though one can recognize it and has a rough notion of its sense, the memory entry may be neither complete nor very strong; one may have a sense of its length and know the initial and final letters but be unable to spell it or speak it. In these circumstances, perhaps we process the form of a word somewhat more "seriously"—in such a way, in fact, as to stengthen and fill in the entry in memory. Resemblance of form between pairs of rare words might effect an increase in the probability of recalling either even if it does not do so for pairs of common words.

Kolers' chapter concludes with a fascinating discussion of the abstract character of orthographic systems, which would be a good thing to read as an introduction to everything else both in this chapter and in the book.

LEVIN AND KAPLAN: GRAMMATICAL STRUCTURE AND READING

Levin and Kaplan describe a nice set of experiments demonstrating the effect of grammatical constraint on the size of the unit processed in reading. They use the eye-voice span, or EVS, which relates to some variables very much as does the size of saccade, but with the difference that the EVS involves a less drastic disruption of the normal reading process than does the measurement of eye movements. To measure EVS, the visual display is turned off at a predetermined point and the subject is asked to report as many words as he can beyond the one he was speaking when the sentence disappeared. EVS, like the size of the reading saccade, increases with the age and skill of the reader and with the redundancy of the material read. There is a strong suggestion, therefore, that EVS reveals the size of the unit processed in reading.

Levin and Kaplan first showed that the EVS usually was of phrase size whether phrases were two, three, or four words long. It appears then that the processing unit is no fixed number of words but is rather a grammatical unit, a phrase. This was about equally true of all their subjects, from third-graders through tenth-graders and adults. Only second-graders did not generally have an EVS of phrase size. They gave some evidence of reading word by word. However, even second-graders made some use of within-sentence constraint; their EVS for words in unstructured lists was shorter than for words in sentences.

A second experiment built on work of Clark (1965) shows that active sentences and their passive counterparts involve somewhat unlike patterns of constraint. In particular, the latter part of the passive, the verb and subject, is constrained by the first part, the object, in greater degree than is the case for corresponding sentences in the active voice. Levin and Kaplan constructed pairs of long sentences that were structurally alike just to the point where the appearance of a *by* phrase in one marked it as a passive. At the corresponding point in the active sentence a prepositional phrase of another sort appeared. Levin and Kaplan predicted that the EVS's for the matched sentences would not differ at points prior to the *by* phrase but would differ at that point because of the greater constraint in the passive sentence. They did find clear effects of just this sort, and I do not doubt that the effects result from the structural differences between the sentences, but I am not clear that they follow from Clark's earlier demonstration. Clark's active sentences followed a subject-verb-object pattern, but, judging from the example in their report, Levin and Kaplan seem not to have used active sentences of this type. In addition, the EVS at the critical point seems to have been between five and six words long and that length carries the grammatical unit well beyond the passivized subject that Clark found was constrained by prior object and verb. It looks as if the structure of the passive involved enough constraint to expand the EVS through the subject and often through a subsequent prepositional phrase.

A third experiment deals with embedded sentences. In preliminary work using the Cloze procedure, the authors found that embeddings were much more strongly expected after, than before, the main verb in English sentences. They, therefore, anticipated that in reading there would be a lower EVS for an embedded phrase before the main verb than for one after the main verb. This prediction was strikingly confirmed. It suggests that expectancies in reading go far beyond word-to-word transitions to include expectancies of high-level grammatical constituents.

The Levin and Kaplan chapter concludes by developing a view of reading as a process of hypothesis formation, directed data sampling, and confirmation or disconfirmation. This is a view very like that found in the other chapters, and Levin and Kaplan anticipate my own reaction to these chapters when they say: "This model of reading, that is, understanding written material, is in its important aspects applicable also to understanding spoken language."

BOWER: READING BY EYE

As I began "Reading by Eye," it seemed to me that the chapter generated its own disconfirming data. Bower, in the first few pages, argues that the seen word is not necessarily transformed into a heard word. He argues that "reading is a visual skill." The trouble was that as I read these sentences they came to me in Bower's familiar Scots accent and that seemed quite a thing for the eye alone to have accomplished. It is an effect I have experienced before; once, after hearing Bärbel Inhelder lecture; another time after attending a conference with Roman Jakobson. I heard the accent only when reading a paper authored by the person in question. It is a curious effect, because I am quite sure I could not have given recognizable imitations of any of the accents. It seemed to slow down reading while it lasted. But it did not last very long. For that reason the effect does not really disconfirm Bower. His thesis is that reading can be visual and with skilled readers often is. He does not contend that it must always be, especially with slow readers.

The evidence Bower offers that is most directly supportive of the thesis derives from two experiments. For the first, Greek text was mutilated so as to replace one letter with another having the same phonetic value (Greek orthography apparently offers rich opportunities for this kind of mutilation). The effect would, I suppose, be a bit like reading, in English text, *ephect* and *phirst* and *phast* and *fisiology* and *fotografy*. Bower found that the reading aloud of such text took about one and one-half times as long (for readers of Greek, of course) as the reading aloud of unaltered text. Translation into English (by Greek-English bilinguals) took about twice as long for the altered text as for the unaltered. Why should it be so if reading involves transformation into a heard word? It should not be if reading through sound is a letter-by-letter affair—and that of course is the point of the experiment. However, reading could involve an auditory transformation without being letter-by-letter. The reader might utilize some parts or attributes of the total printed word as an address for the auditory representation, which as a total pattern is then sounded. For this reason, the experiment is not crucial.

The second experiment utilized the EEG. Subjects saw a periodic light pulse that exactly coincided with a periodic click, delivered by earphone, and so there were two simultaneous evoked potentials, one visual and one auditory. With no change in these circumstances subjects were asked to read text for ten seconds and, afterward, to rehearse the text (sub-vocally by presumption). Bower found that when text was being read the superimposed visual potential was largely washed out, whereas when the text was being rehearsed it was the auditory potential that was washed out. These facts suggest that reading is visual and rehearsal auditory though they are not decisive because of the many uncertainties about how exactly focal attention works.

Bower's second thesis is interesting indeed. He suggests that readers, fast ones at any rate, are able to read sentences from the top down in the sense of being able to judge the syntactic type of the sentence before processing its individual elements. Again there are two experiments. The first is a matching task in which one sentence was briefly exposed by tachistoscope and then followed by another which was to be signaled "same" (in meaning) or "different." The sentence pairs were built up from a set of ten simple active affirmative sentences (SAAD), their negative and passive and negative passive counterparts plus the rotation of lexical items in subject, verb, and object positions. Members of a pair never differed in more than one lexical item. The dependent variable was reaction time. The kind of result that suggests skilled readers can make an early judgment of syntactic type is the following. Consider the pairs:

1. Kennedy will beat Keating. 1'. Kennedy will beat Keating.
2. Kennedy will beat Keating. 2'. Keating will be beaten by Kennedy.

Both pairs call for the judgment "same" and that is the judgment usually made. The reaction times were about the same whether the syntactic forms were identical (as in 1) or different (as in 2). This fact suggests to Bower that the sentence type (active or passive) is first judged and that the logical subjects are then compared.

The reaction times for skilled readers across all kinds of pairs are ordered in a way that suggests subjects followed a certain routine:

(1) Decide on syntactic form of sentence. (2) Use the information to locate deep structure subject. If same in test as target, (3) go to verb stem. If same in test as target, (4) go to deep structure object. If same in test as target, (5) check whether steps 1, 2, 3, and 4 have accounted for all the words in the sentence. At this point, negatives would be (6) discovered. If none left, (7) respond *same*.

I am not persuaded that the matching experiment demonstrates anything about reading. The task, not a usual one, was to judge two sentences the same or different in meaning. The population of sentences created by realizing all combinations of active, passive, negative, and passive negative with rotation of subjects, verbs, and objects surely gave away to subjects its artificiality and perhaps even its formula. Very many of the sentences that would have been used were at least mildly anomalous: *Kennedy surrounded the bridge, A deer will beat Keating,* and so forth. Adult subjects and children, too, are able to create ad hoc routines for coping with such laboratory problems, routines that have nothing to do with normal sentence processing. There is reason to suspect that subjects have done this in certain experiments on the "psychological reality" of tranformational grammar, and I suspect they also did it here.

The second experiment is more persuasive. One hundred sentences were drawn at random, without selection, from *Time* magazine and exposed one at a time for varying brief tachistoscopic exposures. Subjects were encouraged to "give any response they could" and "encouraged to indicate abstract features of the presented sentences." Subjects' responses were categorized in various ways, and "fast readers, after a little practice, were very good at indicating sentence structure. . . ." This is important evidence.

I am somewhat puzzled, however, by Bower's statement that subjects were able to "pick up the structure of sentences before picking up the individual constituents of the sentences." I can easily believe that subjects would learn something about the structure of a sentence from a word or two. An initial *wh-* word such as *what* suggests either a *wh-* question or a nominalization. The word *that* suggests either a predicate-complement or a relative clause. The word *although* suggests a subordinate clause. And so on. But I would have thought that any reader not a linguist would have had no terms with which to name these structures and would have been likely to refer to them by mentioning the diagnostic word. So I wish Bower had given us some examples of the responses he classified as evidence of structural knowledge.

I can see how the subject would learn something about the structure of a sentence from a preliminary scan, but not how he would learn very much about sentences that are a random sample from an issue of *Time.* Here, for instance, are the first three sentences from my random sample of the April 12, 1968, issue of *Time:*

1. "He reported on a poll of Harvard undergraduates, most of whom indicated that they hope their future children will live by a stricter moral code than they have" (p. 60).

2. "Superbly equipped and run by San Francisco's health department, the hospital has a 14-car ambulance service manned by stewards and drivers, both with training and experience equivalent to that of registered nurses" (p. 73).

3. "Come sundown, businessmen who wouldn't be caught dead in the office with anything but a clean-shaven face add paste-ons for a bristling night on the town" (p. 80).

All these contain at least two embedded sentences as well as complicated prepositional phrases, stylistic extrapositions, and so forth. Simple sentences are not very numerous in *Time*. The point is that such words as *that, who,* and *but,* not to mention commas, are cues to sentence structure, but with ordinarily complex sentences they do not reveal very much of the structure.

WEBER: FIRST-GRADERS' USE OF GRAMMATICAL CONTEXT IN READING

This chapter is unlike the others in the set discussed in that it focuses on the beginning reader, the first-grader. It is like the others, however, in calling attention to processes that go beyond visual form recognition and letter sounding. These latter two skills do not, of course, exhaust the competencies of the new reader.

Weber's experiments clearly establish several generalizations, and her method points the way to the testing of others. She shows, to begin with, that first-graders utilize antecedent context when they read. This will be no surprise to teachers of reading who encourage children to guess from context when they can. Spontaneous errors made when the children read aloud in class were analyzed for grammatical consistency with prior context and were found to be consistent about 90 per cent of the time. This shows a degree of reliance on context quite comparable to the adult case (see, for instance, Kolers' related data). Weber's analysis does not actually enable us to tell how much of the effective constraint to attribute to strictly grammatical considerations and how much to semantics nor does it separate out the contributions of varying sorts of grammatical constraint. Finer coding of a large population of errors might yield information at this level of precision or perhaps the information could be obtained with a revised research strategy that involved planting errors of known types in normal text.

When errors were made that disregarded context (only about 10 per cent in all), the similarity between the erroneous word and the displayed word was especially high. If the author had quantified degrees of contextual constraint as she quantified degrees of graphic similarity, she probably would have found a general inverse relation between the two. This is an empirical generalization that is, on one level, easily understood. Because context and visual display, between the two of them, pretty well exhaust the likely determinants of error, when one is absent or low, the other must be high, because the error must be somehow determined. There are additional questions to be asked, however. Does a low degree of contextual constraint automatically result in a more generous sampling of the visual data? Or is it rather the case that, when the visual data sampled happen perfectly to fit a word of very high frequency, then that word is too good a hypothesis to be disconfirmed even by an unaccommodating context?

Weber studied spontaneous self-corrections in children's reading, as well as naturally occurring errors, and for this purpose considered whether errors were consistent with context subsequent to the error as well as antecedent to it. There is a small difference on this point between the better and poorer readers (Table 10–6), which is interesting though evidently not statistically significant. The errors made by the better readers (high group) were consistent with the total sentence, that is, with context on either side of the error, in 68.2 per cent of all cases, whereas the errors of the low group were consistent with the total sentence in 55.9 per cent. Perhaps this difference means that better readers are more likely to have sampled data on either side of the mistake, more likely to attempt to project the total larger syntactic unit. This possibility reminds us of the Levin and Kaplan finding that the processing unit suggested by EVS data is the phrase. It should be possible also, to investigate the size of the processing unit through the study of spontaneous errors and corrections. The sentences Weber's first-graders were reading must have been very short and simple. In longer sentences, and with older subjects, would grammatical consistency in errors prove to be maintained only for units of a certain size, for high-level constituents or phrases or, perhaps, embedded simple sentences?

Finally, errors were much more likely to be corrected when they were inconsistent with subsequent context than when they were consistent with the full sentence. Again comparison with data in Paul Kolers' chapter is in order, and again the first-grader seems to be performing like the advanced reader. However, Weber found that the effect held chiefly for her high group, the better readers. As Weber points out, the near failure of the effect for the low group cannot be confidently attributed to an insensitivity to subsequent context. The children were reading aloud into a microphone with no one else present, and it is perfectly possible that the poorer readers were simply less interested in the quality of their performance.

In general, Weber does not find that poorer beginning readers differ from their more skilled classmates in utilization of contextual constraints. Even more clearly Weber's results do not reveal a qualitative break between advanced readers and beginning readers with respect to the utilization of context.

CONCLUSION

What is the difference between the conception of reading that informs the chapters we have reviewed and the conception that informed the research of earlier times? The earlier research concentrated on just those psycholinguistic processes that are peculiar to reading: the visual identification of graphemes and the translation of graphemes to sound. Because these processes play no part in the perception and comprehension of spoken language, reading seemed a topic sharply distinct from the rest of psycholinguistics. The essays we have reviewed focus on problems that are not specific to reading but common to the processing of both speech and text. Is language stored as form or meaning? In sentence comprehension, what is the size of the processing unit? By what means is data sampling guided? What are the major surface clues to underlying structure? These are the questions to which psycholinguistics generally is directed and so reading research is no longer an isolated field; indeed its bounds have become a little difficult to define.

Letter recognition and letter sounding are the processes that loom large in the task of the beginning reader, and it is the beginning reader that earlier research had chiefly in mind. The researchers whose work we have considered, though they all take the position that there is more than one kind of reading, are (except for Weber) somewhat more concerned with skilled, advanced reading than with the reading of the first-grader. Hochberg and Levin both suggest that the beginning reader proceeds in a unit-by-unit, left-to-right fashion, though, in view of Weber's results we cannot take this to mean that units are processed without regard to context. Bower suggests that, though slow readers may subvocalize, fast readers need not and, reasoning from information-processing rates, seemingly could not. How does the skilled reader operate? I think all our authors would accept the following rough characterization: he engages in directed highly selective sampling of visual data; he combines the initial data with knowledge of semantic, syntactic, and within-word orthographic constraints to construct hypotheses as to the meanings of large units; he samples again, just where and in the degree necessary to choose among competing constructions. To paraphrase Neisser's (1967) captivating metaphor, the skilled reader constructs meaning rather as the archaeologist reconstructs the past—from fragmentary evidence and a lot of general knowledge. This characterization of skilled reading is very like contemporary characterizations of the perception and comprehension of spoken language.

In the last couple of years, psycholinguists who operate with a generative transformational conception of language have given up the notion that the linguists' grammar could literally be a component of the programs by which sentences are perceived and understood (Fodor and Garrett, 1966). The grammar formalizes the knowledge of the native speaker but does not represent the manner in which such knowledge is brought to bear in comprehending sentences. Consequently, it is not reasonable to expect the derivational complexity of a sentence to be an index of the complexity of the psychological processes involved in comprehending it. The problem of sentence comprehension is to supply a semantic interpretation, and the view is now widely held (for example, Fodor, Garrett, and Bever, 1968) that such an interpretation depends on the recovery of the relations marked in the deep structure of the sentence, relations that may be seriously distorted in the surface structure. It is thought (Fodor et al., 1968) that the psychological difficulty of a sentence depends on the number and quality of the clues to underlying relations to be found in the surface structure.

Contemporary research on sentence perception is characterized by an effort to identify some of the main clues to underlying structure and to conceive of heuristics for utilizing such clues. Fodor and Garrett (1967) have shown, for instance, that certain sentences with two embeddings are easier to understand when optionally deletable relative pronouns are present than when they are absent. It is easier to recover the structure of 1 than of 2.

1. The pen which the author whom the editor liked was new.
2. The pen the author the editor liked was new.

To take another example, Fodor et al. (1968) have shown that the presence in a sentence of a main verb that can take predicate complements makes this sentence harder to process than a counterpart in which the main verb is a pure transitive that cannot take complements; 1 below is harder than 2.

1. The box the man the child *knew* carried was empty.
2. The box the man the child *met* carried was empty.

Presumably 1 is harder than 2 because the verb *knew* is consistent with a larger number of deep structures than is the verb *met,* and so in the case of 1 there are more candidate structures to be set aside than in 2.

The two experiments described above are quite similar to the work of Levin and Kaplan on active and passive sentences and embedded sentences and also to Bower's work on the identification in rapid-exposure conditions of structural aspects of sentences. It would be possible to cite psycholinguistic parallels to several other of the reading experiments we have reviewed. We begin to wonder what causes a researcher to characterize his work as a study of reading rather than as a study of language processing in general. The use of text as stimulus material is not the specific distinction. Fodor et al. (1968) present their sentences sometimes in printed form and sometimes in spoken form; the results do not vary much with the form. What is characteristic of the contemporary reading experiment as opposed to the contemporary general psycholinguistic experiment is the special attention given, among components of the total process, to visual reception. Whereas the psycholinguistic researcher is likely to present his sentences complete, printed on cards, and with plenty of reading time, the reading researcher is likely to distort the distal stimulus (Kolers' transformed text and Hochberg's "filled" text), or spread it out in time (Kolers' successive letters), or expose it very briefly (Gibson's and Bower's uses of the tachistoscope), or interrupt it at various points (Levin's EVS span). All these maneuvers are, of course, designed to reveal the nature of the specifically receptive strategies.

Reading researchers and researchers in general psycholinguistics are operating with quite similar conceptions of sentence processing and are similarly engaged in a search for units, structural clues, and heuristics. In our enthusiasm for the knowledge they have gained, we should not forget how fragmentary it is when measured against the goal. No one has offered an explicit formulation of the total process of sentence comprehension for either the reading or the hearing case. What we have is a rough general conception and a collection of isolated clues and conceivable heuristics.

Researchers on reading, many of them anyway, used to spend a lot of time celebrating the cognitive advantages of an alphabetic orthography and arguing about the instructional techniques ("phonics" or "whole word") best calculated to bring these advantages to the young. Speakers of any language are compelled to memorize a very large number of essentially arbitrary associations, the associations pairing semantic readings with phonemic strings. Speakers of a language that utilizes an ideographic or semantic writing (for example, Chinese) are faced with a second such massive learning task when they undertake to become literate. Speakers of a language that uses an alphabetic writing, even as complex and imperfect a one as English, are offered an important economy. If they will learn the general rules mapping spelling to sounds they will be able to spell (approximately) and read all the words they already know in phonemic form. Now that attention has shifted to the advanced reader who only samples the text and seemingly bypasses vocalization, we naturally hear much less about the transfer of knowledge the alphabet permits. There is, however, an interesting possibility of transfer specifically connected with skilled reading. The child who is just learning to sound his letters already knows very well how to perceive and comprehend spoken sentences of great complexity. Presumably he operates on speech with a large number of effective heuristics. The majority of these, with accommodations for the visual medium, are probably applicable also to reading. What kinds of training facilitates the transfer of these higher-order skills? Apparently everyone can process spoken sentences with dazzling skill, but not everyone becomes an advanced reader. We know little indeed of the means by which children acquire those skills that modern reading research has uncovered.

REFERENCES

Brown, R., & McNeill, D. The "tip of the tongue" phenomenon. *Journal of Verbal Learning and Verbal Behavior,* 1966, *5,* 325–337.

Bruner, J. S., & O'Dowd, D. A note on the informativeness of words. *Language and Speech,* 1958, *1,* 98–101.

Clark, H. H. Some structural properties of simple active and passive sentences. *Journal of Verbal Learning and Verbal Behavior,* 1965, *4,* 365–370.

Crovitz, H. F., & Schiffman, H. R. Visual field and the letter span. *Journal of Experimental Psychology*, 1965, *70*, 218–223.

Fodor, J. A., & Garrett, M. Some reflections on competence and performance. In J. Lyons & R. J. Wales (eds.), *Psycholinguistics Papers*. Edinburgh: Edinburgh University Press, 1966, pp. 135–154.

Fodor, J. A., & Garrett, M. Some syntactic determinants of sentential complexity. *Perception and Psychophysics*, 1967, *2*, 289–296.

Fodor, J. A., Garrett, M., & Bever, T. G. Some syntactic determinants of sentential complexity: II. verb structure. Unpublished paper, Department of Psychology, M.I.T., 1968.

Garrett, M., & Fodor, J. A. Psychological theories and linguistic constructs. In T. R. Dixon & D. L. Horton (eds.), *Verbal Behavior and General Behavior Theory*. Englewood Cliffs, N.J.: Prentice-Hall, 1968, pp. 451–477.

Gibson, E. J., Pick, A., Osser, H., & Hammond, M. The role of grapheme-phoneme correspondence in the perception of words. *American Journal of Psychology*, 1962, *75*, 554–570.

Harcum, E. R., & Jones, M. L. Letter recognition within word flashed left and right of fixation. *Science*, 1962, *138*, 444–445.

Hochberg, J., Levin, H., & Frail, C. Studies of oral reading: VII. How inter-word spaces affect reading. Mimeographed, 1966.

Hockett, C. F. Analysis of English spelling. In *A Basic Research Program on Reading*. Cooperative Research Project No. 639, Cornell University and U.S. Office of Education, 1963.

Mayzner, M. S., & Tresselt, M. E. Tables of single-letter and digram frequency counts for various word-length and letter-position combinations. *Psychonomic Monographs Supplement*, 1965, *1*, 13–22.

Mayzner, M. S., Tresselt, M. E., & Wolin, B. R. Tables of trigram frequency counts for various word-length and letter-position combinations. *Psychonomic Monographs Supplement*, 1965, *1*, 13–22

Neisser, U. *Cognitive Psychology*. New York: Appleton-Century-Crofts, 1967.

Sachs, J. S. Recognition memory for syntactic and semantic aspects of connected discourse. *Perception and Psychophysics*, 1967, *2*, 437–442.

Underwood, B. J., & Schultz, R. W. *Meaningfulness and Verbal Learning*. New York: Lippincott, 1960.

Venezky, R. L. A computer program for deriving spelling-to-sound correlations. In *A Basic Research Program on Reading*. Cooperative Research Project No. 639, Cornell University and U.S. Office of Education, 1963.

Venezky, R. L., & Weir, R. H. *A Study of Selected Spelling-to-Sound Correspondence Patterns*. Cooperative Research Project No. 3090, Stanford University, 1966.

GASTON E. BLOM

RICHARD R. WAITE

SARA G. ZIMET

12

A Motivational Content Analysis of Children's Primers

Our initial interest in the research reported in this chapter was stimulated by our clinical work with children who had difficulties in reading. We were much impressed with the greater frequency of this kind of disorder in boys than in girls. This observation, based on limited clinical data, had been made by others; indeed, the sex ratios reported by other investigators ranged from 3:1 to 10:1, boys always having a greater incidence of difficulty. These findings, however, did not hold in all countries or cultures, and this suggested that innate, sex-linked physiological variables were of limited, or at best indirect, importance. We began to wonder what variables were responsible. A variety of variables suggested themselves, including sex differences in childrearing, instructional methods, attitudes toward school and learning, and the content of reading materials.

Our focus of attention was drawn to the materials used to teach American children to read by a number of articles that appeared in the popular and educational press at that time. Prominent among these was one by Bettelheim (1961) and another by Henry (1961). The crux of these writings was that it appeared, on an a priori basis, that the reading textbooks used in the first grade were inappropriate in terms of interest value. They concealed the realities of life in America, hiding not only

---

Supported by the U.S. Office of Education Cooperative Research Project 3094.

188

its difficulties and problems, but also much of its excitement and joy. They featured Dick and Jane in the clean, Caucasian, correct suburbs, in houses surrounded by white fences, playing happily with happy peers and happy parents. They contained a dearth of moral content that could have high interest value. They presented a monstrous repetition of Polly-annish family activities. They offered no new knowledge. They contra-dicted the everyday experiences of children in general, because most American children seldom if ever experienced the affect-less situations depicted in the books. Some of these writers also felt that the stories were so predictable in outcome that little if any of a child's incentive to continue reading was derived from the story content.

We began to look at first-grade reading books in order to get a better understanding of what these writers were referring to. Was there any-thing about the books that could help explain the greater incidence of reading failure in boys? Gradually we arrived at three clinical hunches about the stories. First, we agreed that the descriptions of primers as representative of the upper middle suburban class, unrelated to real-life situations, and overly Pollyannish were essentially accurate. Second, it appeared that the stories depicted activities that in real life are most frequently engaged in by (1) children younger than first-graders and (2) girls rather than boys. Third, it appeared to us that in many stories children's attempts to plan and carry out constructive activities were frustrated by one agent or another. Moreover, from the stories we read it seemed that masculine activities were frustrated more often than femi-nine activities.

We made the assumption that there was a relationship between the kinds of stories used to teach children to read and the development of their ability to read. This assumption is a reasonable one, although attempts to support it scientifically pose noteworthy methodological problems. The results of at least one study (Whipple, 1963) contribute to its validity, although further research is needed. Whipple found differ-ences in measurements of word recognition, oral reading accuracy, and interest appeal between traditional primers and a new multiethnic read-ing text. The results favored the multiethnic reading textbooks. We also believed that the variables included in our clinical hunches (depiction of reality, age, sex, and outcome characteristics of the activities in the stories) were particularly important influences in the development of reading ability. Although some of the research in progress focuses on this assumption, our main interest has been the content analysis of the books themselves.

The work already completed and described below began with the analysis of traditional primers (those used most frequently in American schools) in terms of hypotheses derived from our initial impressions. That is, we sought to establish some indications as to the validity of our impressionistic observations. Following these analyses, our attention turned toward reading books that differed from traditional primers, including books used in other countries, books used in American schools prior to 1950, new series explicitly designed for particular groups of children, and books freely selected from libraries by first-grade children. A number of studies have been initiated and are discussed later in this chapter. Among these, three have been completed that pertain to one type of new, nontraditional book, the so-called multiethnic primer.

CONTENT DIMENSIONS AND CODING MANUAL

The selection of dimensions to be used in the content analyses was based in part on our clinical impressions. That is, particular attention was paid to those aspects of stories that were relevant to the hypotheses we made and to the criticisms of other writers. In addition, it should be noted that both the selection of content dimensions and the generation of hypotheses were based partly on knowledge of developmental factors of special importance for the five- or six-year-old child. For example, the establishment of a more clearly defined sex role identity is of developmental importance in the six-year-old child, and thus the sex of the activities depicted in the story is of interest. Also, the tendency of children this age to identify with peers and adults suggests that the degree of similarity between the child and his environment, on the one hand, and the story characters and their environment, on the other, is a relevant consideration.

Seven content dimensions were selected. In addition, the stories were rated according to reading level as indicated by the publisher in terms of vocabulary range, word complexity, sentence structure, and idea comprehension. The seven content dimensions were

1. Characters. Each story was coded according to its constellation of characters. Ten categories were used, such as "children only," "children and mother," "animals only."
2. Distribution of children. The children in each story were counted according to their family membership (primary family or other family), age (less than six years, six years, more than six years), and sex.

3. Theme. The predominate theme of each story was coded using seventeen categories, including "active play," "pets," "religion," and the like.

4. Age of activity. The dimension refers to the age at which children engage in or would be interested in the main activity depicted in each story. Five categories were used, ranging from "two- and three-year-olds" to "ten- and eleven-year olds."

5. Sex of activity. Each story was coded as to whether its main activity would be one performed preferentially by girls or boys, regardless of the sex of the character(s) carrying out the activity in the story. Because some activities tend to be equally preferred by both sexes, the category "boy-girl" was included in addition to "boy" and "girl." Those stories in which the main activity was coded "boy-girl" were later recoded. The raters were asked to which sex they would assign the activity if they were forced to choose (forced sex ratings). They were instructed here to use the "boy-girl" category only if the forced sex was impossible.

6. Outcome of activity. The main activity of each story was coded as to the nature of its conclusion. Four categories were available to the raters—"success," "failure," "help" (success achieved only with the assistance of someone not involved in the activity's initiation), and "unclassified."

7. Environmental setting. The geographic location of each story was coded, using the categories "urban," "suburban," "rural," "make believe," and "not clear."

When a search of the literature produced no existing scales completely appropriate to the task, four members of the research group devised a coding manual to be used by the raters. They based their judgments on data available in the developmental literature, and, in addition, they made use of their own experiences. (All were parents, two had experience as elementary school teachers, one was a child psychoanalyst, and one was a child clinical psychologist.) Lists of activities appropriate to each age and sex category were compiled. Judgments as to the most suitable category for a given behavioral item were pooled, and for inclusion in the lists complete agreement among the four researchers was necessary.

TRAINING THE RATERS

The four originators used the first edition of the coding manual to code a number of stories independently. Group discussions, revisions, and further discussions followed until the manual appeared satisfactory from the standpoint of its utility as well as its applicability. Two raters who had not been involved previously in the research and who were uninformed as to its purposes and hypotheses were trained in the use of the manual with stories not included in the subsequent studies. They then coded one publisher's series of books (134 stories) independently, and interrater agreements were calculated. These agreements ranged from 86 per cent on one dimension to 99 per cent on another. The over-all percentage of agreement was at 93 per cent.

The raters then proceeded to code stories independently. Periodic re-evaluation of interrater reliability was made, using a criterion of 85 per cent agreement on each dimension. As new raters were employed, they were trained in the same way and subjected to identical evaluations of reliability.

THE STANDARD SERIES STUDIES

Selection of Books

Twelve publishers' series of first-grade reading textbooks were selected on the basis of a national survey conducted by Hollins (1955). Each series consists of about five books graded by reading level, most of which are concerned with the events occurring in a primary family and its neighborhood. These twelve were the most frequently used series in American first-grade classrooms and constituted approximately 90 per cent of the books to which first-graders are exposed. In all, they contained 1,307 stories. In appearance, they are very similar, and they are referred to later as "standard" or "traditional" primers or series.

Tabulation of Data

The coded data on the 1,307 stories were assembled in terms of frequency distributions within each dimension and the interactions between certain dimensions. These distributions and interactions have been reported in part elsewhere (Blom, Waite, and Zimet, 1968). They provide a statistical description of the stories most American children read, or learn to read, in first grade.

The complete findings will not be reproduced here. However, several specific dimensions that were pertinent to our original interests are discussed below.

Theme

Table 12–1 lists the seventeen theme categories in rank order by frequency of ratings. The stereotyped quality of these stories and books is indicated by the large proportion of stories (47 per cent) contained in the first three categories. (In nine of the twelve publishers' series, these three categories account for more than 40 per cent of the stories.) Those stories coded "real life with positive emotions" feature happy endings and, together with those coded "active play," are the kinds of stories frequently described as Pollyannish.

Table 12–1. *Frequency Ratings—Theme.*

	NO. OF STORIES	%		NO. OF STORIES	%
Real life with positive emotions	303	23	Work projects	76	6
			Quiet activities	41	3
Active play	162	12	Pranks and humor	37	3
Pets	152	12	School	35	3
Outings	107	8	Parties	20	2
Imaginative play	94	7	Lessons from life	14	1
Real life with negative emotions	93	7	Aesthetics	7	.5
			Unclassified	3	.5
Nature	83	6	Religion	0	0
Folk tales	78	6			

"Quiet activities," "pranks and humor," "school," "parties," "lessons from life," and "aesthetic appreciation" are all found infrequently. There were no stories at all in which the central theme pertained to religion. The absence of stories about religion and the low frequency of stories about aesthetics and lessons from life is in marked contrast to the content of the McGuffey Readers published prior to the 1830's. Though the absence of religion in modern primers is understandable, the low frequency of other kinds of stories is not. (In seven of the twelve series, no stories were coded "lessons from life.") It is clear that the communication of moral and ethical values is avoided, and, evidently, contemplative, intellectual, and creative activities are considered of less importance than active, happy events. The stories are generally bland, perhaps in an effort to teach reading more efficiently by eliminating interfering stimuli or to avoid public controversy of any sort. In general, there is strong emphasis on vocabulary control and on the mastery of basic skills, and motivational issues are neglected.

Could ethical and cultural values have been represented in the seventy-eight stories coded "folk tales"? Further inspection of these stories indicated that this was not the case. Generally, they contained few stories with human characters. The characters in 77 per cent of them were animals with human characteristics. Ten per cent featured as characters other anthropomorphized figures, including toys, flowers, trains, and pancakes.

Characters

In the character dimension, there are ten categories as shown in Table 12–2. Again, the categories are presented in rank order of frequency. The first three categories constitute 53 per cent of the stories, and, in eight of the twelve series, they account for more than one-half of the stories. This indicates the degree of restriction in the range of character

Table 12–2. *Frequency Ratings—Character.*

Children and animals	$n = 296$	23%
Children and mother	$n = 202$	16%
Children, mother, and father	$n = 188$	14%
Children and other adults	$n = 172$	13%
Children only	$n = 146$	11%
Children and father	$n = 112$	9%
Adults only	$n = 27$	2%
Make-believe characters	$n = 14$	1%
Inanimate objects	$n = 11$	1%

combinations. Four of the twelve series had no stories in which only adults appear. There are fewer stories that include children and father as compared with children and mother. Thus, the emphasis is on restricted patterns of interactions, and only a limited number of stories is provided that would focus the children's attention on adults, particularly male adults.

Distributions of Children

The ratings on the distributions of children dimension are summarized in Table 12–3. Of the 1,307 stories, 1,161 include children. The codings point out the representation of family membership in most stories. The typical family consists of parents, a boy and a girl each about six years, and a younger sister. Older brothers and sisters appear infrequently.

When other child characters appear, they tend to be about six years old or younger. Seldom are older neighborhood children present. If we assume that the child reader tends to identify with the characters in the story, then they would be identifying with age-identical or younger age children. When the data were examined according to combinations of age, sex, and family status (primary family or other), interesting findings emerged. Stories in which only one child is present were few

Table 12–3. *Distribution of Children According to Age, Sex, and Family.*

CATEGORIES	NO. OF STORIES IN WHICH CATEGORY IS REPRESENTED	PERCENTAGE OF TOTAL 1,161
Boy—age 6—family	897	77%
Girl—age 6—family	837	72
Girl < age 6—family	389	34
Boy—age 6—nonfamily	340	29
Girl—age 6—nonfamily	278	25
Boy < age 6—family	69	6
Boy < age 6—nonfamily	64	5.5
Boy > age 6—nonfamily	38	3
Girl < age 6—nonfamily	29	2.5
Girl > age 6—nonfamily	9	.8
Boy > age 6—family	9	.8
Girl > age 6—family	4	.3

(12 per cent). In slightly more than half of the stories, only members of the primary family appeared. Five per cent of the stories excluded the primary family, and 31 per cent included both family and nonfamily characters. In general, these ratings indicated that what is depicted as age appropriate are activities that are shared with others, a kind of other-directed, reactive, yet family-oriented society of children and parents.

Sex, Age, and Outcome of Activities

Three specific hypotheses were formulated prior to the data analysis. They stemmed from our original impressions of the primers and were later stated in terms of the dimensions. The hypotheses were

1. The activities depicted in the stories are more frequently ones that, in American culture, are engaged in by children younger than six years of age than by children older than six.

2. The activities are most frequently those in which, in American culture, girls engage.

3. The masculine activities end in failure more frequently than the feminine activities do.

The results of this particular study have been reported previously (Waite, Blom, Zimet, and Edge, 1967). Briefly, the first two hypotheses (sex and age) were not supported by the data. Approximately the same number of stories were coded "boy" as were coded "girl." A sizable number, 599 out of 1,307, were coded "boy-girl," indicating a decided lack of sex role differentiation in the stories. Forced sex ratings failed to yield differences in frequencies of "boy" and "girl" ratings. The age ratings showed that there were approximately the same number of stories depicting activities appropriate to children older than six years as there were to children younger than six years.

The third hypothesis was tested by examining the interaction between sex and outcome ratings. This interaction, presented in Table 12–4, was statistically significant ($X^2 = 23.8$, $p < .001$). Those activities judged to be masculine (using forced sex ratings) more frequently ended in failure than those judged to be feminine.

Table 12–4. *Relationships between Forced Sex and Outcome Ratings.*

FORCED SEX RATING	SUCCESS	FAILURE	HELP	UNCLASSIFIED	TOTAL
Boy	379	181	56	4	620
Girl	394	135	54	2	585
Boy-girl	64	30	4	4	102
TOTAL	837	346	114	10	1,307

A reexamination of the data disclosed an interesting additional finding. It was found that the first two hypotheses were in fact supported by the data contained in books published between 1956 and 1961. Indeed, these hypotheses had evolved from our original examination of primers published during that period. Thus, the six series published before 1962 tended to feature stories in which the activities were more appropriate to children younger than six years and to girls rather than boys. After 1962, these tendencies were reversed. The interactions between sex of activity and publication date and between age of activity and publication date were statistically significant. Further analysis demonstrated that the third hypothesis (the interaction between sex and outcome) was also supported only in those stories published prior to 1962. (See Table 12–5.)

Table 12–5. *Interaction between Forced Sex and Outcome Ratings According to Publication Dates* (*<1962–>1962*).

FORCED SEX RATING	SUCCESS		FAILURE		HELP		UNCLASSIFIED		TOTALS	
	<1962	>1962	<1962	>1962	<1962	>1962	<1962	>1962	<1962	>1962
Boy	182	197	77	104	18	38	3	1	280	340
Girl	262	132	61	74	26	28	1	1	350	235
Boy-girl	42	22	12	18	4	0	3	1	61	41
TOTAL	486	351	150	196	48	66	7	3	691	616

The fact that the findings were related to the year of publication was surprising. We wondered whether this reflected a deliberate change in the content of stories selected for primers. In the absence at the moment of data relevant to this question (inquiries directed to publishers have been answered with evasions), one might speculate that these differences reflect, directly or indirectly, the reorientation of American education during the late 1950's. During this period, the frequency of reading disability in boys was acknowledged, along with the growing public criticism of reading textbooks put forth in scholarly articles and in the popular press and television. In addition, some recent research on differences in the learning patterns of boys and girls was having an impact. The national support toward greater scientific achievement (the post-Sputnik era) stimulated greater educational efforts throughout schools.

It is also of interest that there was a large proportion of stories coded "boy-girl" both before and after 1962. Developmental studies demonstrate that by the sixth year most children follow interests that are generally preferred by their sex (Kagan, 1964). Boys are caught up in the pursuits of masculine activities, interests, and identifications. They choose male peers as friends and avoid girls. Girls, too, generally accept feminine interests, fantasies, and personality reactions, though perhaps less strongly than boys. It is possible that the lack of differentiation in sex roles in the stories conflicts with the important developmental task of sex role identification. It may be that in their efforts to provide stories that are of interest to both sexes, the authors of these primers have diminished their motivational value for all children. From the standpoint of child development, it would be more consonant to present activities in stories that are clearly differentiated as to sex role. This would mean that, in general, when girls appear in stories, they would perform girl activities and when boys appear they would engage in boy activities. This would be consistent with the reinforcement that various cultural traditions and activities provide in fostering appropriate sex role identification.

MULTIETHNIC SERIES STUDIES

During the past five years, publishers have responded to growing social pressures for reading textbooks that include as characters children of more than one ethnic background. Prior to this time, the characters were almost exclusively limited to white, middle-class people living a suburban life. The need for integrated textbooks has been stated and restated by numerous writers who emphasized not only the necessity of providing better materials for minority group children, but also for educating white children who may receive much misinformation about other ethnic groups. Most of the multiethnic readers currently published have been criticized on the grounds that, except for the skin color of the characters, they are essentially similar to the traditional primers. These criticisms have been mainly impressionistic, but they are important enough to warrant serious examination. Therefore, we carried out two studies of multiethnic series to ascertain how they are similar and different from traditional series, and one study that was a clinical analysis of characters portrayed in one multiethnic series.

First Study

The Sample

The first study focused on a multiethnic urban first-grade reading series that was published in 1964 (City Schools Reading Program). This series resulted from the efforts of individuals associated with a large urban school system to help urban children more readily identify with story characters that represented the types of people seen in multicultural neighborhoods (Marburger, 1963; Whipple, 1963). The authors attempted a deliberate departure from the traditional reading series in more than the skin color of the characters. Efforts were made to develop stories with suspense, surprise, humor, and high interest. Natural, familiar speech patterns and word usage were employed. A large number of active verbs was chosen for the vocabulary. A comparison of this series with the more traditional ones in terms of the reading acquisition, interest, and preferences of children from a variety of socioeconomic and cultural neighborhoods indicated that the urban series was more effective (Whipple, 1963). Whether or not its appeal and effectiveness have continued since its introduction has not been determined.

Method of the Study

The following content analysis dimensions were used: story themes, attributes of characters in the stories, sex appropriateness of the activities, age appropriateness of the activities, and outcome of the activities. In addition, environmental setting ratings and ethnicity ratings (frequency counts of Negro, Caucasian, and other racial characters) were made. The results of this content analysis were compared to those of the previously described traditional series (Blom, Waite, and Zimet, 1967).

Results

The comparisons of theme and character ratings between the two series indicated that the urban series contained the same emphasis as the standard series on Pollyannish stories, with a somewhat greater emphasis on family-centered activities. No statistically significant differences were found in the age of the activities, nor in the sex appropriateness of the activities. Ratings of the character attributes showed a greater frequency of stories in the urban series portraying family and nonfamily members together. Whereas the typical family constellation in the standard series consists of the parents, a boy and a girl, each of about six years, and a younger sister, in the urban series typical family, the younger sister is replaced by a younger brother.

These ratings indicate that in many ways the urban series closely approximates the more traditional series used by schools. The environmental setting ratings support this conclusion, because in this series suburban settings predominate to an even larger degree than they do in the traditional series, although there are fewer rural stories and more urban stories. Qualitative examination of the urban stories revealed that what is being depicted is a Negro family living in a happy, stable, white suburban neighborhood. No Negroes appear other than members of the primary family. Marburger (1963) described the difficulties and frustrations of writing this series of preprimers, which was to focus on the life of a working-class family who lived in a typical, racially mixed neighborhood. The two basic issues confronting this sophisticated and knowledgeable group related to (1) whether to select stories that describe what is or what should be and (2) the avoiding of stereotypes in the characterizations. And yet, despite conscious efforts to avoid the problems associated with these factors, the results of our content analysis indicate that these problems were not adequately resolved.

The outcome ratings in the urban series revealed striking differences between it and the standard series sample. First, the activities in the urban stories end in failure nearly twice as frequently as they end in success. None of the twelve series in the traditional series contains more failure stories than success stories. Second, in the urban series there are about as many activities ending in help as in success. In the traditional series, seven times as many stories end in success as in help. These differences are statistically significant ($p < .001$). Thus, in terms of the outcome dimension, the urban series is distinctly different from each of the other series we studied. An investigation of the relationship between ethnicity ratings and outcome ratings showed no particular relationship between the two dimensions. That is, the preponderance of failure stories is a general phenomenon characteristic of this series and is not correlated with the presence or absence of particular racial groups.

The clear differences between the urban series and the standard series in terms of the outcome of activities are somewhat surprising. If the development of reading skill is related to the content of the stories in reading textbooks, the presentation of a preponderance of failure stories raises questions about the appropriateness of the stories. The first story in the series is a case in point. One must remember that this is part of the first reading book a young child uses. The student opens the book and sees a picture of a Negro child sitting down to read. Before the child can begin to read his books, a second child (Caucasian) tickles him with a small branch. The story goes on to show the Negro child dropping his books and chasing his Caucasian friend. The story ends at that point, with the Negro child's original intention of reading completely frustrated.

Conclusion

We were forced to conclude as the result of our findings that the authors of this important departure from traditional reading series failed to accomplish their aims in several respects. First, they were unable to portray life in a racially mixed, urban neighborhood. What they did do was to present characters of several ethnic backgrounds living in an almost completely white, middle-class neighborhood. They attempted to create early success experiences for first-grade students by shortening the first preprimer of the series. Although this goal was apparently realized, our findings indicated that in the process of meeting this goal the authors created a series of stories that focused on children who were often unable to succeed in whatever they attempted to do.

Second Study

The Sample and Methods

A second study (Waite, 1968) expanded our investigation of multiethnic primers. Six additional multiethnic series were subjected to content analysis, using the same content dimensions described above. They are identified in Table 12–6. Series A is the one investigated in the previous

Table 12–6. *Identification of Series A–G.*

SERIES	PUBLISHER	SERIES TITLE	COPYRIGHT YEAR
A	Follett	City Schools Reading Program	1965
B	Houghton-Mifflin	Reading for Meaning Series (fourth edition)	1966
C	Scott, Foresman	The New Basic Readers Curriculum Foundation Series	1965
D	Harper & Row	The Harper & Row Basic Reading Program	1966
E	Macmillan	The Macmillan Reading Program	1965
F	Macmillan	Bank Street Readers	1965
G	Chandler	Chandler Language-Experience Readers	1966

study. Series A, together with series F and G, represents the results of new and innovative efforts by publishers of reading textbooks. The four other series were published by companies that have marketed traditional series more widely used by school systems throughout the country. Comparisons between series were used to ascertain whether the findings obtained with series A were characteristic of multiethnic series in general. In addition, where the same group of authors wrote both multiethnic series and a traditional series, comparisons were made between their two efforts in terms of the dimensions utilized.

Results

The analysis of environmental setting ratings is shown in Table 12–7. Only series F and G emphasize urban settings. Thus, the authors of

Table 12–7. *Environmental Setting Ratings—Number and Per Cent of Stories in Each Category.*

SERIES	URBAN	SUBURBAN	RURAL	NOT CLEAR	MAKE-BELIEVE	TOTAL
A	22 (19%)	71 (60%)	4 (3%)	10 (8%)	11 (10%)	118
B	3 (2%)	87 (65%)	34 (26%)	9 (7%)	0 (0%)	133
C	8 (7%)	46 (40%)	14 (12%)	42 (37%)	4 (4%)	114
D	2 (1%)	86 (52%)	24 (15%)	40 (24%)	13 (8%)	165
E	2 (2%)	47 (38%)	50 (41%)	23 (18%)	1 (1%)	123
F	48 (70%)	2 (3%)	2 (3%)	16 (24%)	0 (0%)	68
G	80 (81%)	1 (1%)	0 (0%)	13 (13%)	5 (5%)	99
National sample	18 (2%)	499 (38%)	254 (19%)	469 (36%)	67 (6%)	1307

the major publishing companies' series (B through E) have continued to portray children in a nonurban environment. In this respect, they are even more like the all-white standard series sample than is series A. The inner-city child, whatever his ethnic background, is thus reading about children in settings quite unlike those with which he is familiar. On the other hand, the two innovative series (F and G) clearly provide the inner-city child with stories about his own immediate world.

The ethnicity ratings are presented in Table 12–8. "WAS" signifies that all characters in a given story were judged to be of white, Anglo-Saxon background. Because characters of different backgrounds were introduced deliberately into these stories, readers have little or no difficulty in identifying which ethnic groups are involved. These groups would include Negroes; those with Spanish surnames; Orientals; and whites of different national backgrounds. However, the research group experienced difficulty in grouping the characters and labeling according to ethnic background and their combinations. For example, questions arose whether characters belonged to cultural groups or ethnic groups. Neither word is adequate, according to Webster (1961), because the distinguishing attribute of one group is racial, that of another is national background, and others are defined by religion (not included in this particular study). Issues of ethnic background are currently of tremendous national, social, and frequently personal importance, and it is not too surprising that concerns about equality and potential hostility reach even to such an abstract, ivory-tower function of categorization.

Table 12–8. *Ethnic Composition Ratings—Number and Per Cent of Stories in Each Category.*

SERIES	(1) WAS ONLY	(2) ONE NON-WAS GROUP ONLY	(3) NEGRO AND WAS ONLY	(4) OTHER COMBI- NATIONS OF GROUPS	NO REAL PEOPLE	TOTAL
A	7 (6%)	17 (14%)	46 (39%)	35 (30%)	13 (11%)	118
B	105 (79%)	0 (0%)	17 (13%)	0 (0%)	11 (8%)	133
C	56 (49%)	16 (14%)	30 (26%)	5 (4%)	7 (7%)	114
D	66 (40%)	3 (2%)	26 (16%)	50 (30%)	20 (12%)	165
E	107 (87%)	0 (0%)	12 (10%)	0 (0%)	4 (3%)	123
F	3 (4%)	3 (4%)	47 (70%)	8 (12%)	7 (10%)	68
G	0 (0%)	2 (2%)	21 (21%)	67 (68%)	5 (5%)	99

The research group finally developed five categories for rating characters and character combinations to describe ethnic composition. These were: (1) "WAS only," (2) "one non-WAS group only," (3) "Negro and WAS only," (4) "other combinations of groups," and (5) "no real people." The overriding criterion for rating was clear identifiability of the characters. The categories were selected to determine the degree of integration with particular emphasis on Negroes and whites.

The use of the label "WAS" may be somewhat misleading. (It is, of course, a form of the widely used term "WASP." We found it impossible to identify the characters' religions.) A more accurate description might be Northern European white, which would encompass the many possibilities inherent in the illustrations (Nordic, Celtic, Germanic, Gaelic, Baltic, and Slavic, to name a few). However, it became apparent that one could get into trouble whichever way one turned, because the abbreviations of Northern European whites came out NEW, and these characters were anything but new! Rather, they were OLD (Old Line Durables)! The label "WAS" was settled on because it had existing communication value. Moreover, the names of the characters lend credence to the supposition that they were of Anglo-Saxon heritage. There was an abundance of Dicks, Janes, and Mr. Littles and an absence of Pierres, Gretchens, and Mr. O'Briens. Jewish names were never used. The classification "WAS only" is self-explanatory. The second category, "one non-WAS group only," includes those stories in which all characters are of the same non-WAS ethnic background. The third category, "Negro and WAS only," contains characters only from those two groups. The fourth category, "other combinations of groups," refers to those stories in which members of different ethnic groups are present, but the combination is something other than Negroes and white Anglo-Saxons. Finally, the classification "no real people" was necessary to include stories about animals, imaginary creatures, and the like, in which no humans appear.

It is obvious from Table 12–8 that each series approaches the issue of multiethnicity in its own way. In series A, F, and G, people from more than one ethnic group are seen together in most of the stories. Series A and series F contain stories in which only Negroes and whites appear, whereas the character distribution in series G stories is made up predominantly of several ethnic groups. Series B, C, D, and E each have a large number of stories in which only WAS characters appear. Whereas C and D attempt to include other ethnic combinations, B and E (with only 10 to 13 per cent of their stories including characters from groups other than WAS) cannot legitimately be described as either multiethnic or urban. This conclusion is further supported by the environmental setting ratings in Table 12–7, which indicate that 91 per cent of the series B stories and 79 per cent of the stories in series E take place in suburban or rural settings. Obviously, neither of these series was designed to depict accurately children from a variety of ethnic backgrounds living in urban cultures.

Table 12–9 shows the outcome ratings within each series. Series A is unique. No other series had so few stories in which the main activity ended in success. Series B and C also differ from the standard series sample in the same direction, but to a lesser degree. Series D through G approximate or exceed the frequency of success experiences in the standard series. Thus, the findings in the previous study of series A cannot be generalized to all multiethnic primers.

An interesting finding appearing in Table 12–9 is the relatively high frequency of help ratings. With the exception of series G, every series has a greater proportion of stories rated "help" than does the standard series sample. We compared series B through G with the standard series in this regard. There was a significant difference between the multiethnic series and the standard series in the frequency of help ratings ($X^2 = 11.4$, $p < .001$). Examination of the data indicated no correlation between

Table 12–9. *Outcome Ratings in Multiethnic Series—Number and Per Cent of Stories in Each Category.*

SERIES	SUCCESS	FAILURE	HELP	UNCLEAR	TOTAL
A	26 (22%)	64 (54%)	27 (23%)	1 (1%)	118
B	55 (41%)	54 (41%)	17 (13%)	7 (5%)	133
C	59 (52%)	35 (31%)	20 (17%)	0 (0%)	114
D	113 (68%)	22 (13%)	23 (14%)	7 (5%)	165
E	75 (61%)	24 (19%)	18 (15%)	6 (5%)	123
F	49 (72%)	1 (2%)	18 (26%)	0 (0%)	68
G	91 (92%)	4 (4%)	4 (4%)	0 (0%)	99
National sample	832 (64%)	340 (26%)	120 (9%)	15 (1%)	1307

outcome ratings and ethnicity ratings, a finding similar to that for series A alone. That is, non-WAS children in the stories do not succeed, fail, or need help any more frequently than other children. The general emphasis on help is significant and suggests a poorly understood change in emphasis when authors write multiethnic primers. It may very well be, when authors attempt to write stories about children from urban settings with different ethnic backgrounds, that attitudes of limited ability and intelligence influence the content in a general way.

Two series, B and D, were written by authors who had previously written traditional all-white series (Alice and Jerry Basic Reading Program, Harper & Row, 1957; Reading for Meaning, Houghton-Mifflin, 1963). Comparing B with the all-white series written by the same authors, we found that Negro characters were introduced into 13 per cent of the stories and that the stories in general were new and different. Outcome ratings also changed, with the multiethnic series having a lower percentage of success stories. This difference in outcome ratings was statistically significant ($X^2 = 16.3$, $p < .001$). The same comparison was made between series D and the all-white traditional series written by the same authors. Sixty per cent of the stories in series D contained non-WAS characters. Once again, the outcome ratings show a significantly lower incidence of success stories in the multiethnic books ($X^2 = 9.5$, p $< .005$).

Conclusions

Several conclusions were drawn from the results. First, what may appear on the basis of its cover and promotional literature to be a multiethnic first-grade reading book may, on closer inspection, contain few significant characters of ethnic background other than white Anglo-Saxon. Second, including other ethnic groups does not necessarily imply that the environmental setting of the stories is any different than that of the traditional, suburban-oriented series. Third, although multiethnic series are not generally characterized by stories in which the main activity ends in failure, some authors may have a tendency to emphasize lack of success to a greater extent in their multiethnic series than they do in their traditional first-grade reading books.

This type of study, in which the emphasis is on rating scales, frequency distributions, and statistical comparisons, makes it almost impossible to communicate the many attributes that tend to make a reading series attractive, pallid, or unappealing. Suffice to say that series G is new and different, depicting real children in real situations. After having read a large number of Pollyannish stories about essentially the same smiling, unreal children in the same sunshiny, idealized middle-class situations, we found series G to be attractive, appealing, and stimulating.

Third Study

Although our original interest was on the influence of story content on the development of reading skill, it also became apparent that cultural values and attitudes were being conveyed through the content as well. This was strikingly brought to our attention through the content analysis of multiethnic urban reading textbooks.

Waite (1968) approached this problem through a clinical analysis of some character types in one multiethnic urban reading series (series A). He focused on comparisons of white and Negro six-year-old boys and their fathers, in terms of their behavior characteristics displayed in all the stories of the series. Waite found that the Negro boy was depicted as athletic, less intelligent, impulsive, distractible, and as the object of humor. In contrast, the white boy was presented as reflective, more intelligent, and socially secure. The fathers of these two boys also showed definite individual characteristics. The white father had greater economic resources, displayed consistent masculine behaviors, and offered assistance to the Negro father. In comparison, the Negro father had fewer economic resources, performed feminine tasks or assumed feminine responsibilities in nearly half of his appearances, and accepted help from the white father.

Waite (1968) indicated that although the authors of this multiethnic urban series (series A) responded to an urgent social need to write textbooks that depicted whites and Negroes in social interaction, the characteristics they chose for the Negro males reflect the stereotypes and prejudices that exist about them. Though the conscious intent of the authors was socially responsive, prejudicial values and attitudes clearly emerged in spite of conscious attempts to avoid them.

HISTORICAL STUDY OF SEX ROLE MODELS

The large proportion of stories coded for both boys and girls together in both the standard and multiethnic series suggested an area for further exploration by Zimet (1968). She was interested in finding out what models of sex role behavior were portrayed in the primary reading textbooks used by previous generations of American school children.

Methods of the Investigation

Six contiguous time divisions were established, covering the years from 1600 to 1966,[1] after a careful examination of the literature describing sex role behavior patterns and expectations for adults and children over this span of years. The six time boundaries included (1) trends away from a previous behavior standard; (2) the predominant behavior standard; and (3) trends toward a new standard of behavior expectancy. Using the same source of information, criterion lists were devised for each of the six periods consisting of (1) the play activities participated in by boys, girls, and both boys and girls together; (2) behavior expectancies for boys, girls, and boys and girls together, under and over five years old; and (3) behavior expectancies for male and female adults.

The coding dimensions used in the earlier studies required some modifications and expansion in order to tap the sex role variables more adequately. In other words, in addition to those categories mentioned for

---

[1] Period 1: 1600–1776; period 2: 1776–1835; period 3: 1835–1898; period 4: 1898–1921; period 5: 1921–1940; period 6: 1940–1966.

the standard series,[2] each story was rated as to adult male and female roles, outcome of adult roles, outcome for children characters, aggression and dependency themes, agents of help and frustration; sex-directed references to learning and school; occupational references; and ratings of the age and sex appropriateness of the content and illustrations.

Three primary reading textbooks representative of each of the six periods were selected for coding, making a total of eighteen readers in all. Because sex role behavior was being coded, one male and one female were trained as raters. Interrater reliability was computed at 95 per cent agreement, after which the books were divided between the two raters and coded independently.

Results and Discussion

A diffuse sex role model was presented in varying and increasing degrees from colonial days to the present. This model was expressed through the portrayal of adult males and females performing similar roles and of boys and girls playing at the same activities.

The lack of specificity in sex role is consistent with the diffuse model described in the behavior criterion lists for each of the six periods. It should be noted, however, that a sex-differentiated model is also described in this list. Thus, on the one hand, differences between the sexes are minimized in a society that prides itself on its egalitarianism. On the other hand, the culture continues to expect different behavior from the two sexes. The model selected for presentation in these textbooks has been the diffuse one, and therefore such a model of behavior is incomplete.

In addition to the consistent pattern of sex role diffusion that shows up from 1600 to 1966, another consistent and complimentary pattern appears to evolve. Textbook authors began to increase the number of female characters in the stories as formal education was opened up to girls (between 1776) and 1835). This trend continued so that by 1898 and up through 1966 girl characters actually outnumbered boy characters in the texts. Despite this dominance of females in the stories, a distinct female behavior identity was avoided. The diffuse sex role characterization prevailed.

A possible explanation for the minimizing of sex differences may be found in the desire to present materials that would be acceptable to a heterogeneous classroom grouping. It remains a curious matter, how-

---

[2] Family composition and forced sex ratings were not included.

ever, that other alternatives were not attempted. Thus, one might also speculate that the neutral, nonsex-linked male and female behavior described in the stories was an unconscious effort to deny the existence of sexuality in children.

This same explanation may also account for the similar treatment in our culture today of boys and girls under five years old. They are dressed alike, have the same toys, and play together at the same activities. By presenting these less mature models of behavior in stories meant to be read by children over five years old are we not also ignoring the tendency of older children to look down on behavior that was appropriate the year before? A prime insult is to be accused of "acting like a baby."

There was an extremely high frequency of dependency themes in the total sample of books coded, especially in those from 1921 to 1966 (periods 5 and 6). This behavior was rewarded overwhelmingly for both sexes and for all age levels, and thus helped to reinforce the less mature behavior model described above. A feminizing quality is also present in the positive characterization of a male dependent model. Dependency is characteristically associated with females.

Adult characters dominated the texts during periods 1 and 2 (1600 to 1835). They were portrayed as idealized models of religious and ethical behavior and in this sense an adult-centered model was presented. Between 1835 and 1921 (periods 2 through 4), adult characters practically disappeared from the texts and were displaced by children and animals. Adult characters entered the books again in sizable numbers during the last two periods (1921 to 1966), but this time they (both males and females) were presented as facilitators of their children's wishes, interests, and needs, without distinct interests and needs of their own. Thus a sex-diffuse, child-centered model of adult behavior was portrayed.

Because it is primarily from adult models that sex role behavior is learned, it was important to examine the characterizations of adults in the books to see what standard they were communicating. The child-centered adult model communicates an attitude that the adult exists for the child's pleasure only. The sex-diffuse adult model also presents a very limited view of male and female behavior. Let us assume, however, that the adults are also being assessed by the child reader on the basis of their personality characteristics. Unfortunately, the range was limited here to those of congeniality and affability and also made no distinction between the sexes. Although these examples of behavior were consistent with the egalitarian and nurturant standards and expectations of society, they excluded the sex distinctions and the broad range of behavior manifested by adults in our culture. To this extent, the texts fell far short of fulfilling the role of an acculturation medium.

Both adults and children, males and females, were successful most of the time in whatever they set out to do in those books coded from 1835 to the present (periods 3 through 6). During this time span, life for both sexes and all age levels was presented as being carefree, without sorrow, pain, and conflict and may be characterized broadly as Pollyannish. The preoccupation with Pollyanna themes in the textbooks may well be a reflection of the protective attitude that developed toward children as a result of seeing them as unique beings. Keeping children from negative experiences as well as from the realities of the adult world could be accomplished through presenting this kind of vapid story content. The predominance of stories in a rural and suburban setting may be attributable to this same protective attitude, because the bad life was equated with the city and the good life with the country or the suburbs.

Aggression themes were rarely present. When they were in evidence, the aggressors were more often animals rather than humans (periods 3 through 6, 1835 to 1966). This finding is a prime example of the avoidance of negative affect in the reading texts. The presence of aggression themes appeared to be for the sole purpose of convincing children that only animals experienced such feelings or exhibited such behavior. The aggressive behavior was detached enough so that the child would not copy it and yet plausible enough for him to accept the moral that aggressive behavior led to punishment.

Only one socioeconomic and cultural group was represented in the total sample of texts examined and thus only one possible social class model of sex role behavior was presented. The avoidance of socioeconomic and cultural differences is similar in a sense to the avoidance of sex differences and the denial of aggression as a human trait. We are saying, in essence, that by ignoring them or diffusing them we are doing away with the evils or inequities associated with them. This is the old story of treating the symptom rather than the cause. By dealing with aggressive drives directly we can better understand both the direction they can take us and the direction we can take them. Similarly, the extent to which sex labels, cultural labels, and socioeconomic labels produce inequities in our society—the inequities should be eliminated, not the differences.

Perhaps in this sense, what was left out of the content of these primary reading texts is as important to examine as what was left in. The exclusion of the plurality of sex role models that exists in American society suggests that these texts ignored the differences in cultural backgrounds and socioeconomic conditions that account for these differences. It is interesting to speculate whether this was an attempt to unify a diverse people under the white Anglo-Saxon middle-class model in the spirit of egalitarianism or if this was a reflection of the attitude toward the role of education as a selector and sustainer of tradition.

LIBRARY SELECTION STUDY

Having identified several motivational variables in the basal reading series, we were curious to discover how closely some of these characteristics coincided with the actual reading interests and reality/fantasy experiences of children. Free book selections from the school library for sixty first-graders in a suburban, middle-class community have been tabulated. The possible choices (639 books) were coded along the dimensions described earlier in this chapter. The results of this study are being prepared for publication (Wiberg and Trost, 1970). Some of the preliminary analyses are of interest. The story content of the library books (639 books) differed markedly from the story content of the national sample of primers (1,307 stories in twelve publisher series). In the library sample, there were significantly more stories displaying boy activities and depicting urban environments. In contrast, the national sample contained significantly more stories with children and mother, children and father characters. They also had more girl activities, failure outcomes, and suburban environments.

When the story content of books checked out of the library was compared to those not checked out, significant differences were found. The books selected had themes of folk tales, pranks, and nonsense, and character categories included "animals only" and "make believe." Girl-activity stories were frequent. (This was probably owing to the fact that girls checked out books more frequently than boys.) Stories about other environments (foreign countries, seashore, and so forth) were also checked out. In contrast, the books not chosen had story themes of outings and Pollyannish real-life events and children-only characters. Ambiguous sex activities, that is, what both girls and boys would do, were also not selected. In addition failure outcomes and not clear environments (those not identifiable as suburban, urban, or rural) were among the books not checked out of the library.

In the selected library books, there were differences in content preferences between first-grade boys and girls. Boys selected boy-activity content and theme content of pranks and information whereas girls selected pet themes. Girls did not have significant differences in terms of sex activity.

These preliminary findings of the library selection study indicate that children's preferences of story content are markedly discrepant from the content that is contained in first-grade reading textbooks.

Application of the Research

One of the practical consequences of this research has been the development of a motivational guide for selecting stories of interest to children learning to read from the coded basal reading series (Zimet, Blom, and Waite, 1968). This guide is aimed at facilitating the development of a program of differentiated primary reading instruction by those teachers, curriculum consultants, and clinicians directly concerned with organizing and implementing such a program. For example, the users of this index will in effect be saying, "Given the characteristics of this child, I think he will be attracted by stories whose themes are work projects and whose characters are solely children." This represents an attempt, therefore, to match the story to the child.

The categories used to construct the index were carefully devised according to principles appropriate to the development of the child in our present cultural setting. Information about the stories includes:

1. Level. The stories are grouped by publisher and then listed according to reading difficulty level. There are nine levels that have been specifically defined by the various publishers.

2. Stories. The stories are grouped by publisher and copyright date. Each story selection is identified further by a number, story title, the title of the book in which it may be found, and the page number.

3. Age. Each story is classified according to the age at which children would typically perform the activity and/or would be predominantly interested in the activity or theme depicted.

4. Sex. Each story is given a rating that indicates that predominantly boys or predominantly girls do the activity or have interest in the theme. Because both boys and girls share interest in some activities, a third category, "boy-girl," is also included.

5. Outcome. The outcome of the plot of the story is classified in terms of success, failure, and help.

6. Theme. The predominant activity or theme of each story was categorized according to fifteen possible theme choices.

7. Environment. Both the physical appearance of the situation and the context of the story were used as criteria in establishing where the activity of the story took place, in an urban, suburban, or rural setting. When the setting was not clearly definable, it was rated as "not clear." Other settings, such as foreign country, jungle, and make-believe, were specifically written in.

8. Characters. The characters of each story or plot were placed into one of the following categories: "children only"; "children and animals" (no adults); "animals only" (no real people); "make-believe characters but no animals or people"; "inanimate objects" that are either personified or described without real people or animals as characters; "adults only"; "children and mother"; "children and father"; "children and mother and father"; and "children and other adults."

9. Sex/Outcome. The close relationship between success in reading and the sex of the child prompted the inclusion of this category in the index. It is possible to locate a story appropriate to a boy and/or a girl in which the outcome of the plot ends in success or failure. Therefore, whenever sex and outcome are of special concern, this reference is useful.

10. Cultural composition. The cultural composition of the characters depicted in the stories was classified into four categories and was defined as follows: (a) nonintegrated conventional—only middle-class, Anglo-Saxon characters present; (b) nonintegrated other cultures—only one cultural group present but differs from the conventional, middle-class, Anglo-Saxon characters usually found; (c) integrated bicultural—refers to conventional, middle-class Anglo-Saxon characters with Negro characters; (d) integrated multicultural—refers to the presence of two or more cultural groups, which may or may not include the standard, middle-class Anglo-Saxon characters.

NEW DIRECTIONS

Multiethnic primers have been praised and criticized for a variety of reasons. However, we wondered whether or not the interests, real and fantasy, of children from different backgrounds differed enough to warrant experimentation with separate primers. As a beginning venture in this area, we have started collecting stories made up by kindergarten-age children. Among the groups we are working with are lower- and middle-class urban Negro children, Spanish-surnamed children from a large urban area, and Spanish-surnamed children from migrant workers' families. These stories will be coded according to the dimensions previously described and compared with stories obtained from WAS middle-class children and with the primer data already available.

In the future, we plan to study directly the influence of content variables in stories on reading acquisition. The design of such studies will be factorial; the independent variables will be socioeconomic cultural groups, content of primers, and sex of pupils. These studies will be feasible because there are three cooperative school systems that have a sufficient number of classrooms that include a predominance of children from one socioeconomic cultural group. We will be able to study the effects of using multiethnic primers as compared with traditional all-white primers. Other comparison studies will include an investigation of the effects of varying specific content dimensions such as sex role appropriateness. Dependent variables will include rate of reading acquisition, measurements of attitudes, and reading preferences.

Cross-National Study

An examination of the results from our analyses of both the contemporary and historical American primary reading texts has identified characteristics popular to values assigned to the American middle-class culture. Although the earlier texts communicated these values in a more obvious and direct manner than do contemporary texts, studies by other investigators (Child, Potter, and Levine, 1946; Holmes, 1960; McClelland, 1961) support our contention that the modern readers communicated these values as well but on a more covert, inferential level. The findings of these other investigators indicate that elementary reading textbooks accurately reflect national characteristics, modalities, attitudes, and values. However, the reading textbooks used by them for these analyses were at higher grade levels than the first grade.

Following this lead, a cross-national study of a sample of first-grade reading textbooks from twenty foreign countries as well as from the United States (for public and parochial school use) is in process. In addition to evaluating parameters already examined in the American contemporary first-grade texts, means of identifying and scoring the presence of cultural values in the stories are being devised.

At this time, we have developed a series of thirty-six attitude scales that can be carefully defined and scored with acceptable interrater reliability. The series of thirty-six scales have been divided into three groups: cultural posture (n = 11), other-directed posture (n = 15), and inner-directed posture (n = 10). Cultural posture includes such scale items as traditionalism, family togetherness, and nationalism. Other-directed posture has such scale items as caring and nurturing, conformity, and independence. Inner-directed posture has such scale items as ambition, alertness, and intelligence. In addition to assessing the presence or absence of attitudes in a story from its verbal and illustrative content, the rater characterizes an other-directed or inner-directed attitude in terms of who displays the attitude according to sex, age, and character.

Recently, Wiberg and Blom (1970) have completed a pilot study of stories (sixty randomly selected stories from various publisher series) from the United States, West Germany, and Great Britain. This study has demonstrated the feasibility and applicability of our content analysis methods to both English and translated materials. However, it should be recognized that there are limitations in using translated materials and in employing scales based on American standards.

Nevertheless, some preliminary findings from this pilot study are of interest. From the original dimensions on which the content of American first-grade textbooks were analyzed, we found that there were more successful outcome stories in West Germany and Great Britain than in the United States. Ratios of success:failure were as follows: United States 2:1, Great Britain 4:1, and West Germany 8:1. All three countries had a similar high number of stories identified as what both boys and girls are interested in doing. Boy activities, successful in outcome, were found in about equal frequency for all three countries, but female successful outcome activities were strikingly more frequent in both Great Britain (22:1) and West Germany (28:0) than in the United States sample (3:1). It would appear then that the higher success outcome findings in England and West Germany were contributed by girl-activity stories.

As regards the findings from the attitude scales, Table 12–10 indicates the over-all frequency distributions of the three groups of attitudes in the primers of West Germany, the United States, and Great Britain. Over all, more attitudes are shown in stories from Great Britain than the two other countries; this difference is particularly large for inner-directed attitudes.[3] It can also be seen that West German stories display a strikingly greater number of cultural attitudes compared with U.S. stories.

---

[3] "n" indicates the number of times an attitude or an attitude group appeared in the sample of sixty stories.

Table 12–10. *Distribution of Attitude Frequencies According to Groups and Countries.*

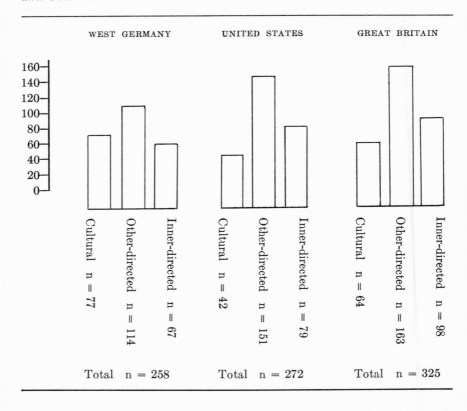

Table 12–11 indicates both the high and low frequencies of attitude scales in the three countries. As can be seen from the table, cultural attitudes of traditionalism, family togetherness, education, and display of food were in high prevalence in the West German stories. Attitudes of family togetherness (cultural), work and care and nurturing (other-directed), and intelligence (inner-directed) were high among U.S. stories, whereas attitudes of display of food and death and infirmity (cultural), caring and nurturing and physical aggressiveness (other-directed), and cleanliness and ambition (inner-directed) were high among stories from Great Britain. From Table 12–11 it can be seen that religion and education were seldom represented in stories from the United States and Great Britain, although these attitudes were high in frequency in West German stories. On the other hand, intelligence is displayed infrequently in the German stories and very frequently in the U.S. stories.

Table 12–11. *High and Low Attitude Frequencies According to Countries.*

WEST GERMANY	UNITED STATES	GREAT BRITAIN
HIGH FREQUENCY ATTITUDE SCALES		
traditionalism n = 9	family togetherness n = 11	display of food n = 28
family togetherness	caring and nurturing n = 45	death, infirmity n = 11
n = 13	work n = 19	caring and nurturing
education n = 9	intelligence n = 15	n = 35
religion n = 8		physical aggressiveness
display of food n = 26		n = 22
cleanliness n = 12		cleanliness n = 13
		ambition n = 17
LOW FREQUENCY ATTITUDE SCALES		
disobedience n = 1	physical weakness n = 2	education n = 0
intelligence n = 4	religion n = 0	religion n = 2
dirtiness n = 2	education n = 4	

The characterization of an other-directed or inner-directed attitude according to who displays the attitude (sex, age, and character) also provides interesting data. For example, physical aggressiveness (other-directed) was found in the following frequencies: Great Britain (n = 22), United States (n = 13), and West Germany (n = 12). Though one might say that stories from our random sampling show a high frequency of physical aggressiveness in Great Britain, interesting results appear when physical aggressiveness is characterized by sex, age, and character for the three countries. Table 12–12 indicates that in stories from the U.S. primers physical aggressiveness is displayed almost entirely by animals and imaginary animals and is not clearly related to sex or age. (This finding is consistent with the results from the historical study.) This in contrast to the stories from Great Britain and West Germany where no females alone are shown portraying physical aggressiveness.

These preliminary findings from a pilot study of primer stories from the United States, Great Britain, and West Germany indicate both similarities and differences in content characteristics as measured by our primary dimension scales and our new attitude scales. At this point, we find national differences, but we are not certain as to whether these

Table 12–12. *Physical Aggressiveness According to Sex, Age, and Character.*

	GREAT BRITAIN	UNITED STATES	WEST GERMANY
1. *Sex*			
male	9	2	5
female	0	1	0
indeterminate*	13	10	7
2. *Age*			
child	9	2	7
adult	4	0	0
indeterminate*	9	11	5
3. *Character*			
human	8	0	6
animal	8	9	5
imaginary	0	0	0
imaginary animal	2	3	0
inanimate	1	0	0
indeterminate*	3	1	1

* Indeterminate: either more than one category displays the attitude or the category cannot be determined.

findings reflect true national differences or whether they are the result of differences in the way educational programming is carried out in these countries. We will therefore try to interpret our findings in the light of other cross-national studies from these countries. Many similarities in findings would be expected, of course, because these three nations have many values in common. We plan to apply our methods of analysis to primers from countries where contrasting values and attitudes clearly exist.

Though we see the attitude scales themselves as providing valuable information on socialization differences among countries, we are also interested in those attitudes that may promote and be related to learning and reading. It is our contention that attitude variables together with motivational variables exert a powerful force on reading acquisition.

CONCLUSION

The reading textbook is the traditional means through which reading skills are taught. But more than that, it is also the first text placed in the hands of the child entering school. Though considerable national attention has been focused on the need for providing appropriate socio-cultural models in the reading materials, less attention has been given to coordinating these models with appropriate developmental ones and to examining the motivational influence they exert on the learning process itself. And yet it is assumed that in reading a story, the child symbolically goes through the action that is described and that, consequently, his social attitudes will be influenced by the behavior patterns portrayed in the many stories he reads.

Thus, the content of reading textbooks has two functions to perform: (1) an instrumental one and (2) a socializing one. The degree of success textbooks achieve instrumentally may well depend on their success as a socializing agent. What is needed is an investigation into how content actually affects children's attitudes and their acquisition of reading skill. Once we gain more insight and understanding in this area, it may be possible to apply our knowledge of child development to the writing of textbooks that are equally effective for acculturation and for teaching reading.

REFERENCES

Ashton-Warner, S. *Teacher.* New York: Simon & Shuster, 1963.

Bettelheim, B. The decision to fail. *Saturday Review,* 1961, *69,* 377–412.

Blom, G. E., Waite, R. R., & Zimet, S. G. Ethnic integration and urbanization of a first grade reading textbook: a research study. *Psychology in the Schools,* 1967, *2,* 176–181.

Blom, G. E., Waite, R. R., & Zimet, S. G. Content of first-grade reading books. *The Reading Teacher,* 1968, *21,* 317–323.

Books for Schools and the Treatment of Minorities. Hearings before the Ad Hoc Subcommittee on De Facto School Segregation of the Committee on Education and Labor, House of Representatives, Eighty-ninth Congress, 1966.

Byers, L. Pupils' interests and the content of primary reading texts. *The Reading Teacher,* 1964, *17,* 227–233.

Carrillo, L. W. *Informal Reading-Readiness Experiences.* San Francisco: Chandler, 1964.

Caswell, H. L. The nature of good teaching. In A. Crow & L. D. Crow (eds.), *Vital Issues in American Education.* New York: Bantam, 1964, pp. 29–38.

Chilcott, J. H. An analysis of the enculturation of values as illustrated in primary readers, 1879–1960. Paper presented at California Educational Research Association Meeting, March 1961.

Child, I. L., Potter, E. M., & Levine, E. M. Children's textbooks and personality development: an exploration in the social psychology of education. *Psychological Monographs,* 1946, *60,* 1–54.

Commager, H. S. Foreword, *McGuffey's Fifth Eclectic Reader,* 1879 Edition, New York: Signet, 1962.

Edge, S. A review of the literature relating to sex differences and reading disability, Parts I and II. Unpublished term papers, University of Denver, School of Librarianship, April 1963.

Flesch, R. *Why Johnny Can't Read—and What You Can Do about It.* New York: Harper & Row, 1955.

Gates, A. I. The word recognition ability and the reading vocabulary of second- and third-grade children. *Reading Teacher,* 1962, *15,* 443–448.

Gray, W. S. Physiology and psychology of reading. *Encyclopedia of Educational Research.* 3rd ed.; New York: Macmillan, 1960, pp. 1096–1114.

Harris, J. M. The expressed reading interests of first grade boys and girls and the adequacy of current basic readers in meeting these interests. Doctoral dissertation, Cornell University, 1955.

Henry, J. Reading for what? *Claremont Reading Conference. Twenty-fifth Yearbook.* Claremont, Calif.: Claremont Graduate School Curriculum Laboratory, 1961, pp. 19–35.

Hollins, W. H. A national survey of commonly used first grade readers. Unpublished data from Alabama Agricultural and Mechanical College, Normal, Alabama, 1955.

Holmes, M. B. A cross-cultural study of the relationship between values and modal conscience. In W. Muensterberger & S. Axelrad (eds.), *The Psychoanalytic Study of Society,* Vol. 1. New York: International Universities Press, 1960, pp. 98–181.

Kagan, J. Acquisition and significance of sex-typing and sex role identity. In M. L. Hoffman & L. W. Hoffman (eds.), *Review of Child Development Research,* Vol. 1. New York: Russell Sage Foundation, 1964, pp. 137–166.

Klineberg, O. Life is fun in a smiling, fair-skinned world. *Saturday Review,* 1963, *46,* 75–77.

Lamb, E. N. A study of the reading interests of poor reading achievers at the second-grade level. Unpublished data from San Diego State College, 1955.

Larrick, N. The all-white world of children's books. *Saturday Review,* 1965, *48,* 63–65, 84–85.

Loban, W. D. *The Language of Elementary School Children.* Champaign, Ill.: National Council of Teachers of English, 1963.

McClelland, D. C. *The Achieving Society.* New York: Van Nostrand, 1961.

McKee, P., Harrison, M. L., McCowan, A., & Lehr, E. *Reading for Meaning.* Boston: Houghton Mifflin, 1963.

Marburger, C. L. Considerations for educational planning. In A. H. Passow (ed.), *Education in Depressed Areas.* New York: Teachers College Press, 1963, pp. 298–321.

Norvell, G. W. *What Boys and Girls Like to Read.* Morristown, N.J.: Silver Burdett, 1958.

O'Connell, M. *The Alice and Jerry Basic Reading Program.* New York: Harper & Row, 1957.

Peller, L. Reading and daydreams in latency boy-girl differences. *Journal of the American Psychoanalytic Association,* 1958, *6,* 57–70.

Smith, R. C. Children's reading choices and basic reader content. *Elementary English,* 1962, *39,* 202–209.

Strickland, R. G. The language of elementary school children: its relationship to the language of reading textbooks and the quality of reading of selected children. *Bulletin of the School of Education, Indiana University,* 1964, *34,* No. 4.

Trace, A. S., Jr. *Reading without Dick and Jane.* Chicago: Regnery, 1965.

Waite, R. R. Further attempts to integrate and urbanize first-grade reading textbooks. *Journal of Negro Education,* Winter 1968, 62–69.

Waite, R. R. Some character types in Negro primers: a psychoanalytic study. Paper presented to the Denver Psychoanalytic Society, February 1968.

Waite, R. R., Blom, G. E., Zimet, S. G., & Edge, S. First-grade reading textbooks. *Elementary School Journal,* 1967, *67,* 366–374.

Walcott, C. C. *Tomorrow's Illiterates.* Boston: Little, Brown, 1961.

Webster's New Collegiate Dictionary. Springfield, Mass.: Merriam, 1961.

Whipple, G. *Appraisal of the City Schools Reading' Program.* Detroit: Detroit Public Schools Division for Improvement of Instruction, Language Education Department, 1963.

Whipple, G. & Black, M. H. *Reading for Children Without–Our Disadvantaged Youth.* Newark, Del.: I.R.A., 1966.

Wiberg, J. L., & Blom, G. E. A cross national study of attitude content in reading primers. In press, *International Journal of Psychology,* 1970.

Wiberg, J. L., & Trost, M. Comparison of content of first-grade primers and free choice library selections. In press, *Elementary English,* 1970.

Zimet, S. G. Sex role models in primary reading texts of the United States: 1600–1966. Doctoral dissertation, University of Denver, 1968.

Zimet, S. G., Blom. G. E., & Waite, R. R. *A Teacher's Guide for Selecting Stories for Children–The Content of First-Grade Reading Textbooks.* Detroit: Wayne State University Press, 1968.

13 WILLIAM LABOV

The Reading of the -*ed* Suffix

It is generally agreed that we do not understand the process of reading, or what happens when a child does or does not learn to read. Even more generally, we are at a loss to provide a theoretical understanding of mistakes or of partial learning. We learn a great many things perfectly on one exposure—like the name of a street or a new friend—and never forget. Why is this not the case with the letters of the alphabet or the rules for reading them? Anyone can observe that children continue to make mistakes long after they have given clear evidence of knowing about a rule; they may give a large number of correct responses that plainly indicate that they know the rule, and yet they continue to deviate from it unpredictably. Granted that children have not learned the rule in its full adult form, we must still ask—what kind of rule have they learned?

One possible answer is that this failure to produce consistent results is merely a matter of "performance" and therefore lies outside the study of linguistic (or reading) "competence." A large number of miscellaneous factors intervene between the child's competence at reading and his output: lapses of memory, failures of attention, temporary confusion of categories, and so on. However, this method of disposing of the problem does not seem either promising or helpful. There is nothing to say about

The work reported here was supported by the U.S. Office of Education as Cooperative Research Projects Numbers 3091 and 3288. The findings reported here are the products of the joint efforts of Paul Cohen, Clarence Robins, and John Lewis, as well as the author. For a fuller treatment of methods and modes of analysis, and discussions of other phonological and grammatical variables of nonstandard Negro English, see Labov, Cohen, Robins and Lewis (1968).

the child's knowledge of reading before he is introduced to the letters of the alphabet; after he becomes a competent adult reader, his skills are well beyond our present powers of analysis. For us, the heart of the reading problem lies in the learner's variable performance—rule-governed behavior that is not absolutely regular. If linguistics can contribute nothing to this, it is very little help indeed.

In several years of work on nonstandard English (NNE) spoken by Negro children in the urban ghettos, we have observed a sharp contrast between their fluent and skillful use of oral language and their slow and erratic behavior in reading. The over-all pattern is one of reading failure rather than reading difficulty. The primary cause for this failure appears to be the conflict between the vernacular culture and the middle-class culture of the schoolroom rather than any linguistic differences between their dialect and standard English. Yet, there do appear to be some correlations between particular reading difficulties and particular linguistic rules within the dialect that help illuminate the type of variable performance that we have described here. There are regular linguistic rules that are variable—that do not determine the behavior of the speaker precisely, yet that ensure that over a number of utterances certain important distinctions will be firmly made. This chapter will concern the correlation between such a rule and one kind of particular reading problem—the reading of the *-ed* suffix.

The case of the *-ed* suffix is especially useful because it gives us a direct view of reading in the full sense of the term—deciphering meaning from symbols on the printed page and projecting this meaning on other elements that have been deciphered. We examine sentences of the type *When I passed by I read the posters.* The reader's pronunciation of the word *passed* does not tell us whether or not he has read the *-ed*, because there is a general rule of the sound pattern of the language here that simplifies the cluster *-st* in a high percentage of the cases before a following consonant. Teachers who judge the correctness of the child's reading by his pronunciation will be deceived: if he says *passed* as [pæst] it does not mean that he has read the *-ed* successfully; if he says it as [pæs] it does not mean that he has failed to read the *-ed*. It is of course most important for teachers to begin to distinguish between differences in pronunciation and mistakes in reading (Labov, 1966). In this case, correct reading is signaled by the pronunciation of the unique homograph *read* in the next clause. If it is pronounced [rɛd], rhyming with *bed,* the child has given evidence that he has deciphered the meaning of *-ed* and has projected this meaning onto the word *read*. If it is pronounced [ri:d], rhyming with *seed*, the subject has given evidence that he has not read *passed* correctly. The ability of adolescent Negro boys to perform this task is well below their general reading ability. A few succeed in doing quite well in reading *-ed*, and the linguistic differences between them and others will be a useful point in our examination.

SOURCES OF THE DATA

The primary data for this analysis is derived from long-term studies of adolescent male peer groups in south central Harlem. Contacts with these groups were maintained outside the adult-dominated environments of the school and the home, for our main purpose was to make accurate recordings of the basic vernacular under the same social controls that are effective in the interchanges of everyday life and also to examine reading behavior under the most favorable circumstances. Our studies of the preadolescent "Thunderbirds" and "Aces," the adolescent "Cobras" and "Jets," and the late adolescent "Oscar Brothers" were conducted within the following paradigm:

1. The group was located and contacted by our participant-observer living in the area. Several individual members and leaders were interviewed by him in face-to-face sessions.
2. Several outings and field trips were conducted with the group as a whole. At group sessions with video-tape and multitrack recording, records were obtained of each individual in spontaneous interaction with his peers.
3. Individuals were interviewed in face-to-face sessions that included a wide range of contextual styles, readings, word lists, and a variety of subjective evaluation tests.
4. Our participant-observer maintained contact with the group over a long-term period. This added greatly to our knowledge of the history and internal structure of the group.

We also conducted a preliminary survey of fifty preadolescents (ten-to-twelve years old) in vacation day camps. Many of these boys were not members of any peer groups that represented the vernacular culture, but they showed varying degrees of influence of the standard American culture in their linguistic forms and social behavior. We have shown elsewhere (Labov and Robins, 1969) that these nonmembers contrast sharply in their reading achievement with the members of the central peer groups. Here we will be concerned with the connection between a particular reading skill and a particular linguistic rule that holds for all individuals, regardless of group membership.

READING TESTS AND DECIPHERING THE *-ED* SUFFIX

At the end of the individual interview, a number of formal tests were given. These included reading a list of nine sentences. The sentences were at the second- or third-grade level of difficulty, and the subjects, ranging from ten to seventeen years old, were in the fourth to eleventh grades. Almost everyone had difficulty in reading these sentences; most boys made many mistakes, and a good number could not read the words at all. The reading skills of this population are very low, as has been reported in other studies and in official reports. A great many cannot reasonably use reading as a tool for learning. We were able to examine the school records of some of these boys,[1] and we found that the reading performance on our tests was only slightly better than scores on the Metropolitan Achievement Reading Test. For our peer groups of the vernacular culture, test scores ran from two to five years below grade. Nonmembers of the vernacular peer groups showed somewhat better scores, averaging about two years below grade.

The nine sentences in our test were:

1. Last month I read five books.
2. Tom read all the time.
3. So. . . I sold my soul to the devil.
4. When I passed by, I read the posters.
5. Don't you *dare* hit your *dear* little brother!
6. When I liked a story, I read every word.
7. They cost a nickel yesterday, but today they cost a dime.
8. Now I read and write better than Alfred does.
9. I looked for trouble when I read the news.

Sentences 4, 6, and 9 were designed to examine the reader's competence in deciphering the *-ed* suffix on the printed page. As noted above, one

[1] We are deeply indebted to Dr. William H. Bristow of the Bureau of Curriculum Development, to Dr. Samuel D. McClelland of the Bureau of Educational Research, and to the superintendents and principals of the schools concerned for their invaluable assistance in obtaining these important data.

cannot use the pronunciation of the NNE speaker as he is reading aloud
in order to decide whether he is reading -*ed* properly. For this reason,
we utilized the unique homograph *read* in these sentences.[2] If the reader
has correctly read the -*ed* suffix, he will transfer the past tense meaning
to the verb *read* in the next clause and pronounce that word [rɛd].
If not, he will pronounce it either [riːd] or [rɛd]—most likely the latter,

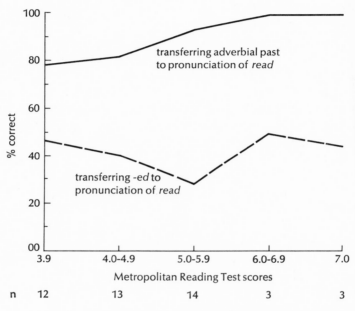

Note: upper line: % correct for sentences 1, 2, and 8;
lower line: % correct for sentences 4, 5, and 9

Figure 13–1. *Correlation between Metropolitan Reading Test
scores and reading of the –ed suffix for forty-six NNE speakers.*

because it is the more common form. Therefore, success in this task
was indicated by the pronunciation [rɛd] in all three of the test
sentences.

Several other factors must be taken into account. It is possible that
the reader would decipher "past tense," but that he would not remember
this when he came to the next clause. For this reason, the distance

---

[2] We are indebted to Joshua Waletzky for the device of using the homograph
read to test -*ed* reading.

between the two verbs was made as short as possible. Second, a reader might have no ability to transfer meanings in general, and not simply be unable to do this for tense signals. In order to check on this, we included sentences 1, 2, and 8. In sentence 1, the reader uses the past tense signal *last month* to derive the correct pronunciation [rɛd]; in sentence 8, he uses the adverb *now* to yield [riːd]. Sentence 2 is more difficult; even speakers of standard English do not use this unmarked context to give an automatic pronunciation [rɛd], and NNE speakers are particularly confused because in their present tense there is no third singular -*s*. Therefore, *Tom* [riːd] *all the time* is a perfectly normal NNE sentence. In any case, we would expect that readers who could interpret *read* correctly in context would get numbers 1 and 8 without difficulty.

There was a very high level of success in transferring tense information from lexical features to the pronunciation of *read* in sentences 1, 2, and 8. Figure 13–1 shows the performance on these three sentences as a function of Metropolitan Achievement Test score for forty-six NNE speakers. Even at low levels on the Metropolitan, performance is quite high.

Successful use of the -*ed* suffix was much more limited and did not correlate with general reading ability. Figure 13–1 indicates that performance on sentences 4, 6, and 9 is rather poor at all reading levels. Although some reading skills are being acquired by these subjects, the reading of the -*ed* suffix is plainly not being learned.

CONSONANT CLUSTER SIMPLIFICATION IN NNE

We have seen that the reading of the -*ed* suffix is not correlated with general reading skill. One might attribute difficulty in reading the -*ed* to the fact that this suffix is frequently not pronounced by NNE speakers. However, there is no direct correlation between the overt pronunciation of this suffix as [t] or [d] and the decipherment of the past tense suffix as shown in the pronunciation of *read*. There is a connection between the more general pattern of consonant cluster simplification and reading -*ed,* but it appears at a higher level of abstraction from actual performance. To show this connection, it will be necessary for us to present some of the data on the deletion of final -*t,d,* and construct from this data a variable rule that determines the phonetic output of NNE. First, we will consider the general nature of the process of consonant cluster simplification and the specific process of -*t,d* deletion.

The phonological process with which we will be concerned in this section is the simplification of final consonant clusters in words such as *belt, hold, find,* and *passed.* This is not a rare or isolated phenomenon, but a process that occurs in many languages over long periods of time. Before the actual data on the NNE situation is given, it will be helpful to present some general considerations on the nature of this process.

There is a general tendency in the evolution of Indo-European languages, and especially the Romance and Germanic branches, to lose information at the ends of words. This tendency shows up most sharply in the treatment of consonant clusters, but it can also be observed with final sonorants and unstressed vowels. In addition to the more general trend, there appears to be an inherent articulatory difficulty in the pronunciation of final clusters of the CVCC type, and even more so in CVCCC forms. In every language family, syllables of the type CV and CVC are the favored forms, as opposed to CVCC or CVCCC. The latter are less frequent, and in the course of linguistic development, they are frequently reduced to the former.

In many phonological variables of English, the over-all effect is to lose final consonants. In most cases, this tendency is reduced when the next word begins with a vowel. Final liquids /l/ and /r/, which are normally vocalized, are frequently or regularly preserved as consonants before a following vowel. In effect, they are converted to initial consonants in the surface phonetic structure. When words such as *haul,* in isolation usually [hʊ·ɪ] in NNE, are found in sequences such as *haul away,* the CVC form becomes in surface phonetics CVCVCV [hʊləweɪ]. Similarly, following vowels will serve to convert CVCC forms to simpler ones, so that *last* does not show a cluster in the final phonetic form of *last of all:* CVCC becomes CVC[CVCVC]. Thus there are two routes to the reduction of CVCC to CVC: either (1) one of the two consonants is vocalized or dropped or (2) the final consonant is reassigned to a following syllable. That is not to imply that such a process is normally obligatory. It merely reflects the general tendency toward the simplification of consonant clusters.

On first approach to NNE, the existence of this tendency for simplification seems to be overwhelming. All the processes noted above are active. First members of clusters are vocalized (*r, l,* sometimes nasals) ; and second members are frequently dropped (*t, d,* sometimes *p, k, s, z*), when they are not reassigned to following syllables. Furthermore, we find some speakers who go to extremes in their reduction of syllable form and maximize the general tendency to lose final consonants, es-

pecially apicals. Thus, one illiterate sixteen-year-old speaker from North
Carolina:

> Every time I say a work [wərk] or sump'm I try to make it—be'er [bɛɛ]
> . . . corre' [cɔrɛʔ] myself every time I, you know, make a ba'—ba' spea'
> [bæ bæ spiʔ].

However, these tendencies are not so general as to allow us to set up
a general variable (KKL) "consonant cluster simplification." Our ultimate view of the matter shows that the tendency toward such simplification is highly differentiated. There is a specific rule applying first to
all stops following sibilants: -*sp*, -*st*, and -*sk*. Then a general rule follows
for all other clusters ending in the apical stops -*t*, *d*.[3] A much weaker
process applies to apical fricatives: many of the extreme cases of simplification of final -*s*, *z* clusters are not regular rules of NNE at all, but
cases where the vernacular has no morpheme /z/ corresponding to the
SE third singular, possessive, and adverbial morphemes. At a much lower
level than the simplification of clusters, there is another operation
to weaken and delete final single stops after a vowel. Finally, we note
that some clusters are simplified by processes operating upon the first
member, never the second. This is almost always the case with -*ts*, where
an assimilation rule converts the stop to a fricative, and it is always
the case with nonapical nasal plus stop, as in *jump* or *bank*. The nasal
may be completely vocalized, but the stop in these combinations is never
lost. Despite these limitations on the universality of a consonant cluster
simplification rule, the effects of the general processes outlined above
are always relevant in one way or another. In the analysis of variables
that appear to be purely syntactic at first glance—such as the deletion
of the copula—we find that consonant cluster simplification is in the
final analysis one of the two most important constraints on the variable
rules.

In general, we find that consonant cluster simplification is a phonological process that intersects with grammatical processes, operating on
a number of formatives to produce highly reduced surface forms. In

---

[3] The selection of /t/ or /d/ as second member of the cluster is determined
by the voicing assimilation rule after a morpheme boundary, and after obstruents
there is also agreement of voicing in monomorphemic forms. The opposition /t~d/
is free to carry lexical information after liquids and nasal /n/ in monomorphemic
forms, as in *welt, weld; heart, hard;* or *tent, tend.* Another way to analyze the
conditions for application of the consonant cluster simplification rule is to consider
only clusters with the same voicing throughout, as suggested by Wolfram.

this chapter, we will consider clusters ending in *-t,d*—the class that intersects with the class of words with *-ed* suffixes representing the regular past of weak verbs. We will be interested in the form of consonant cluster simplification in which the final *-t,d* is detected, and we will not be concerned with the retention, vocalization, or deletion of the first member of the cluster; we will refer to this type of simplification as *"-t,d deletion."* The effect of this phonological process will be to reduce the frequency and stability of the morphological form. Even though the *-ed* suffix is an inherent element of NNE, well represented in the language of each speaker, the form of the variable phonological rule is indeed correlated with the decipherment of the printed *-ed* in reading.

INHERENT VARIABILITY AND REGULARITY OF *-t,d* SIMPLIFICATION

The first statement that must be made about *-t,d* clusters is that they are variables. We have no NNE speakers in any context or at any age level who do not show some intact clusters. This is true not only of clusters in words such as *passed*, with an underlying morpheme boundary [pæs#d], but also in monomorphemic words such as *belt*/belt/. Furthermore, the extraordinary regularity of the processes, and the regularity of the internal constraints involved, show that these final *-t,d*'s cannot be regarded as erratic borrowings from SE. Borrowings are in fact marked by erratic patterns, or rather the absence of patterns. For example, there seems to be no basis at all in NNE for a third singular *-s*. The *-s* ending does appear occasionally in NNE, but in odd and unpredictable ways: not only does it appear after first and second person pronouns, and after plural pronouns, but attached to nonfinite verb forms as well. Thus, we have sporadically *I trusts my friends. My brothers plays in it. You get the break . . . You gets the break. You mean how does he gets away? . . . and neighbors woulds call the cops. . . . the guys that . . . bes around the park with us.* But no such hypercorrections appear with the *-t,d* variables. We have no recorded cases of *-t,d* being added to present forms, and surprisingly enough, very little evidence of *-t* or *-d* being added to SE forms in *-s* to produce hypercorrect monomorphemic forms. All of this illustrates the sharp difference between a regular, systematic variable in NNE and irregular, unsystematic borrowing from SE. A typical example of the regularity of this process can be seen in Table 13–1, a simple listing of the proportions of *-t,d* deleted in final clusters for eleven members of the Jets.

Table 13–1. *Proportion of -t,d Deletion in Clusters for Eleven Members of the Jets in Single Interviews.*

	MONOMORPHEMIC		PAST TENSE	
	BEFORE CONSONANT	BEFORE VOWEL	BEFORE CONSONANT	BEFORE VOWEL
Stanley	19/20	7/10	2/6	0/14
Rednall	25/26	5/9	2/5	0/3
Hop	18/21	4/9	5/7	1/3
Larry	36/38	2/8	5/9	0/25
Vaughn	35/42	4/11	4/12	1/16
Doug	28/30	4/8	1/3	0/3
Tyler	16/17	4/7	1/5	0/2
Its	9/15	1/1	1/4	0/3
Stevie	21/21	2/4	7/11	2/13
Turkey	11/13	0/1	3/3	2/13
Rip	11/12	1/2	2/7	1/8
TOTAL	229/255	34/70	33/72	7/103
Per cent $-t,d$	90	49	46	07

The data serve to illustrate the meaning of the terms *"inherent"* and *"systematic"* applied to variability. In the first column, we see that simplification of monomorphemic forms before consonants is almost complete, but that in almost every case there are a small percentage of unsimplified forms. Only two individuals show a sizable number of unsimplified forms. It is worth noting here that the two individuals, Vaughn and Its, who show distinctly lower simplification for $KD_{mm-}K$, are also unusual in that they are good readers. Vaughn, who came from Washington Heights one year earlier, is a full member of the group who has exceptional ability in the verbal skills of middle-class culture; he is the only member who is an excellent reader by middle-class high school standards. Its fills the role of an extremely slow and nonverbal member of the group, but has apparently been strongly influenced by school sub rosa. His grammar shows a number of departures from NNE in the direction of SE, and his reading skill, though several years behind grade, was high enough to surprise other members of the group.

The second column figures are closely grouped around the 50 per cent mark, despite the small numbers involved. The third column, for past tense clusters before consonants, shows more variability. In most cases the percentage is somewhat lower than in the second column. However, in all but one case it is much lower than the first column. The fourth column, past tense clusters before vowels, regularly shows the lowest proportion of simplification. We will examine the relationships which appear here in more detail below.

It is important to emphasize that regularity is consistent with variability. One might be tempted to hope that further examination of the data would ultimately eliminate variability and allow us to predict or account for each utterance. However, all our experience has led us to believe that such hopes are illusory. The relatively rare cases of monomorphemic -*t,d* in final clusters are not predictable at any one point in the verbal exchange. What is predictable is that in every hundred cases, roughly five to ten will not be simplified.

We find it difficult to explain the extraordinary regularity of -*t,d* deletion. It is likely that a great many small factors that influence simplification have mutually cancelling effects, so that even with such small numbers as shown in the right-hand side of Table 13–1, the characteristic proportion appears. On the other hand, certain major constraints, which we have distinguished below, can easily be separated from this background variability.

Another aspect of the regularity of the -*t,d* simplification is that the basic relationships are repeated in group after group, across neighborhoods and age levels. The rule for -*t,d* simplification to be presented below is a part of a fairly uniform NNE grammar that prevails from preadolescence to early adulthood. Certain quantitative changes take place, and there is some reordering of the variable constraints, but the fundamental structure remains the same. Furthermore, the same basic relationships, at different quantitative levels, apply to all other dialects of English.

VARIABLE CONSTRAINTS ON -*t,d* SIMPLIFICATION

By far the most important effect on -*t,d* simplification is the presence of a preceding consonant, that is, when we are dealing with a cluster rather than a single stop after a vowel. A comparison of clusters and single consonants is shown in Table 13–2. In single interviews, the average percentage of -*t,d* deletion is 55 per cent, of single consonants 15 per cent. In group sessions, the difference is even greater—83 per cent as against

12 per cent. Although only a small amount of the available data on single consonants was analyzed, it is obvious that the loss of single consonants is a minor effect, operating at much lower levels than the simplification of clusters. Whereas the effect of a following vowel is seen with single consonants as well as clusters, the frequency of deletion does not seem to be sensitive to the stylistic context. We will not consider this lower-level activity further, except to note that its existence underlines the generality of the over-all process—that consonant cluster simplification is the most favored case of the tendency to lose information at the ends of words.

Table 13–2. *Effect of a Preceding Consonant vs. Preceding Vowel on -t,d Deletion for Eleven Adolescent NNE Speakers.*

	MONOMORPHEMIC −t,d		PAST TENSE −t,d	
	____#K	____#V	____#K	____#V
Consonant preceding (KD)				
ratio −t,d deletion	228/257	49/99	40/108	15/115
per cent	90	50	38	14
Vowel preceding (VD)				
ratio −t,d deletion	29/124	4/91	11/50	2/59
per cent	22	04	22	04

Table 13–2 also illustrates the effect of a following vowel on -t,d deletion. In this limited body of data, we find that a following vowel is a major factor in reducing the loss of the final consonant in both clusters and single cases, although it is not so strong an effect as that of a preceding vowel. This finding is consistent with the logic of our original presentation of the mechanism of consonant cluster simplification.

The third major constraint on simplification is the effect of a morpheme boundary preceding the -t,d. Words such as *mist, past, bold* and *find* are simple "monomorphemic" stems, in which the final consonant has the same status as the other vowels and consonants. It is true that the -t or -d can distinguish these words from others, and when it is missing there is the possibility of homonymy.

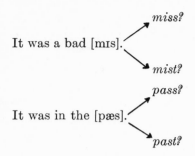

It was a bad [mɪs].
→ *miss?*
→ *mist?*

It was in the [pæs].
→ *pass?*
→ *past?*

At the same time, the possibility of confusion is quite remote; it would be rare that other context would not be present to identify the form that was intended. This is not the case with words such as *missed, passed, rolled,* or *fined.* Here the final *-t,d* of the standard pronunciations [mɪst, pæst, roʊld, faɪnd] represents a separate meaningful element, the past tense morpheme *-ed.* Although there are many adverbial signals of time and other context that indicate past, it is quite common to find this single consonant the only sign of the past meaning. When it is deleted, forms such as the following are frequently ambiguous:

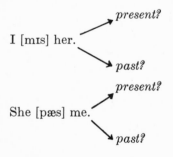

I [mɪs] her.
→ *present?*
→ *past?*

She [pæs] me.
→ *present?*
→ *past?*

We can represent this systematic difference between the two sets of forms by the following abstract representations:

mist	/mist/	missed	/mis#d/
past	/pæst/	passed	/pæs#d/
bold	/bōld/	rolled	/rōl#d/
find	/fīnd/	fined	/fīn#d/

The morpheme boundary is represented by the double cross #, which separates inflectional endings from their stems. It is characteristic of such suffixes that they do not affect the phonological form of the stem.

Thus, there is no change in the stem that identifies the past tense: the only overt signal is the single consonant that follows the #.

Because the *-t,d* that follows the # boundary has no effects on the stem and is the only signal of the past tense, it plainly has a very different status than the *-t,d* of *mist* or *past* or *bold*. Speakers of NNE recognize this status in their differential treatment of clusters that contain the boundary # and those that do not. For almost every speaker, and for every group, we find less *-t,d* deletion when the *-t,d* follows this type of morpheme boundary.

There is no question here of the category of the past tense being affected. The small number of irregular verbs of the type *give, gave; go, went* are extremely high in text frequency. Whereas white speakers often use the "historical present" in narrative, with forms such as *Yesterday he gives me a nickel*, NNE speakers do not do this. There are some irregular verbs such as *say, said* where the present/past distinction is not well fixed: it is quite characteristic of NNE to use *say* in the past. But for the irregular verbs that do make the distinction, we find that NNE invariably uses the past form in past contexts, the present form in present contexts.

The two major constraints on *-t,d* deletion are thus (1) the restraining effect of a following vowel and (2) the restraining effect of a morpheme boundary. We can break down the class of words with final *-t,d* clusters into four subclasses:

(KD^k_{mm}) monomorphemic clusters before following consonants
(KD^v_{mm}) monomorphemic clusters before following vowels
(KD^k_p) past tense clusters before following consonants
(KD^v_p) past tense clusters before following vowels

Figure 13–2 shows the proportions of clusters in these four categories in which the final *-t,d* is deleted, for five peer groups of NNE speakers in single and group style. In addition, a group of seventeen working-class adults is shown. These speakers are one-quarter of the random sample of adults interviewed in the Jet and Cobra areas.

There are two sets of lines in each diagram; the upper pair shows the deletion of final *-t,d* before consonants, the lower pair before vowels. There are twenty-two comparisons, then, in which we can observe the effect of a following vowel restraining the operation of the rule, and there are no contrary cases. In all but one case—the upper broken line for the Cobras—the lines slope downward to the right, showing that

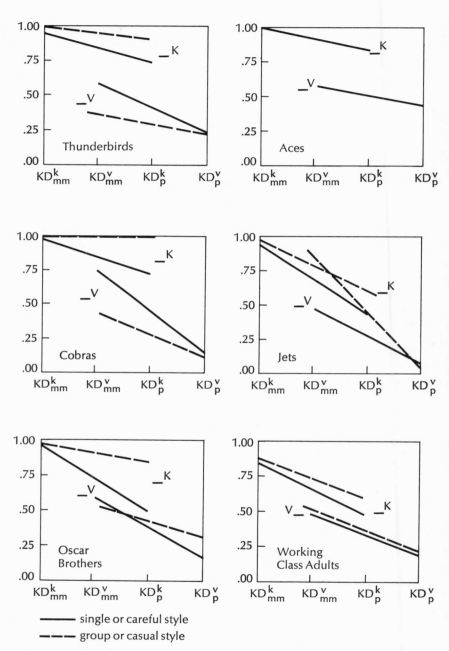

Figure 13-2. *t,d cluster simplification for NNE peer groups and adults in two styles.*

the effect of the morpheme boundary is to reduce the deletion of the final -*t,d*. Thus, there are twenty-one cases where this relationship can be observed. There is also a stylistic regularity that can be noted; in the five cases where we contrast single and group style, there is more -*t,d* deletion before consonants in single than in group style. For the Thunderbirds and Cobras, this effect is reversed before vowels; the Jets, Oscar Brothers, and working-class adults show a tendency to retain the same effect before vowels. We are not concerned here with the stylistic shift in itself, however, but with the fact that the fundamental relationships are repeated in the two styles and that this systematic variation appears in the basic vernacular.

In each group, and in each style, the basic relations are preserved: the effect of a following vowel is to reduce -*t,d* deletion, and the effect of the morpheme boundary is in the same direction. It is this type of regularity that we term "systematic" or "inherent" variation in the NNE vernacular.

THE RELATION OF THE -*t,d* DELETION RULE TO THE READING OF THE -*ed* SUFFIX

Because the chief variable constraints on the -*t,d* deletion rule are so uniform, it would seem at first glance that the form of this rule would have no relation to the relative success or failure of different NNE speakers in reading the -*ed* suffix. However, there are several aspects of the rule that show variation from group to group and even from person to person. First of all, the relative strengths of the two main variable constraints may vary. In the actual frequencies of consonant cluster simplification, we can see this relative strength in the relation of the cross-products, that is, where one constraint is favorable and the other unfavorable to the operation of the rule. Thus, if the effect of a following vowel is predominant, we would get a pattern of simplification of form A:

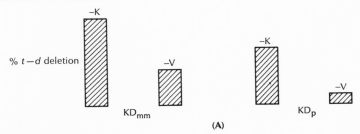

(A)

On the other hand, if the effect of a morpheme boundary (signaling the past tense) is predominant, then we would see a pattern such as:

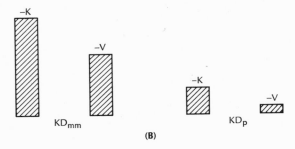

(B)

When these relationships are examined in the six subsections of Figure 13–2, it appears that there is considerable variation in the various groups. In the older groups—the Oscar Brothers and the working-class adults—there is a marked difference between casual or group style and single or careful style. In the latter, the effect of the grammatical boundary is stronger than in the former, and for the Oscar Brothers, the single interviews show a reversal of the relative positions of the two constraints. That is, they follow pattern A above in group style and pattern B in face-to-face interviews. This reflects the general fact that when they give more attention to speech, they show the influence of Standard English rule forms. As we have shown in other studies, white middle-class speakers delete the *-t,d* mainly in such monomorphemic clusters as *just now*—the effect of the morpheme boundary is absolute in preventing simplification. As NNE speakers become older, the effect of the past-tense boundary becomes stronger in their careful speech.

We can observe the same general tendency when we compare isolated individuals with peer group members. In many ways, the rule structure of isolated individuals contrasts with that of peer group members and is closer to that of standard English. For example, if we compare the Thunderbirds with isolated boys in the same low-income apartment house, we see the contrast shown in Table 13–3. Thus, the isolated individuals

Table 13–3.

	KD_{mm}^k	KD_{mm}^v	KD_p^k	KD_p^v
Thunderbirds(8)	94%	59	74	24
Lames(4)	89	51	26	08

show a much stronger effect of the grammatical constraint that predominates over the effect of a following vowel, just the reverse of the Thunderbird rule.

We can, therefore, profit from an examination of the relative position of the two variable constraints in the speech of our subjects who read the nine sentences. Table 13–4 shows the results for forty-nine individuals,

Table 13–4. *Predominance of Grammatical over Phonological Constraints on -t,d Deletion vs. Success in Reading the -ed Suffix.*

VARIABLE CONSTRAINTS ON $-t,d$ DELETION	NO. OF SENTENCES WITH PAST TENSE MEANING DERIVED FROM *-ed* SUFFIX			
	0/3	1/3	2/3	3/3
Following vowel predominant	15	18	7	5
Constraints equal	9	9	5	2
Past tense predominant	13	7	3	9
No. subjects	16	17	10	6

including thirty-two members of the peer groups and seventeen isolated individuals from the same area. The values of KD^v_{mm} and KD^v_p are compared in all styles for which sufficient data were available in group sessions, in single interviews, and in reading other text besides the nine sentences—a total of 103 points where such comparison might be made. The subjects are divided into four groups, depending on whether they read the word *read* correctly in one, two, or three of the sentences. Good performance on the three sentences was rare, as noted above. There are only six subjects who fall into the 3/3 category, and only ten are found to have succeeded in two out of three cases. If the *-ed* suffix is not identified, it is quite possible for someone to pronounce the word *read* as [rɛd] just the same, even though it is the less favored form, and one cannot make any sharp distinction between 0/3 and 1/3. The fact that does emerge from Table 13–4 is that there is only one group that shows the past tense constraint as predominant and that is the 3/3 group. Even though there is considerable variability within all groups, the predominance of the effect of the relative position of the grammatical constraint does show some correlation with reading performance.

We are still dealing with a weakly determined and fluctuating effect, quite different from primary variable constraints themselves. More precise data can be obtained by seeing how deeply the past tense constraint itself governs the speech of each subject. One can have a relatively vague effect that appears only when large numbers are taken in hand, or when various other effects are cancelled out; or one can have a relatively powerful effect that, though variable, controls behavior in each style and in each phonological environment. We can examine the past tense constraint in four phonological subclasses in the single interviews:

1. Vowel preceding the -t,d
2. Underlying l preceding
3. s preceding
4. Other voiceless consonant preceding

We can also study the data from other stylistic subclasses:

5. Group sessions
6. Reading of text other than sentences discussed above
7. Reading of word lists and minimal pairs

The data in the last three categories are too limited to allow the detailed breakdown of the single interviews. But in each of the seven subcategories above, we can make a separate comparison of KD^k_{mm} vs. KD^k_p and KD^v_{mm} vs. KD^v_p. There are thus fourteen possible points of comparison, although the data do not provide a definite answer in all of them for most of the forty-nine subjects. Table 13–5 shows the results: we find that there is one group for which there were no cases of the grammatical constraint reversed, so that $KD_{mm} < KD_p$: the group of speakers who were able to decipher the past tense meaning of -ed three out of three times.

It was observed above that the constraint of a preceding morpheme boundary operates uniformly on almost every individual and on every group. The totals of Table 13–5 show that this is indeed a very strong tendency even in such small subcategories as 1 to 6 above. It was reversed in only 17 per cent of these cases. By contrast, Table 13–4 shows no such clear-cut orientation toward the ordering of the cross-products KD^v_{mm} and KD^k_p, although we have seen that individual groups do lean strongly in one direction or another. Table 13–5 clearly demonstrates, then, that the grammatical constraint of the variable rule is most firmly

Table 13–5. *Consistency of Grammatical Constraint on -t,d Deletion vs. Success in Reading the -ed Suffix.*

EFFECT OF PAST TENSE BOUNDARY ON *-t,d* DELETION	NO. OF SENTENCES WITH PAST TENSE MEANING DERIVED FROM *-ed* SUFFIX			
	0/3	1/3	2/3	3/3
Grammatical constraint holds	52	41	16	25
No grammatical constraint	18	23	15	7
Grammatical constraint reversed	13	22	5	0
	83	86	36	32
Average reading score	4.7	4.6	4.7	4.7

fixed in the behavior of that subgroup that reads the *-ed* suffix most competently. The second best subgroup, who read the *-ed* suffix two out of three times, did not do so well—in fact, there are no clear-cut differences between any of the other groups. One would not expect to find any regular distribution across the 0/3, 1/3, 2/3 groups, because guessing might produce any of these patterns if the reader knows that there are two readings of the homograph *read*. If the reader has a firm grasp of the fact that *-ed* signals the past tense, then he should be able to reproduce the pronunciation [rɛd] in all three sentences 4, 6, and 9, for it was shown in Figure 13–1 that the ability to transfer a past tense meaning in general to the pronunciation of *read* runs far ahead of the ability to decipher and decode the *-ed* signal.

From the last line of Table 13–5, it is again evident that there is no correlation between general reading skill and the ability to decipher the *-ed* suffix as a signal of the past tense. This finding strengthens our inference that it is the form of a specific linguistic rule rather than a general deciphering capacity that differentiates the four groups of speakers.

Table 13–5 has significance for our general understanding of the process of reading, for it shows that the process of deciphering signals on the printed page can be controlled by underlying linguistic rules of an abstract nature. But these findings also have significance for our understanding of linguistic structure and the nature of linguistic rules. We have provided behavioral evidence to support independently the body of data that lies behind variable rules derived from speech. Note that the 3/3 group did not show the command of the *-ed* meaning by an invariant refusal to delete the *-t,d* in *tried, passed,* or *rolled.* On the contrary, the deletion of this final consonant is not uncommon in their speech patterns. Their competence is shown in the fine-grained adjustments they make in the frequency with which *-t,d* is deleted when it forms a part of the stem, and when it is a past tense signal.

COMPARISONS WITH WHITE NONSTANDARD SPEAKERS

If the findings of Table 13–4 and 13–5 have an explanatory value in dealing with reading difficulties, it must follow that speakers of other English dialects, who have different *-t,d* deletion rules, should have less difficulty with sentences 4, 6, and 9. We can make such a comparison through the records of the white Inwood group, which was included in the over-all investigation reported here to allow us to contrast white working-class peer groups in Manhattan with Negro peer groups.

The Inwood groups are located in upper Manhattan, in a neighborhood where the chief contact of white with Negro boys is in school. In the residential neighborhoods, the Inwood boys belong to named groups and informal hang-out groups that are entirely white.

We applied the paradigm of group study described above to a preadolescent Inwood group, comparable to the Thunderbirds, and to an adolescent group that was comparable to a subgroup of the Jets. There were four members in each group, including two pairs of older and younger brothers—a common pattern in the Jet and Cobra areas as well.

The *-t,d* deletion pattern of the Inwood groups operates at a considerably lower level than for the NNE groups. Both the preadolescent and adolescent groups show approximately the same level, at about 30 per cent lower than Table 13–4, which may be summed up in the aggregate figures of Table 13–6.

Table 13–6.

	(KD_{mm}^k)	(KD_{mm}^v)	(KD_p^k)	(KD_p^v)
Ratio of deleted to total *-t,d* forms	93/138	8/45	8/34	2/62
Per cent deletion	67	19	23	03

This is pattern B cited above, and it is worth noting that this is quite close to the pattern of middle-class Negro speakers. Our sample of twenty middle-class residents of middle-income apartments shows -*t,d* deletion, as in Table 13–7.

Table 13–7.

	(KD_{mm}^k)	(KD_{mm}^v)	(KD_p^k)	(KD_p^v)
Ratio of deleted to total -*t,d* forms	52/76	4/27	7/39	5/39
Per cent deletion	69	15	18	13

Both patterns represent strong constraints on the deletion rule, so that the great majority of deleted -*t,d*'s are in monomorphemic stems before consonants, where they are most easily reconstructed.

The reading of the Inwood groups was considerably better than the NNE groups, although several of the preadolescents were poor readers (one refused to read altogether). The preadolescents did not do at all well in reading the -*ed* suffix: none of the three who read the nine sentences gave the correct pronunciation of *read* as [rɛd]. This suggests that there is an inherent difficulty in reading the -*ed* suffix for boys of the nine- to thirteen-year-old range and that consonant cluster patterns of preadolescent groups only partly explain their behavior in reading. However, the results with the teen-age Inwood groups were quite different than with the Jets and Cobras. Three of the four read sentences 4, 6, and 9 perfectly. Of the twenty-three NNE adolescents, only three did so. The comparison, shown in Table 13–8, is striking.

Table 13–8.

	0/3,1/3,2/3	3/3
Inwood teenagers	1	3
Jets and Cobras	20	3

Table 13–5 indicates that over-all reading level does not account for differences in the reading of the -*ed* suffix. This comparison of adolescent Negro and white speakers confirms the conclusion that the variable rule for -*t,d* deletion is a controlling factor in this aspect of reading performance.

IMPLICATIONS FOR THE GENERAL STUDY OF RULE-FORMATION IN LEARNING TO READ

This chapter should not be read as a suggestion that mechanical or structural interference between SE and NNE is a major factor in reading failure. As indicated in the opening pages, it is our conviction that cultural and social conflicts are more important matters. Structural interference between NNE and SE is probably critical when it produces misunderstanding and unresolved conflict between the student and the teacher, when the teacher's behavior reflects her ignorance of the chief characteristics of NNE. Repeated pronouncements that the *ee* in *beer* sounds different than the *ea* in *bear*, that the *-st* in *past* sounds different than the *-ss* in *pass*, will undoubtedly contribute to the eventual confusion and defeat of the student and the loss of confidence in the alphabetic code that is reflected in third, fourth, and fifth grade reading failure. But these problems are not the inevitable results of deep-seated linguistic differences; we are dealing principally with a complex set of relatively superficial differences in phonological rules, such as the difference between patterns A and B.

The direction of this investigation, therefore, is to utilize a particular difference between NNE and SE to illuminate a particular difficulty in reading, and so eventually to explicate the processes that control success in learning to read. We are all aware of the fact that students' performance is often erratic, and mistakes continue to occur long after it is evident that the student has grasped and knows the general rule. It is indeed puzzling that it is so difficult to attain 100 per cent accuracy in the application of a given rule.

However, variable rules of the type discussed here may throw a different light on the matter. If they indeed reflect something about the speaker's knowledge of the language—and there is every reason to believe that they do—it is clear that one can have firm knowledge without categorical rules. There is no question that reading the *-ed* suffix requires categorical behavior: that it must be taken as past every time it is encountered affixed to the main verb. But there is no reason to believe that the student will automatically construct a categorical rule in an area where he has been using variable rules throughout his career as a native speaker of English. The patterns of Table 13–4 and 13–5 are quite consistent with the patterns of Table 13–2. It is conceivable that a speaker on NNE will formulate, well below the level of conscious awareness, rules that do not require the categorical performance demanded for reading and writing. If this is the case, it is clear that we need in the educational process either a technology designed to build categorical rules from the outset, before variable rules can be formed, or a means of transforming variable rules into categorical ones more rapidly than has been done in the past.

One may, of course, retain the hope that each individual variation in the pronunciation of *-t,d* or in the reading of *-ed* can be explained. If we take into account additional factors—the tempo of speech, pitch, stress, stylistic context, the particular phones involved, the shade of semantic meaning concerned, the relative functional load of the *-ed* in this sentence, the relative energy or fatigue of the speaker, the hearing conditions for the listener, the power relations between speaker and listener, and any of a hundred other variables—we may indeed drive the level of explanation down in the direction of individual speech acts. In the same way, one might ultimately hope to account for the air pressure in a room by the combined force of the individual impacts of all the molecules of air. It is a question of how fruitful such efforts would be in the delineation of linguistic structure and of how the results of such labors might contribute to our knowledge of the more abstract levels of the rule system. We believe that the major variables that we have described here are a part of a relatively small set of constraints that play an important part in linguistic behavior. Variable rules of the form given here expand our knowledge of linguistic structure and fit into a series of variable and categorical rules of NNE phonology that determine the surface forms of the language. Such variable rules have a complex internal structure that allows us to trace change and evolution within systems as well as the relations of systems in contact such as SE and NNE portrayed here.

REFERENCES

Labov, W., Cohen, P., Robins, C., & Lewis, J. *A Study of the Structure of the Non-Standard English Used by Negro and Puerto Rican Speakers in New York City*, Final Report of Cooperative Research Project No. 3288, Section 3.2. (New York: Columbia University, 1968).

Labov, W. Some sources of reading problems for Negro speakers of non-standard English. In A. Frazier (ed.), *New Directions in Elementary English* (Champaign, Ill.: N.C.T.E., 1966), pp. 140–167.

Labov, W., & Robins, C. A note on the relation of reading failure to peer group status. *The Teachers' College Record*, 1969, *70*, 395–406.

VERA P. JOHN

VIVIAN M. HORNER

TOMI D. BERNEY

14

Story Retelling: A Study of Sequential Speech in Young Children

To acquire language is to become independent of the immediate surroundings, while becoming more deeply tied to them. The young child becomes a functioning member of his community (characterized by specific cultural, technological, and ideological features) by learning to speak its language. But, at the same time, the acquisition of speech is a critical step toward the child's intellectual maturity and independence. In learning to fuse the knowledge of his senses with the sequential flow of his words, the child becomes independent of the immediacy of his material and social world; he learns to plan, to fantasy, to outwit, to invent, to resist.

Most studies of language socialization have failed to reflect the dynamics of this intricate process. The common approach, particularly on the part of psychologists of language, has been to measure the rate of verbal growth. Linguists' efforts to characterize language development in children have concentrated largely on specifying rules for the emerging grammatical structures and have tended to impute to the young child

Preparation of this report was partially supported by National Science Foundation Grant GS–90 and Project Literacy.

Many individuals have contributed to this research. I particularly want to thank Mrs. Kae Dakin, Mr. Marshall Peller, Mr. Richard Brodie, and Mrs. Esther Fink.

246

an innate language acquisition mechanism. Psychological studies, based on word counting, vocabulary tests, and the measurement of mean sentence length, have been characterized by linguists, for example, Chomsky and others, as trivial. By the same token, behaviorists have been dissatisfied with the nativist assumptions that underlie the theory and methods of the new grammarians. The current controversy may result in the impasse of the heredity-environment debate of an earlier era, unless fresh attempts are made by all students of language to develop more viable theories and methods.

AN APPROACH TO LANGUAGE ACQUISITION

A biological schema, though elucidating certain aspects of the mastery of syntax, is of limited value in the study of the semantic and functional aspects of language acquisition. Skinner's notion of a single-factor reinforcement theory to account for the acquisition of complex language behavior is equally inadequate. The enormous impact of both of these approaches can be seen, perhaps, as a reaction to eclecticism, as a hunger for elegance of thought and "useful" theories. But language acquisition cannot be explained by a unitary statement of underlying processes. As Ervin-Tripp has stated in a recent review article (1966), "the basis of the child's most important and complex achievement (language) still remains unknown."

In our view, several levels of language processes need to be identified prior to the development of a comprehensive theory of acquisition. One criterion that may aid in identifying the significant levels of language organization is the study of different effects of the same conditions on various aspects of language. For example, Courtney Cazden has suggested a distinction between the critical role of direct tuition in the acquisition of vocabulary and the relative lack of importance of specific instruction in the acquisition of syntax (1968). If indeed, the referential and syntactical levels of language are to some extent independent, then one crucial problem is to discover whether there are different processes of acquisition for each of these levels.

The notion of "specificity" in the development and training of different levels of language organization has been explored elsewhere by John (1967). This chapter deals with a single aspect—the emergence of connected discourse. When exposed to the flow of speech of those around them, young children listen to and ultimately acquire language. This is not a passive process, as postulated by the early associationists. On the contrary, it is an active process of hypothesis building and testing. It consists of transformations (in the broadest sense), neologisms, radical simplifications, repetition of just-heard messages, all of which are manifested during the emergence of thematic, connected speech. Most significantly, it is a creative process rivaling, as the Russian linguist Gvozdev (1967) put it, "the productions of the poet and artist in subtlety and originality." Story retelling, a novel method of gathering connected speech samples from young children, provides a basis for the study of this process.

The examination of protocols of young children who are beginning to produce a coherent account of events witnessed, or tales told to them, reveals several interesting features. Very young children produce one-word phrases. Children who are inexperienced in the production of thematic and connected discourse retell a story by simply labeling the sequentially presented pictures. As they grow more experienced, hesitations, redundancies, and incomplete phrases provide clues to the translation necessary for externalizing children's "thoughts."

In light of such observations, the assumption is advanced that though the final act of stringing words into phrases in the presence of an audience may appear smooth, it is the result of sometimes conflicting processes. To speak is to unite, temporarily, intrapersonal demands (that is, linguistic, cognitive, and emotional) and social forces impinging simultaneously on the speaker. The production of speech in response to this interplay of demands is particularly difficult for the young child.

Even adults in their language display signs of the multiple processes that may occur simultaneously during the act of speech. Bever (1967) described fluctuating attention during speech perception. He differentiated between outward social attention and inward attention to a just-heard message at the end of a phrase unit. Frieda Goldman-Eisler (1964) and others have distinguished between the short pauses preceding automatic or overlearned phrases and the longer pauses preceding newly elaborated messages requiring time to think and plan. The lengthy travail of language acquisition, as stressed by Brown, Vygotsky, and others, is in part a reflection of this interplay of the inward and outward aspects of speech.

In the study of the emergence of connected discourse, a critical problem is to discover how a child manages to fuse an internalized story, or an original idea, with the verbal expression required of him in a particular context. If our formulation is correct, and speech is a process of unifying diverse and at times conflicting processes, then the study of story retelling by young children may provide new theoretical perspectives relevant to the fusion aspect of speech.

Some of the recurrent stimuli impinging on the young child are the patterned discourses of his elders. The manner in which the child selects, transforms, and stores these streams of words is as yet unknown. One way to gain insight into the process is to require that children externalize that which they have just internalized. Memory and imitation, or retelling in the case of more complex inputs, involve some modification of the original stimuli. It seems reasonable to assume that, during the internalization process, what has been heard undergoes simplification into a sequence of key symbols. During recall, a simplified, internal version is reexpressed in communicative language.

Story retelling, then, is thought of as the act of joining some internal shorthand with the production of both newly elaborated and overlearned phrases, tailored to a particular audience. It is a complex process, acquired slowly, and conditions of rehearsal presumably contribute greatly to its smoothness and effectiveness. In our research, descriptive work on retold stories is accompanied by the development of "minitheories" of language acquisition. Our focus is on psychological, rather than linguistic, processes.

THE STORY-RETELLING METHOD

The commonsense notion that we speak in words has been the guiding framework for most of the early studies on the acquisition of language. The normative studies of the 1930's and 1940's, developed independently of linguistic considerations, aimed at monitoring verbal growth and were methodologically grounded in single-word approaches. A variation on this approach that was suggested by Vygotsky (1962), but never adequately implemented, is that word meaning be used as a significant unit in the study of the interrelatedness of language and thought.

The word is a useful unit for studies of referential behavior and verbal mediation. However, studies of vocabulary have been substituted, inappropriately, for the broader and more urgently needed studies of verbal and communicative skills. Perhaps the traditional use of a series of unrelated words, pictures, or objects in eliciting language had value from a psychometric point of view; but these methods have been unrepresentative of the communicative context of language learning.

For the reasons mentioned above, traditional techniques of language assessment have been found wanting by contemporary workers, particularly by the psycholinguists influenced by generative grammar. Structural units, rather than words, have been proposed as an alternative. The "pivotal construction" is an example of one such unit used in current research on the syntax of young children. But even this unit reveals, on close examination, the problems inherent in a unitary approach. The unmarked grammar of the young child relies on numerous paralinguistic and extralinguistic features for communicative effectiveness. Functionally, then, a systematic analysis involving all these features is required for an analysis of the child's language as a communicative process.

Though the emotional, evocative power of words, as Sylvia Ashton-Warner has reminded us, is a force that children and their teachers can grasp, the weight of tradition is with those who have stressed the greater importance of the orderliness of language. The chaining of words into recurrent structures and the well-established strategies followed by effective communicators have to be mastered by young children during their early years. Telling and reading stories to young children are time-tested methods of language socialization aimed, perhaps, at achieving this latter goal. In our search for methods of eliciting representative sequential samples of speech from young children, we chose stories because of their critical role in exposing children to language routines.

We have asked children to retell these stories because of our concern with how children translate what they hear into their own words. The organization and ultimate recall of a standard story read or told to a young child are carried out in a manner characteristic of that child, but similarities of production may be found among children as functions of age, experience, setting, and social background.

The empirical research to be reported is descriptive, focusing on the technique itself and the study of patterned variation in retold stories related to socially significant antecedent variables.

We chose the age range of four to seven, favored by many developmental theorists, for the examination of the emergence of connected speech. Through use of standard children's stories, we are able to minimize diversity in input. We then attempt to discover the patterned regularities of the retold stories.

Briefly, the procedure of story retelling is as follows. The child is told that, after the story has been read, he will be asked to retell it. The child is then read a story while he looks at a sequence of pictures corresponding to parts of the text. Once the reading is completed, the child is shown the illustrations and retells the story. Each picture is presented separately and in its proper story sequence. (Young children are unable to retell the story without the sequential presentation of the illustrations as cues.) The examiner, who is trained to avoid prompting, records the retold story.

The emphasis in analysis has been on examining the retold stories as "patterned verbal output." At least two types of patterning are considered: linguistic and cognitive. Children transform the story into their own words, reflecting their level of syntactic and vocabulary development. In addition, they selectively recall features of the original story and impose their own organization. Though not all features of the retold stories are quantifiable, we have developed a number of indices that relate to such patterning.

Linguists find our methods too controlled, whereas psychologists find them not controlled enough. The former have raised the problem of limited variability in speech samples elicited in a standardized setting; they have suggested that such a procedure allows too much opportunity for imitative speech. Psychologists, on the other hand, have raised the thorny problem of quantification of continuous speech. The story-retelling method is open to both criticisms if it is viewed either as an attempt to elicit a representative corpus of the child's language or as a standardized test of language proficiency. Our intent is neither of these. Rather, we are developing a technique for obtaining protocols of continuous verbalization in naturalistic settings.

By standardizing the setting and the procedures, the protocols are comparable across children and across time. Such a technique is not intended to meet the full needs of both the linguistic and psychological disciplines; rather it is devised to allow for the limited developmental study of language acquisition in a manner that meets some of the demands of both fields. Based on the preliminary analyses of the many protocols we have assembled, we have sketched out a developmental model of the sequential stages in the production of thematic, connected discourse.

DEVELOPMENTAL STAGES IN STORY RETELLING

The story-retelling method is useful as an approach for describing major steps in the acquisition of connected, fluent language. Protocols revealed a developmental shift from the simple labeling of sequentially presented pictures to the effective reproduction of an organized story with thematic content. We have violated the usual tradition of reading very short and simple stories to young children. We have purposefully chosen stories to create a "stimulus overload," so that children would not remember the stories verbatim.

The developmental model that has emerged from analyses of story-retelling protocols is outlined below:

Stage 1. Sequential Picture Labeling

Some of the youngest and least experienced children with whom we worked (aged three and one-half to four) retold the beginnings of Curious George[1] in the following way: Picture 1. The child says, *George.* 2. *Hat.* 3. *George* . . . (short pause) . . . *George.* 4. *Bag.* 5. *Hat.* 6. *Bag.* And so on.

One little girl whose protocol consisted of these noun phrases retold little of the story read to her beyond the monkey's name. Some of the children, though able to produce phrases of greater length in conversation, were limited to one-word labels in their retelling performance. Among these simple responses were occasional phrases such as *to the zoo* or *sitting down,* but these did not occur often.

These children displayed close attention to the story when it was read to them. Nevertheless, they subsequently failed to retrieve it for retelling. If their overt performance is an indicator of the covert processes, the input-output coordination necessary for this task is as yet undeveloped in these subjects It is intriguing to note that the actual verbal productions in this first stage are so similar to the holophrases of much younger children just learning to talk.

Stage 2. The Skeleton Story

An example of a protocol that illustrates the second stage is as follows: Picture 1. *Once upon a time was a monkey.* 2. *What you call it?* 3. *He got the hat on his face.* 4. *And he in the bag.* In this stage, children still tend to utter one phrase per card, but these are no longer holophrastic. There is evidence of some sequential linking of the events described in the story and those depicted in the illustrations. A number of these short retold stories reveal a stylistic unity and appeal in their rhythm and simplicity.

Stage 3. The Embroidered Story

In this phase, many of the preschool children introduced new elements, or embroidered on the stories read to them. One four-year-old Negro

---

[1] H. A. Rey, *Curious George* (Boston: Houghton Mifflin, 1941), was used in most of the story-retelling research.

girl in Harlem says in response to the second picture in *Curious George*, *He put his hat on, and look for a cowboy.* (In the printed story, George is still in the jungle.) To the next picture, the little girl says, *And he got his hat, and he go out, and then tell his mommy, "goodbye."* (The monkey's mother is absent in the printed version.) Many of the younger children weave a tale half-remembered, half-invented in their retellings.

Among the first-grade children, we found less evidence of imaginative but narratively irrelevant elaborations. More than half of these children produced longish stories, reflecting, however, a strain for accuracy in retelling. Their stories contain many fillers, hesitations, phrase segments, or what we have called "runner-up" sentences, redundancies, and elaborations, which are ingenuously in context. An example of an elaboration is, *And they took the monkey into the prison all alone, alone.* The runner-up phrase is illustrated with this example, *The little men was selling some kind of—I mean—the balloon man was selling balloons.*

The largest group of children tested to date retold these stories in this manner, with two to three phrases per illustration. Such output is about one-fifth of the length of the original stories.

The children's performance at this stage is of great theoretical interest. In story retelling, children are deprived of an active interlocutor. The examiner does not correct or cue the child's responses. Thus, the resulting performance resembles what Ervin-Tripp (1966) has called an "expressive monologue." The child's behavior at this stage can be likened to the acquisition of any new sequential skill (for example, skating, bicycle riding) replete with false starts and overcorrections. As yet, corrective feedback is absent from his performance.

Stage 4. Accurate and Concise Story Retelling

An example of this phase of story retelling is as follows: Picture 1. *George. He went, was up in a tree.* 2. *And the man with the big yellow hat said, "That looks like a good monkey." He put his hat down on the ground.* 3. *And George wanted to put it on his head.* 4. *It covered his whole head so he can't see. And the man put a bag on him.* 5. *And took him into a little boat, put him into a little boat and took him to a big boat.* 6. *He said, "You're going to like it in the zoo."* 7. *Then George came off the ship onto land and the big man with the yellow hat did too.* 8. *He felt very tired and he went to sleep.* 9. *The next morning the man telephoned the zoo and went out and George wanted to call somebody too. He called the fire department.* 10. *And the fire,*

the fireman ran to the telephone. There was no answer, and he didn't
know where the call came from.[2]

SOCIAL CLASS DIFFERENCES IN STORY RETELLING

The first study using the story retelling technique (1963–1964) was
concerned with social class as an antecedent variable in the development
of language proficiency. The subjects were ninety Negro children, attending the first grade in New York City public schools. The sample was
selected to represent three social class groupings: lower lower, upper
lower, and middle class. The population of the study was balanced for
age, sex, and birth order. All subjects were selected from the top two
academic groupings of their class, thus selecting a group of children
who were relatively homogeneous in academic standing. This group was
of particular interest because it permitted us to study subtle differences
in language behavior without the confounding effects of grosser intellectual differences. In comparing their performances in the SRA Primary
Mental Abilities Test, no social class or birth-order differences emerged
on the perceptual subtest, but significant social class differences were
obtained on the verbal subtest, as shown in Table 14–1.

Table 14–1. *Mean Raw Scores on SRA Perceptual and Verbal Subtests
as a Function of Social Class in First-Grade Children.*

| | SOCIAL CLASS | | | | |
	1	2	3	F	p
Perceptual	109	113	112	1.30	NS
Verbal	173.05	179.08	190.48	6.86	.01

1 vs. 2 = 6.02; not significant
2 vs. 3 + 11.40; significant at $p < .05$
1 vs. 3 = 17.42; significant at $p < .01$

Of the ninety children in this study, sixty were tested individually
by the story-retelling method. The book used was *Curious George*. We

---

[2] This is the first half of the retold story, transcribed here in ordinary orthography.

examined differences in the quantity and quality of the retold stories as a function of the child's social class membership and birth order.[3]

The analyses, to be summarized below, refer to output, accuracy and measures of "techniques of production." Among the difficult problems of quantifying retold stories is the choice of a unit. The unit chosen for the quantitative aspects of these studies is the phrase. Empirical criteria of pause length, juncture phenomena, stress contours, and minimal units of meaning were used in specifying a phrase unit.

MEASURES OF VERBAL OUTPUT

The most obvious question to be asked in a study of sequential speech is whether children drawn from varied backgrounds vary in their over-all verbal output. In the study of first-grade Negro children, no significant relationship was found between socioeconomic status and verbal output, as shown in Table 14–2.

Table 14–2. *Number of Phrases as a Function of Social Class.*

| | SOCIAL CLASS* | | |
	1	2	3
Mean	68.88	72.75	64.42
Range	40–124	40–120	36–102
SD	22.3	22.7	21.1
N	24	24	12

* Social class 1—lower-lower class Negro children
Social class 2—upper-lower class Negro children
Social class 3—middle class Negro children

The wide range in story length is significant when related to variations in story quality. First-grade children produced stories that correspond to the third and fourth stages of development described above. These children tended to give either accurate and concise stories or their renditions were labored and redundant, thus contributing to length without quality. (These features of their retellings will be examined further by means of other measures.)

---

[3] A preliminary summary of the findings of this study was published in an article entitled, "Children and Language Acquisition" (John, 1967).

MEASURES OF ACCURACY IN STORY RETELLING

The excellence of a retold story can be judged according to many different attributes, including accuracy, organization, and imagination. Of these, we have found that accuracy is the easiest to quantify.

The unit of analysis used was always the phrase. Accuracy was thus determined by counting the number of text-based phrases in a particular retelling. Text-based phrases are those that can only be elicited when the subject is familiar with the actual text of the story. We have included in this definition only first instance text-based phrases; that is, we have excluded those responses that are based on previous responses of the subject, such as redundancies and elaborations. We also excluded labels of picture details that were not included in the text and fillers, such as half-phrases.

Of the text-based phrases, we differentiated stimulus-derived (SD) phrases, and story-relevant inferred (SRI) phrases. The former category refers to text-based phrases that are depicted in the illustrations, such as

A man with a yellow straw hat.
It covers his eyes.
Put him in a bag.
They took him to a big ship.
They looked on a big map.
They locked George up.

The SRI category refers to retold items based solely on the text, such as

He was curious.
It was too heavy.
George was very happy.
He slept.
They thought it was a fire.
He sneaked out.

It is nearly impossible for very young children to retell a story without illustrations as cues. Consequently, the production of phrases not based on the illustrations (SRI items) is thought of as a more demanding cognitive task than the production of the directly cued SD phrases.

The inferred items measure, it is suggested, the child's skill in retelling a sequentially organized continuous story.

The prediction was made that SRI scores would vary significantly with social class and birth order. One-half of the prediction, that related to social class, was confirmed.

Problems of unitizing plagued us in the earlier phases of this research. Repetitions of phrases and poor approximations of text-based sentences created scoring difficulties. The findings reported in this chapter are based on a revised scoring method. Because our main interest lay in the way in which children actually used the total number of phrases they emitted, accuracy scores were based on the percentage of the total number of phrases that were SD or SRI phrases.

Table 14–3. *Mean Percentages of SRI Phrases to Total Phrases as a Function of Social Class.*

		SOCIAL CLASS			
	1	2	3	F	p
N	24	24	12		
Mean	14.98	15.96	23.36	3.82	.05

1 vs. 2 = .98; not significant
2 vs. 3 = 7.40; significant at $p < .05$
1 vs. 3 = 8.38; significant at $p < .05$

The differences between the performance of lower-class and middle-class children is clearly shown in Table 14–3. There are several ways to interpret the findings. One is to state that the verbal superiority of the advantaged child is a pervasive one; he excels in all language tasks. A second interpretation, and one that more closely fits our findings, is that advantaged children show specific verbal strength, but fail to differ from their disadvantaged peers on many tasks and measures of verbal proficiency.

In this study, middle-class children did not excel over low-income children in the proportion of cued, text-based phrases (SD items). The lack of differences in total verbal output was mentioned above.

About a third of the retold phrases cannot be categorized as accurate, text-based units. Among the units thus classified (called nontext-based items) are those of redundancy, fillers, out-of-context elaborations, labels of pictorial details. Middle-class children tended to retell concisely and appropriately. In contrast, the low-income children tended to produce stories that lack the smoothness required in the task-oriented setting of story retelling. A global score of nontext-based items (as described above), divided by the total number of phrases, is presented in Table 14–4.

Table 14–4. *Mean Percentages of Nontext-based Phrases of Total Phrases as a Function of Social Class.*

| | SOCIAL CLASS | | | | |
	1	2	3	F	p
N	24	24	12		
Mean	41.34	36.14	28.60	4.47	.05

1 vs. 2 = 5.20; not significant
2 vs. 3 = 7.54; not significant
1 vs. 3 = 12.74; significant at $p < .01$

Nontext-based items are of four general types: redundancies, fillers, elaborations, and labels of pictorial details. Redundancies, as the name implies, include such repetitions as *And he was curious. And he was curious.* Fillers include such phrase segments as *And he, and he.* Elaborations include *After eating some bananas* (in the picture, the meal was a hot one with soup) and *He was tired up* (George is getting caught; tiredness is not mentioned). Included in labels of pictorial details, we find such items as *Fireman house.*

The findings presented in Table 14–4 are an interesting corollary to those in Table 14–3. There appear to be highly verbose children in both the middle and lower classes. It would seem, however, that verbose lower-class children exhibit much interference in their attempts to retell a story accurately. Verbose middle-class children, on the other hand, exhibit behavior that is highly relevant to the required task.

Many of the low-income children retell stories as if they are straining for accuracy. This process was described above in stage 3 of story retelling. Their stories are filled with fillers, hesitations, phrase segments, redundancies, and elaborations. Middle-class children also give these, but to a lesser extent.

The importance of the conditions of rehearsal in the acquisition of complex, sequential responses was mentioned earlier in this chapter. Opportunities for frequent rehearsals of sequential speech may be limited in certain kinds of families. However, the children who have prolonged contact with, and gain encouragement from, adults who are effective communicators themselves, learn the important skill of "self-editing." These children, who have acquired functionally appropriate verbal strategies, are often the offspring of small, middle-class families in which learning and intellectual preoccupations are a shared family pursuit. The impact of such a verbally nurturing environment is reflected in certain features of the children's sequential language, such as appropriateness, conciseness, and task orientation. It is of interest that a great number of low-income children have retold excellent stories in this study. We do not know whether this performance is owing to unusually favorable home conditions (in spite of poverty) or to some other as yet unexplored variables.

THE SEQUENCE OF DEVELOPMENT OF SEQUENTIAL LANGUAGE

The strings of words spoken by children may appear to be a smooth process in most social situations. However, it is here thought of as the temporary unification of various ongoing processes in and around the speaker. These processes in fact may be contradictory and may deeply influence the character and amount of a child's speech.

In this study, the empirical findings illustrated the various stages of development in the production of sequential speech. We witnessed this general process from the point of view of a cognitively taxing task presented to young children, and we evaluated the resulting speech patterns and production at several types of performance.

The youngest children tested by this method and those handicapped by bilingualism (see John and Berney, 1968) retold the stimulus story by sequentially labeling the illustrations. They did not, in most cases, integrate, or remember the story when the story illustrations were presented to them in a serial order. Although they were old enough to produce the basic syntactical structures of their native language, their performance was immature in terms of syntax and content. In a sense, they behaved in the way shy young children respond to a strange situation amid strangers: they answered with one-word phrases. Cognitive stress and social stress may thus have a similar effect in reducing the complexity of language in young children.

A skeleton story emerged in the next stage of story retelling. The child linked one phrase with one picture; he retrieved a sequence of actions. His output was short; he was telling a story simply. But he succeeded in integrating the three-pronged process involved in thematic productions: (1) the internalized story, (2) the linking of the illustration with some version of the remembered text, and (3) the production of words in the presence of a listener. At this stage, the child's production is reminiscent of the telegraphic speech of young children who capture some critical but unelaborated core of what they have heard, like an office memo.

The older children in this study, whose performances were reported in detail, were drawn from a culturally homogeneous setting. They were similar to one another in many ways. The sixty Negro first-graders of New York City were in the top half of their classes. Although they were drawn from three socioeconomic groups (lower lower, upper lower, and middle class), they revealed but minor differences in performance on a nonverbal test of intelligence.

However, the effects of social class were reflected in several features of their retold stories. Low-income children tended to strain for accuracy in their retelling. In what we have categorized as the third stage of story retelling, these children revealed some of the mechanics of production of sequential speech. Middle-class children more readily produced a smooth flow of thematically connected and relevant words. Thus, six-year-olds in this study differentially exhibited behaviors commonly found in 'the third or fourth stage of the development of story retelling.

The social class differences described above were not pervasive, however. On some indices, such as output and stimulus-derived phrases, the three socioeconomic groups were quite similar. Consequently, our study would suggest caution against the facile and premature conclusions about the verbal impoverishment of the low-income child.

To date, two studies have been completed using the story-retelling technique.[4] The populations from which the two samples were drawn differed from each other in many respects. Thus, our results reflect both the differing experimental emphases and the dissimilar populations studied.

---

[4] The second study described above is reported in the final report for Office of Economic Opportunity Research Project No. 577 and is entitled "Analysis of Story Retelling as a Measure of the Effects of Ethnic Content in Stories" (John and Berney, 1967).

The population of the second study included 142 preschool children of the following ethnic groups: Negro, Puerto Rican, Mexican, Sioux Indian, and Navajo Indian. Forty-six children did not speak English. They represented a range of social class from lower lower to middle class. Though, as shown above, no differences in verbal output were found in a homogeneous group of first-graders, significant differences appeared for a heterogeneous group of preschoolers. The paucity of verbal output of the Indian children was particularly impressive. Negro children, as a group, gave longer and more action-packed stories. The retellings of the Indian children were largely descriptive and included little action. Bilingual Navajo children tended to function at stage 1 of story retelling (labeling), whereas monolingual children tended to function at stage 2.

Pre- and posttesting now under way using a story-retelling technique has yielded some interesting tentative findings. As young children attend school over a period of time, the material included in their retellings becomes more relevant. There are fewer elaborations and less associative material. It would thus seem that greater task orientation occurs as a function of education.

The studies described above have demonstrated that the social conditions in which language is elicited is a critical factor in interpreting findings of variations in verbal output. A lack of attention to this significant variable accounts, perhaps, for the many misleading statements in which educators and psychologists speak of the "wordlessness" of the low-income child, a finding not supported in our research.

The story-retelling method has shown its strength. Critical in the future, however, is its use in conjunction with specific hypotheses; otherwise, it will be open to reliance on ex post facto interpretations. Our endeavors in the development of the story-retelling technique were joyous and intriguing experiences. However, they were but a beginning, an introduction to the need to specify the development of sequential language in young children.

REFERENCES

Bever, T. Paper presentation to Psycholinguistic Circle of New York, Fall 1967.

Cazden, C. Some implications of research on language development for preschool education. In R. D. Hess & R. M. Bear (eds.), *Early Education*. Chicago: Aldine, 1968.

Ervin-Tripp, S. Language development, In M. L. Hoffman, & L. W. Hoffman, (eds.), *Review of Child Development Research.* New York: Russell Sage Foundation, 1966, vol. 2, pp. 55–105.

Goldman-Eisler, F. Discussion and further comments. In E. H. Lenneberg (ed.), *New Directions in the Study of Language.* Cambridge: M.I.T. Press, 1964, pp. 109–130.

Gvozdev, A. N. Quoted in D. Slobin, "Early Grammatical Development in Several Languages with Special Attention to Soviet Research." Mimeographed, 1967.

John, V. Children and language acquisition. In A. Frazier (ed.), *The New Elementary School.* Association for Supervision and Curriculum Development, N.E.A., 1967.

John, V., & Berney, T. D. Analysis of story retelling as a measure of the effects of ethnic content in stories. Final report, Office of Economic Opportunity, Project Number 577, 1967.

John, V., & Berney, T. D. Analysis of story retelling as a measure of the effects of ethnic content in stories. In J. Hellmuth (ed.), *Disadvantaged Child.* Seattle: Special Child Publications, 1968, vol. 2.

John, V., and Goldstein, L. The social context of language acquisition. *Merrill-Palmer Quarterly,* 1964, *10,* 265–275.

John, V., & Moskovitz, S. A study of language change in integrated and homogeneous classrooms. Progress Report No. 2, O.E.O. Grant No. 2440, 1968.

Rey, H. A. *Curious George.* Boston: Houghton Mifflin, 1941.

Vygotsky, L. S. *Thought and Language,* E. Hanfmann, & G. Vakar, trans. Cambridge, Mass.: M.I.T. Press, 1962.

15   JOANNA P. WILLIAMS

From Basic Research on Reading to Educational Practice

Reading is without a doubt one of the most important and essential skills that a child must learn. Lacking the ability to read, a child cannot be successful in school. Indeed, any nonreader, young or old, is handicapped in trying to get along in the world. Yet more than one-tenth of the population of the United States is considered "functionally illiterate," that is, they have not reached a fourth-grade reading level. Moreover, many people who do achieve reasonable proficiency do so only with difficulty and a great expenditure of time.

Is this inevitable? Clearly, reading is a complex skill, involving many different aptitudes and competencies, and there are bound to be substantial differences among individuals in reading level. It does seem reasonable, however, that many of the difficulties encountered in the acquisition of this skill could be alleviated, and many cases of reading failure eliminated, through the development of more effective techniques of instruction.

Throughout the years, a multitude of ideas concerning the best way to teach reading have been proposed and debated. The history of reading instruction seems always to have been characterized by indecision and conflict—in part owing to the enormous value placed on reading in our society. Unfortunately, most of the programs and methods (which sometimes amounted to nothing more than short-lived fads) have been devised and promoted on the basis of intuition alone, with little or no empirical data to justify them.

Today's demands are great for instructional programs that are both effective and efficient. New and innovative programs abound, and there are immense numbers of publications—both professional and in the mass media—that focus on problems in reading. Current enthusiasm has led to the acceptance (at least on an experimental basis) of techniques that in previous times might have seemed unusual: for example, an artificial orthography such as *i/t/a/* can receive wide field testing and generally favorable publicity at the present time.

Paralleling all of this practical activity is the increased attention being given to research on reading. A large proportion of educational research has always been devoted to reading, and recently this interest has been spreading: more and more investigators whose main focus is on other areas have become involved in research related to reading. In fact, the *1968 Yearbook on Innovations in Reading,* published by the National Society for the Study of Education, devotes an entire chapter to a discussion of relevant work in allied disciplines.

This research activity has been sparked enormously by national concerns. One of the most dramatic effects following Sputnik in 1957 was the change in attitude toward formal education during the preschool years. Previously, there had been a great deal of work in the area, but it had never been emphasized until we began the race for space; then the advantages of early learning began to be extolled. As would be expected, one of the issues most closely studied has been early reading. Much of the work in reading in the last decade, in fact, has centered around issues in beginning reading, and in Durkin's (1968) words, a great deal more thought has been given to when instruction should take place than to other basic questions, such as how. The war on poverty has also provided impetus to the study of reading. The disadvantaged person is almost by definition a nonreader, and our nation must work steadily and rapidly to provide adequate instruction in this area (as well as in many others).

Thus, as is often the case, social needs have played a large role in providing motivation for educational research and development. It is largely because of the awareness of the gravity of the problem on a national scale that there is greater acceptance of classroom innovations, increased support of research, and acceptance of contributions from those who are not reading specialists.

Before discussing the educational implications of some of the basic research reported in this volume, it would be helpful to review briefly other types of reading research. A great deal of the work done on reading over the years has focused on what at first glance appears to be a very simple question: what characterizes the most effective reading program? For a long time, most investigators attempted to answer this question directly, that is, by taking two (or more) programs and comparing their effectiveness in typical classroom settings. The difficulties with this sort of study—the little possibility of adequately controlling the many crucial variables, the limitations of the test instruments used in evaluation, the lack of follow-up studies beyond the end of the first year of instruction—have received much discussion lately. Recently, a carefully organized and coordinated series of such studies was conducted (Bond and Dykstra, 1967), supported by the U.S. Office of Education (U.S.O.E.). Each of twenty-seven investigators, located at various universities, compared two or more reading programs in first-grade classrooms. One of the programs in each instance was one of the currently popular basal reader systems; the comparison programs represented a large variety of methods. Some of the projects included instruction and/or follow-up testing through the third grade. For a variety of reasons, not all the studies could be included in the over-all evaluation: for example, one or two had elected to study special populations, such as Mexican-Americans. There were uncontrollable practical difficulties, such as complications in coordinating plans with local school boards, dropouts (teachers as well as students), and so forth.

The results of this massive effort indicate no over-all superiority for any one particular program or for any general type of program. Though we hope that further assessment of the data (interactions between method and pupil characteristics, for example) will prove instructive, one summing-up sentence is used by supporters and detractors of this type of investigation alike: above all, it is the teacher who has the greatest effect on pupil achievement.

It seems likely that more research efforts along these lines will yield similar outcomes. First, we know how difficult it is to do this type of study well. The best experimental design and the most elegant statistical techniques will not overcome the practical problems. Second, there are now many studies of this type. All the methodological criticisms, though just, are not so overwhelming that consistent trends in the data would remain hidden. Extreme care in methodology and control, so that a manipulation will be effective in demonstrating the presence of even small differences, can be crucial in theoretically based research. However, in educational research, we are generally interested in manipulations that will make a difference in the natural setting—typically, a classroom in which we will have little control over those variables we have tried to identify and isolate. Thus, if the effects of a manipulation are so small that they cannot be seen even when great pains are taken with control, we can hardly be dealing with a crucial variable.

Chall's recent comprehensive study of such research up until 1965 (Chall, 1967) and the outcome of the recent U.S.O.E. studies make it abundantly clear how little we have learned from this comparative approach. Though many of the criticisms Chall makes of the older studies are, of course, not true of the recent research, it is a matter of some chagrin that even with sophisticated organization and design, little more trustworthy information has been gained from the latest work.

The emphasis during the last few years on individualization of instruction, conducted in large measure within the context of programmed and computer-assisted instruction, has led to new types of curriculum development. There are many such experimental programs presently under development, for example, the Brentwood Project at Stanford University, the Oakleaf Project at the University of Pittsburgh, and the work at the Southwest Regional Laboratory in Los Angeles. In general, the initial steps in the development of these instructional programs are similar to those of more traditional, classroom-oriented programs. That is, the basis of the program is intuition, judgment, and logic. Then come systematic tryouts and field tests; the outcomes are evaluated on the basis of student performance, and the program is modified on the basis of the evaluation. Presumably each field test/evaluation/modification cycle leads to a successive approximation to the ultimate goal, the optimal program. In this model, the results of subsequent revisions are judged in relation to this goal.

This is no different in principle from what a good teacher does, although to be sure the sequence of lessons is more explicitly formulated and described, the testing is done under more formalized, specified conditions, and the evaluation is more complete and objective. Moreover, the stress on precise specification of the instructional materials and the provision for complete and detailed records of each student's performance as he goes through the program (Atkinson and Hansen, 1966) provide important and valuable data for evaluation of small segments of the program and reworking of specific aspects that seem to need extra attention.

It will be several years before any of these curricula are developed to the point where a more general evaluation is possible. But the time will come, I am sure, when we plan a comparison of several of these individualized curricula in a natural setting, similar to the recent assessments of more traditional first-grade curricula. It is just a little bit sad to contemplate the justifications, rationalizations, and accusations that we will hear if and when it appears that no one of them is distinctly superior to the others in a nationwide, well-organized, objective appraisal.

Let us turn now to work of a more basic nature, as presented in this volume. For the most part, the chapters have been prepared by psychologists and linguists who have not been prepared professionally in matters concerning reading instruction, but whose backgrounds and interest in learning, language, and other related areas have led them to investigate problems of reading. The questions they raise and the descriptive and experimental work they do represent an approach that is clearly different from the ones discussed above.

This work is predicated on the belief, as is all basic research, that a more complete understanding of the phenomena in question is itself a worthy goal. Carroll (1968) has cited the work initiated and encouraged by Project Literacy as a notable instance of what he calls "basic educational research."

In attempting to justify this research in terms of educational practice, of course, we should keep in mind Hilgard and Bower's (1966) observation that there is an additional criterion that is critical in the evaluation of applied research: its relevance to the educational enterprise. The potential applications of any outcomes of basic science, and the ultimate usefulness of basic discoveries, are, of course, unpredictable. We can, however, specify what seem to be today's questions and speculate as to the relevance of the questions as well as to the probability of finding worthwhile answers to them.

In general, what kinds of gains can we legitimately expect from basic studies of the reading process? First, let us consider direct influences. One important outcome might be a set of principles and generalizations that would be genuinely and immediately helpful in preparing instructional materials and methods. There are few, if any, principles at the present time! Or perhaps we can look to the development of useful technology, possibly the outcome of the current interest in providing reading instruction via programmed and computer-assisted instruction.

Such relatively direct effects are hard to come by, however. A much larger set of outcomes are indirect, but they may prove very valuable in the long run. First of all, people involved in instruction, notably the classroom teachers, will become more aware and sensitive to their pupils and to their task. As Labov points out, the middle-class teacher who understands the variations between lower-class Negro dialect and standard English will be better equipped to deal with his Negro pupils. He need not speak his student's dialect himself in order to perform adequately as the teacher, but he must be able to recognize, so as to reinforce appropriately, the child's comprehension of written material as he translates from the printed page into his own dialect. Also, a teacher may well be aided in diagnosing the sources of any individual child's difficulties after a consideration of basic data (Williams and Levin, 1967). For example, he might note that the child exhibits a regular and identifiable pattern of errors in word recognition, and if so, he may try to determine how his errors relate to the variety of cues that form the basis for word recognition (as specified, for example, by Marchbanks and Levin, 1965). Hopefully, if a diagnosis is successful, the teacher may then be able to identify appropriate remedial techniques. At the least, he may be able to avoid devoting time and effort to instruction that is irrelevant to the pupil's deficiency.

Second, as basic research on reading becomes prevalent, more and more students during their graduate training will undertake such work. There is probably no better preparation for a career in an applied field than a strong foundation in basic research in a related discipline—especially, as Carroll (1968) points out, at a time when applied research seems to be yielding diminishing returns—which certainly is true today in reading.

How may the current trends in reading research be characterized? In recent years, there have been many important shifts in research. As is obvious from much of the work reported in this volume, there is a growing interest in theory—especially the cognitive theory of psychology, and in linguistics, the theory of transformational grammar. Noam Chomsky's provocative thesis that English orthography closely represents an underlying abstract level within the sound system of the language and that it is, in fact, a very useful system for representing the spoken language has already proved highly influential. Moreover, another Chomsky, Carol (1970), is a good deal more sanguine about the implications for teaching reading and spelling that follow from this point of view. There is also renewed interest in collecting descriptive data. Weber's analysis of first-graders' errors in reading and Venezky's comprehensive mapping of the regularities between orthography and sound are excellent examples of this type of study. Not that they are atheoretical in conception, but the main focus is on the collection of a body of data, rather than on testing hypotheses.

There is another type of study, not represented in this volume, which deserves mention if only because it has recently been so popular. Though it can be classified as both basic and theoretical, it is closer to educational concerns than most of the theoretical work. It can be described as an attempt to look directly at controversial issues and to assess directly the value of assumptions made by curriculum specialists or writers of instructional materials. One of the main contributions these "laboratory analogues" can make is to redefine a complex question or an assumption so that it is in a testable form. Sometimes the restatement is enough to shed new and useful light on an old question.

So far, many of these studies concern the beginning stages of reading. For example, Bishop (1964) was interested in a standard and critical issue—the role that component spelling-sound relationships play in reading. She approached the question in a novel manner, and in a sense her experiment can be classified as a simulation study. College students were taught to read CVCV Arabic words in which there was a simple one-to-one relationship between a single letter and its sound correlate. Two training conditions were used. In the letter-training group (L), subjects were required to associate the graphic forms of twelve individual letters with their appropriate sounds. In the word-training group (W), eight CVCV words made up from the same twelve letters were presented. A control group (C) spent a comparable amount of time on an unrelated task. Then the subjects were asked to learn eight transfer (CVCV) words constructed from the initial set of letters. Group L learned this task in the fewest number of trials. Group W was next, and group C took the greatest number of trials, indicating that there was some transfer value resulting from both kinds of training, but that there was more transfer in the letter-training group. When tested on the twelve individual grapheme-phoneme correspondences, both training groups displayed some proficiency, but the letter-training group did better. Interestingly, more than half the word-training subjects reported that they had attempted to form individual correspondences during training, and these subjects were in fact the ones who performed well in learning the transfer words. Bishop concluded that though knowledge of correspondences was not necessary for reading words, it was necessary for transfer to new words. She criticized word training on the grounds that it did not ensure that the subjects would learn the component correspondences.

In generalizing from this type of study, one must keep in mind the differences between the classroom and the experimental situation. For one thing, Bishop's subjects were proficient readers, who, presumably, were aware of the basic notion of correspondence. An important question left unanswered by her work is whether young children who have not mastered reading would perform in the same way. In a similar study, Jeffrey and Samuels (1967) found that letter training also led to superior performance on the transfer task in a kindergarten group. Indeed, in this study, none of the word-training subjects were able to abstract the individual correspondences from the words, providing additional support for arguments in favor of direct training of grapheme-phoneme correspondences.

Sometimes assumptions made by scholars and/or primer writers have been accepted wholeheartedly with no critical appraisal nor objective data to support them. For example, Bloomfield and Barnhart (1961) and other proponents of linguistics reading methods recommended that only simple, single grapheme-phoneme correspondences be presented to the beginning reader. Evidently this untested assumption seemed commonsensical enough to go unquestioned until Levin and Watson (1963) challenged it with what seemed to be an equally commonsense point of view. That is, they argued that a child must learn that there are variations in correspondences (in English) and that if he is presented with multiple correspondences early in instruction, he will be more likely to develop a useful problem-solving approach to the reading task (that is, a "set for diversity").

In a test of these contradictory points of view, fifth- and sixth-graders learned multiple correspondences in a modified paired-associates paradigm (Williams, 1968). Two methods were used: "successive," where only one of two phonemes that mapped to a particular grapheme was presented for the first half of the training trials, and the other phoneme for the last half of training, and "concurrent," where both phonemes associated with each grapheme were presented on each of the six trials. Asked how many sounds went with each form, subjects were much more accurate at identifying as multiple correspondences the ones that were trained concurrently. Presumably, then, in attempting to read new words, children would more readily identify such graphemes as multiple and so try out more than one phoneme for them, thereby making it more likely that they would succeed in reading the word.

Further support for Levin and Watson's "set for diversity" hypothesis came from analysis of the errors on another test, in which the subject was to identify all the phonemes that were associated with each grapheme. Here, there were fewer omissions on concurrent items than on consecutive ones. These effects were large, and they persisted over two variations in the procedure (which equated (1) the number of presentations of each type of correspondence and (2) the strength at the end of training of the two successive correspondences). A second important question, of course, is how much of the material was actually learned. In terms of this simple performance criterion, there were again differences in favor of concurrent training, but here the effect was small and unstable. Further work indicated that first-graders, tested early in their first semester of reading instruction, on a similar task (in which the stimuli were homographs), showed a similar pattern.

Admittedly, more research is needed in order to apply such findings to actual instruction. For one thing, few programs teach letter-sound correspondences in isolation. Indeed, the very notion that the grapheme and especially the phoneme are the appropriate units to consider in the development of correspondences is now open to question. Further work is in progress, focusing on spelling patterns presented in the context of words. At present, however, in the absence of sufficient data on which to base a final decision, it would seem reasonable to provide at least some variation—some kind of concurrent training—when presenting multiple correspondences, whatever the units selected. Certainly, the data indicate that critical questioning of some of the time-honored recommendations of Bloomfield and others is desirable.

In another study, Atkinson and Hansen (1966) considered the perennial controversy over whether nonsense materials should be presented during initial stages of instruction. Fries (1963) and other proponents of linguistic reading programs recommend strongly that only meaningful items be used. Five-year-olds were taught to associate the appropriate sounds to a series of seventy-seven CVC items made up of eleven consonants and the medial vowel *a*. Thirty-one of these letter patterns formed meaningful words. Over all learning trials, there were very small differences between the mean proportion of correct responses on the meaningful items (.908) and on the nonmeaningful items (.891), and for some individual patterns the direction of the difference was reversed. The authors concluded that children can learn to associate regular pronunciations of nonsense items to spelling patterns fairly easily, and in fact, for some patterns, nonsense associations appear to be easier to learn. One of the important features of this study was that it was done within the context of an actual (computer-assisted) instructional situation. For this reason, the difficult question of the extent to which the findings can be generalized back to the classroom, if not entirely eliminated, is at least minimized.

The type of research represented by these three studies will not take the place of purely descriptive data nor of attempts at theory-building. However, it does serve an important role, in that it requires the explicit statement of the question at hand in terms that can be tested and evaluated.

"Research on reading" now has a broader, more comprehensive scope of investigation than it did ten years ago. Early contributions from the allied disciplines were concerned primarily with only a few topics. In fact, one of the first and most influential contributions was to define the term "reading." Whereas many reading specialists (instruction- and research-oriented) had tended toward a soup-to-nuts definition of reading, including simple letter-discrimination and recognition skills, association of appropriate sound values to the letters, comprehension, appreciation of good literary style, and so forth, the new trend was toward a much narrower definition. What was distinctive about reading? In what essentials did reading differ from talking or thinking? The answer proved simple. The one definition encompassing only those aspects of reading that did not overlap with other processes described reading as the ability to "decode" from an unfamiliar orthographic code to the already mastered speech code.

Most recently, however, the pendulum has swung in the other direction. Decoding is necessary but not sufficient, and other aspects of reading—notably, of course, comprehension—have been attracting attention. The emergence of such interests undoubtedly reflects the very strong influence of cognitive psychology. Reading now tends to be tied to information processing and other related concepts. Definitions also seem to be growing more general and less focused on what is unique to reading: for example, Neisser's (1967) definition of reading as "externally guided thinking."

One general description of skilled reading runs through this entire volume. The reader samples the cues on the printed page, and, using these partial cues together with previous knowledge both about printed pages and about the world, he forms hypotheses (expectations), which are confirmed or disconfirmed by subsequent samplings. The fact that this definition is more specific to the reading process per se than is Neisser's makes it more useful. To be sure, a glance at the history of reading research (Huey, 1908; Woodworth, 1938) reveals the great stress placed on the "active" nature of reading and the complexity of the processes involved. The simplistic explanations prevalent recently reflect the preoccupation of scientists with more simple phenomena, which has led to the almost complete abandoning of reading as a research area.

It is clear that whatever the definition of reading, the process(es) involved for the proficient reader and for the beginner do not completely overlap. Language has a hierarchical structure, and whether we are considering the processing of speech or of text, the identification of the processing units is of prime concern. It seems obvious that there are different types of units and different levels of units, depending not only on the characteristics of the reader—his proficiency, his purpose, and so forth—but also on the nature of the material to be processed. The specification of these units, intraword and beyond, and how they are structured, will continue to be a central focus of the research in this area.

What units should be considered in the development of teaching materials? Though fully satisfactory answers to this question are obviously far in the future, it is worth noting that recent work (that of Gibson and of Venezky, for example) may well lead to a significant advance in the classic phonics vs. whole-word controversy, simply by focusing attention on the importance of the unit(s) and on the often overlooked idea that the word and the letter do not constitute the entire range of possibilities.

Current notions of what it means to read will lead to greater stress on meaning, language development, critical thinking, and other topics that only a few years ago were often considered to be quite outside the province of reading. As Brown has observed, a great deal of recent work in psycholinguistics, heretofore largely ignored by those interested specifically in reading, is of central importance.

It would be unfair to say, however, either that enough work on decoding has been accomplished or that interest in this topic has completely dwindled. Rather, those people who were involved in perceptual learning and decoding aspects of reading have for the most part continued to work in these areas. It has been other investigators who have taken up the interest in the later stages of reading. This recent emphasis on cognitive processes has led to a decline in interest in questions that are not clearly related to cognition. Interest in writing, for example, is minimal, even though writing is itself a crucial skill that is intimately related to reading, and even though many beginning reading programs emphasize "kinesthetic" methods of one sort or another (Williams, 1965). Perhaps the next few years will see some changes here.

As would be expected, interest has shifted to the adult, skilled reader.

Certainly, many of the issues arising from cognitive theory are more pertinent to the reader who has some proficiency, that is, an individual for whom decoding skills have become fully established and automatic. Moreover, a good bit of work on the visual discrimination processes and decoding processes has already been accomplished, and it is to be expected that there would be a major push to do the same kind of initial mapping out with respect to the other aspects of reading.

I am concerned about this shift in interest, in that findings may not relate very closely to the behavior of the beginning reader, let alone to any ultimate concern with instruction in beginning reading. In the past, justifications for preferring one reading method to another often have been made on the basis of data from proficient adult subjects, and it has long been recognized that some of the generalizations are faulty. For example, a justification for using the whole word as the unit in beginning reading was partially based on data indicating that adults can recognize equally well isolated letters and letter combinations that make meaningful words. Recent discussions by Carroll (1970) and Smith (1971) corroborate the view that there is a critical distinction between the acquisition stage and the mature reading stage. Indeed, the analysis of the differences between the processes found in the development of reading skill and those found in proficient reading is certain to be one of the most challenging research problems.

Other recent interests also seem to be leading away from questions of literacy training. The notion, for example, that speaking and writing are both derived directly from underlying linguistic structures—as opposed to the more common view among linguists that speech is primary and that writing is simply (or complicatedly) a representation of speech—is most provocative. Moreover, there seems to be a strong possibility that what is true today may not have been the case when, presumably, written language was developed. Throughout the course of its evolution, the relationship between spoken and written language may well have changed drastically (see chapters by Gibson, Shurcliff, and Yonas and by Francis).

Such questions are tremendously fascinating and obviously deserve study. But what about the five-year-old? Will he gain from a more systematic and sophisticated understanding of the correspondences that occur between speech and writing? And if so, when?

Partly because of the disappointment in comparisons of classroom methods some investigators are putting faith in the possibility that important effects may result from manipulations of motivational variables.

This attitude is seen primarily in the renewed emphasis on the importance of the role of the teacher in the classroom setting. Blom, Waite, and Zimet's analysis of primers is another manifestation of this concern. Moreover, we are beginning to acknowledge that, especially in the case of the disadvantaged, many of the most essential early learnings are indeed motivational in the broad sense of the term: ability to focus attention, to delay gratification, to persist in a task; also the development of achievement motivation and the development of interest in scholarly activities.

One advantage the field of reading holds is that there is usually no conflict about the need for teaching this skill; all the conflict concerns how best to meet the goal. There is an important distinction between this area and others, notably the social studies and even mathematics, where the concern for choosing what to teach means that less attention is given to method. Blom, Waite, and Zimet's analysis of the content of primers, however, and their discussion of the hidden lessons in motivation and character development that are incorporated in materials designed primarily to help a child gain skill, indicate an area where, indeed, there are controversial choices to be made. Essentially, what types of motivation are permissible? That is, what content may we use that will be effective for arousing motivation for reading without compromising any other desirable basic learnings, including the acquisition of "appropriate" values and attitudes?

Blom et al. recommend that differences in sex roles as seen in our culture be defined more explicitly in early instructional materials. This seems to echo the intent of one publisher, who, describing a recent edition of his house's best-selling basal reading series, says, "Many stories have been written to attract and hold the interest of boys, who largely make up our slow reading and retention groups. Boy activities, in sports, building things, in teasing girls, expressing male superiority, have a terrific appeal for boys—and will be of interest to girls also." I, for one, find this a very poor policy. Certainly the many far-reaching implications of this seemingly simple point of view will have to be studied at length before they are well understood. Moreover, when the implications are in fact known, who is to make these value decisions? Hopefully not the psychologist, linguist, nor other basic scientist, at least not alone—and definitely not the publishers!

What is it, really, that we expect basic research to accomplish? A homely analogy may be instructive. There are many ways in which a person can lose weight; he can exercise, he can worry, or best of all, he can stop eating. Any one of a wide variety of diets will prove effective—if it cuts down on the calories, and if it suits the particular dieter. At the same time, a diet must be balanced: often the current fashions and fads in weight-reduction programs are extreme, so that not only are they ineffectual, but sometimes actually harmful.

No one expects research on the topic in itself to lead to weight loss or even to effective reducing programs. The research does accomplish a great deal, however: it furthers the study of obesity and related areas (the basic science goal), and it helps people to understand how weight is gained, what a calorie is, and the importance of a balanced diet (the dissemination and motivational goals). Moreover, specialists can thereby develop effective and efficient diet programs. Indeed, individuals can make their own diets; they can plan a long-term regime and also make sensible moment-to-moment decisions at the table: ordering appropriate foods, refusing second helpings, and so forth.

In the same way, the knowledgeable and experienced teacher can draw on the best of what is known from research to develop and evaluate instructional programs and to make the multitude of quick judgments as to technique and treatment required in any classroom every day.

Teaching is an art, William James pointed out many years ago. Whatever method is used, whatever materials are provided, the teacher's own knowledge and sensitivity count heavily. How is the pupil's motivation to be aroused and sustained? How is his attention to be focused? How closely attuned to the child's responses is the teacher, and how well can he provide appropriate reinforcement contingent on the desired output? Until we actually have at our disposal that mythical all-wise computer, or those scarcely less mythical "teacher-proof" materials, we shall all have to be very grateful to the teacher, who, among his many other virtues, can understand and appreciate the implications of basic research and put them to good use in the classroom.

REFERENCES

Atkinson, R. C., & Hansen, D. N. Computer-assisted instruction in initial reading: The Stanford Project. *Reading Research Quarterly*, 1966, *2*, 5–25.

Bishop, C. H. Transfer effects of word and letter training in reading. *Journal of Verbal Learning and Verbal Behavior*, 1964, *3*, 215–221.

Bloomfield, L. & Barnhart, C. L. *Let's Read: A Linguistic Approach*. Detroit: Wayne State University Press, 1961.

Bond, G. L., & Dykstra, R. Coordinating center for first-grade reading instruction programs, Final Report, U.S. Office of Education Project No. X–001. Minneapolis: University of Minnesota, 1967.

Carroll, J. B. Basic and applied research in education: definitions, distinctions, and implications. *Harvard Educational Review*, 1968, *38*, 263–276.

Carroll, J. B. The nature of the reading process. In H. Singer & R. B. Ruddell (eds.), *Theoretical Models and Processes of Reading*. Newark, Delaware: International Reading Association, 1970.

Chall, J. *Learning to Read: The Great Debate*. New York: McGraw-Hill, 1967.

Chomsky, C. Reading, writing and phonology. *Harvard Educational Review*, 1970, *40*, 287–309.

Durkin, D. When should children begin to read? In H. M. Robinson (ed.), *Innovation and Change in Reading Instruction*, Sixty-seventh Yearbook of the National Society for the Study of Education. Chicago: University of Chicago Press, 1968, No. 2, pp. 30–71.

Fries, C. C. *Linguistics and Reading*. New York: Holt, Rinehart & Winston, 1963.

Hilgard, E. R., & Bower, G. H. *Theories of Learning*, New York: Appleton-Century-Crofts, 1966.

Huey, E. B. *The Psychology and Pedagogy of Reading*. Cambridge: M.I.T. Press, 1968 (original edition, 1908).

Jeffrey, W. E., & Samuels, S. J. Effect of method of reading training on initial learning and transfer. *Journal of Verbal Learning and Behavior*, 1967, *6*, 354–358.

Levin, H., & Watson, J. The learning of variable grapheme-to-phoneme correspondences: variations in the initial consonant position. In *A Basic Research Program on Reading*, U.S. Office of Education Cooperative Research Project No. 639. Ithaca: Cornell University, 1963.

Marchbanks, G., & Levin, H. Cues by which children recognize words. *Journal of Educational Psychology*, 1965, *56*, 57–61.

Neisser, U. *Cognitive Psychology*. New York: Appleton-Century-Crofts, 1967.

Smith, F. *Understanding Reading: A Psycholinguistic Analysis of Reading and Learning to Read*. New York: Holt, Rinehart, & Winston, 1971.

Williams, J. P. Reading research and instruction. *Review of Educational Research*, 1965, *35*, 147–153.

Williams, J. P. Successive vs. concurrent presentation of multiple grapheme-phoneme correspondences. *Journal of Educational Psychology*, 1968, *59*, 309–314.

Williams, J. P., & Levin, H. Word perception: psychological bases. *Education*, 1967, *87*, 515–518.

Woodworth, R. S.. *Experimental Psychology*. New York: Holt, Rinehart, & Winston, 1938.

INDEX

Aborn, M., 128, 132
alphabetic (phonetic) system, 113, 114–115
Anderson, I. H., 120, 121, 124, 132
Anisfeld, M., 59, 72
Ashton-Warner, S., 219, 250
Atkinson, R. C., 266, 271, 276

Barnhart, C. L., 34, 42, 270, 276
Bender, David, 146n
Berko, J., 32n, 42
Berney, T. D., 246–262
Bettelheim, B., 188, 219
Bever, T., 135, 146, 184, 187, 248, 261
Biemiller, A. J., 60, 73, 84, 89
Bishop, C. H., 269–270, 276
Black, M. H., 221
Bloch, Bernard, 14n
Blom, Gaston E., 188–221, 275
Bloomfield, Leonard, 20, 29, 32, 33, 33n, 34, 42, 270, 276
Bond, G. L., 265, 276
Bower, G. H., 267, 277
Bower, Thomas G. R., 134–146, 173, 178–181, 183, 185
Bristow, William H., 225n
Brodie, Richard, 246n
Brooks, V., 76, 80, 89
Brown, L., 80, 89
Brown, Roger, 164–187, 273
Bruner, J., 57, 73, 170, 186
Buswell, G. T., 76, 85, 89, 120, 121, 132
Byers, L., 219

Carillo, L. W., 219
Carroll, J. B., 267, 268, 274, 277

Caswell, H. L., 219
Cattell, J. McK., 57, 72, 121, 132
Cazden, Courtney, 247, 261
Chall, J., 266, 277
characters, preception of, 91–101
Chilcott, H. L., 219
Child, I. L., 214, 219
Chomsky, Noam, 3–18, 20, 29, 30, 43–52, 54, 55, 136, 146, 153n, 162, 268, 277
Clark, H., 125, 132, 177, 186
Clark, W., 84, 89
cognitive search guidance, 75–76, 77, 86–88, 169
Cohen, Paul, 222n, 245
Coleman, E. B., 148, 162
Commager, H. S., 220
Conrad, R., 84, 89
content analysis, motivational, of children's primers, 188–221, 275
context, grammatical, first-grader's use of, in reading, 147–163, 181–183
Cooper, F. S., 60, 73
Crovitz, H. F., 170, 172, 173, 187
Curme, G. O., 103, 118

Dakin, Mrs. Kae, 246n
deaf subjects, utilization of spelling patterns by, 57–73, 164–167
dialects, 13, 14, 29
Diebold, A. R., 57, 72
Doehring, D. G., 62, 72
Durkin, D., 264, 277
Dykstra, R., 265, 276

-ed suffix, reading of the, 222–245
Edge, S., 196, 220, 221

279